LIGHTING DESIGN

An Introductory Guide for Professionals

Published in the Americas by John Wiley & Sons, Inc
605 Third Avenue
New York
NY 10158–0012

First published in the United Kingdom by
The Design Council

Printed and bound in Hong Kong by
Dai Nippon Co (HK) Ltd

Every effort has been made to ensure the accuracy
of the information given in this book. No responsibility
can be accepted for any errors or omissions, or for the
use to which the information is put.

Library of Congress Cataloging in Publication Data
available

ISBN 0–470–22083–X

LIGHTING DESIGN

An Introductory Guide for Professionals

Carl Gardner and Barry Hannaford

John Wiley & Sons, Inc

New York Toronto

Contents

Introduction

At a time when lighting is increasingly recognized as an indispensable part of any architectural or interior design scheme, the literature available for interior designers and architects to help them through the maze of new lighting technologies, light sources and luminaires and the effects that can be achieved with them, is minimal.

Many books on lighting design originate in the USA and deal exclusively with US standards, equipment and environments. While much of what we have to say will apply to lighting design in the USA there are differences between the two design cultures which have to be recognized. As a profession, lighting design in the USA has a high profile, is well organized, and has a great deal of cross-over of expertise from theatre lighting. As a result, US lighting design technique is probably more sophisticated than in Europe, though paradoxically lighting technology in the USA lags behind that in Europe. In general it is European manufacturers who have led the exapansion of lighting sources and equipment. Consequently, some lamps referred to in this book may not be in common use in the USA.

Other publications tend to be glossy coffee-table books with little specialist information; books produced by manufacturers, which, while useful, are inevitably partial; or over-technical, drily presented handbooks aimed more at lighting and electrical engineering experts than at designers or architects looking for some guidance. Many more popular books seem to have been written for the residential market than for the professional and contract sector. This is despite the fact that domestic consumers, in Britain at least, have been notoriously retrograde in their appreciation of interior lighting and have put little investment into lighting their homes. While there is now some useful technology transfer from the contract sector into the domestic market (dimmers and low-voltage lighting, for example), this book is primarily concerned with the commercial, professional sector.

An important aspect of well-conceived lighting for the professional is the way that it can highlight in a complementary, fully integrated manner, the main features and themes of the built design. Effective lighting, with the appropriate sources, in the right combinations, all correctly mounted and controlled, can show off an architectural or interior design scheme to maximum effect. Conversely, wrongly chosen, poorly designed and badly managed lighting can wreck an otherwise effective installation. Such effects, whether positive or negative, can have a powerful psychological impact on users and observers. In exterior contexts, not only do people feel safer in well-lit environments, there is evidence that better illumination can reduce crime (see Painter 1988 and Philips 1991).

Lighting design involves very much more than the aesthetic enhancement of commercial and public environments. It can serve several other functions that relate directly to the economic management of a scheme. Good lighting design has a role to play in conserving energy and reducing power consumption and building maintenance costs. Within the retail and leisure sectors, programmed lighting schemes can be used to manage and control entire environments, perhaps to encourage customer circulation or to direct attention to product areas and to boost sales. Within working environments, harmonious, individually controlled lighting has been shown to increase user satisfaction, reduce absenteeism due to migraines and eye strain, and boost working efficiency (see Boyce 1989). In many cases the investment in good design and superior luminaires and sources amounts to a fraction of the value of a company's major investment, its staff. Yet many managements are often ignorant of the financial benefits or indeed legal requirements (for example the new EC directives) involved in interior lighting.

Interior designers and architects have grasped many of these issues. Similarly, lighting budgets within building and interior schemes have risen considerably in recent years. But knowledge about lighting technology and design technique hasn't grown accordingly amongst those same professionals; indeed few seem to have kept pace with the possibilities of today's technology. Unless a practice has its own lighting specialist – a situation that applies in only a handful of large firms – or is in a position to bring a specialist lighting consultancy onto the project at an early stage, it tends to have to depend on manufacturers or suppliers for information. This is undesirable, especially in terms of giving the client an independent, professional service.

In their approach to lighting, designers and architects are often fixated on the hardware itself – the aesthetic style and form of the product – at the expense of the potential effects. This approach, undoubtedly accentuated by the coverage of lighting design in the design press, which often is similarly preoccupied with form rather than content, has been responsible for the erroneous specification of lighting products. We hope this book will go some way towards redressing this imbalance.

This then is the context in which the book is written. It is intended as a wide-ranging, readable primer and source book to many of the latest projects, developments, technologies, equipment and issues in this expanding field. It is not a book for the DIY residential sector; nor is it a technical guide for engineers; nor is it an academic study of light; nor a detailed, step-by-step guide to lighting design, although we do offer general advice and guidance on the principles and problems associated with the subject. The book is popularly written and deliberately keeps statistical charts and jargon to a minimum. It is aimed at professionals within the commercial and contract design world, such as interior designers, architects and facilities/premises managers. It will also serve as a useful reader for interior design and architecture students looking to plug the gaps in their current education. Although the technical content of the book may be familiar to most electrical services engineers, they too might benefit from a study written from a design perspective.

Most importantly, we don't intend that the book should usurp independent lighting consultants. Indeed we hope that the often complex questions raised, and the advice offered, will make professionals regard lighting designers' work even more highly, and will encourage them to call on their services more often and at an earlier stage in project planning. To date, despite the importance of their craft, the work of lighting design professionals has, in our opinion, been underrated. And, despite the best intentions, project lighting has often been treated as an afterthought, an add-on extra or a decorative luxury.

Structure of the book

Chapter 1 is a general discussion of light and the terminology related to it and the specialist terms used within the lighting design industry.

Chapters 2 and 3 focus on lighting technology. Here we survey and explain the proliferating range of light sources and luminaires (technical terms, which are highlighted in the text, are explained in the Glossary) available to professionals. In these sections we have two aims: first to discuss the way these technologies function, their possible applications and misapplications, the broad effects achievable with them, and, most importantly, their advantages and disadvantages. Second, we attempt to illustrate, in a semi-catalogue form, some of the main types of product available from the major manufacturers. While designers and other specifiers are constantly bombarded with literature outlining the 'improved' features and capabilities of new lamps and luminaires, there is little critical guidance on the disadvantages of particular categories of lamp or luminaire. We start from the assumption that there is no such thing as the 'perfect' lamp or luminaire. A central concern of this book is our attempt to detail, where possible, the main disadvantages, as well as benefits, of particular products, systems or lighting design approaches.

In chapters 4 and 5 we look at the growing trend towards the creation of one-off tailor-made lighting systems, and the uses of lighting controls. The largest section of the book – chapter 6 – contains illustrated case studies of some of the most interesting and/or influential lighting design schemes from around the world. These case studies illustrate many of the lighting design themes, techniques and effects available to professionals, across a broad range of indoor and outdoor environments. Within this section, wherever particular sources, luminaires or other pieces of technology are used, these are cross-referenced to other parts of the book, where they are assessed more fully.

Given the special nature and growing popularity of exterior lighting, we devote chapter 7 to its main principles and problems.

In chapter 8 we consider energy conservation and other environmental concerns, and assess how lighting design can play its part.

In chapter 9 we discuss what lighting designers do, how they work, and how you can work best with them.

In chapter 10 we speculate about the future and how lighting design might look in the early years of the next millennium. What are the new technologies currently in development or coming on stream? How might they effect lighting design and the look of our built environments in the coming years?

Towards the end of the book we provide a glossary of lighting and lighting design terms; references and a select bibliography; technical appendices; and a list of trade organizations, lighting consultancies and manufacturers.

One area we have not covered in any great detail is the issue of technical codes and standards pertaining to lighting and lighting design. There are two main reasons for this omission: first, there is an extensive literature already available, published by CIBSE (see the Bibliography), which is indispensable reading for any would-be lighting designer. Second, the subject is in a state of flux: with the advent of the Single European Market national standards (such as British Standards) will be subsumed under common European standards (EN). These may or might not vary from those presently applying to individual European nations. We refer readers to the British Standards Institute or CIBSE (see Addresses) for up-to-date clarification.

A final caveat. We don't claim that the book is an objective guide to lighting design today (or tomorrow). We are neither academics nor scientists. In fact we feel that too much emphasis has been put on science, rather than design, in previous studies of lighting design. Inevitably in a book jointly conceived and written by a design writer/editor and an experienced lighting consultant, our tastes, preferences and opinions have influenced the way we have selected and shaped our material. This, we feel, gives the book much of its edge and interest. It should be read or consulted in the same critical spirit. Our aim is to encourage professionals to think about and use lighting in an informed, critical, and creative manner, rather than repeating the clichés and mistakes of the past.

Carl Gardner
Barry Hannaford

London April 1993

The nature of light

Before discussing the various types of artificial lighting source available in the commercial lighting sector, we provide some elementary information about the nature of light, and give a brief run-down of some of the terminology used by lighting designers and engineers to describe and quantify light and light output.

What is light?

Light is a form of electromagnetic radiation and is the major medium through which we discover the world around us. The world is made visible when light, either emanating from the sun or artificially created, falls on objects. Some of this light energy is reflected back into the eye and is decoded by the brain, to discern the particular size, movement, distance, shape, colour and form of the object(s) concerned. The nature of the light falling on our surrounding environment – its brightness, the angle at which it falls, and so on – can have a profound effect on how we perceive it. For example, we know that a landscape lit by bright sunshine looks totally different from the same landscape lit by 'grey' light from a dull, overcast sky.

Not only does the world look different, everything else being equal, this changed perception can have a strong psychological effect on viewers, even causing shifts from

a happy optimistic mood to one of sadness, melancholy or even depression. There is now a clinical term, SAD ('seasonal affective disorder'), to describe the condition suffered by some people, particularly those living in northern latitudes. During the shorter days of winter, when daylight is limited and sunlight is minimal or even non-existent, people can feel sluggish, depressed and physically run-down. Exposure to substitute artificial daylight for periods each day has been shown to have a beneficial effect on SAD sufferers and is sometimes used as a clinical treatment. The exact mechanisms of this psychological and even physiological malaise are, as yet, not fully understood. That the quantity and quality of light have profound and varied effects (some of which may as yet be undiscovered) on the feelings and emotions of human beings (and other living things) is now indisputable (see Boyce 1981 and Shepherd *et al.* 1989).

For the purposes of this book we maintain that there are broad similarities between our response to natural lighting and to artificial lighting within buildings. As many office or factory workers probably spend more time under artificial light than in natural light, particularly during the winter months, we can begin to see the considerable responsibility we have to achieve optimal conditions for them.

The power of light to influence perception, mood and even the outward behaviour of people, is one of the most important aspects of designing with light. For anyone working in the field – lighting designers, interior designers, architects and engineers – this puts paid to any purely functional view of light, whereby illumination is viewed as simply a means of helping people to see the goods on offer or to stop them falling over the furniture. Virtually any kind of light, provided it is in sufficient quantity, will enable people to orient themselves, to recognize objects, and to

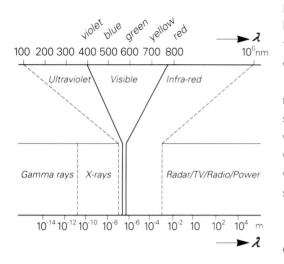

Figure 1 The electromagnetic spectrum

Courtesy: GE Lighting

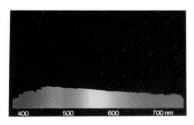

*The spectral composition
of natural daylight*

Courtesy: Osram

walk about without doing themselves physical damage. But clearly lighting can go beyond that, to help people feel good about their environment, their work and possibly even themselves.

Light, like other forms of electro-magnetic radiation such as heat, radio signals, and X-rays, is transmitted in waves which have a characteristic and unique wavelength. Visible light is emitted from a very narrow range in the electromagnetic spectrum, between 380 and 760 nano-meters (nm) (1 nanometer = 1 millionth of a millimetre). At longer wavelengths, energy is transmitted as infra-red (heat radiation) and radio waves; at shorter wavelengths, it is transmitted as ultra-violet 'light', X-rays and gamma rays (Figure 1).

Within the narrow band (380-760nm) of visible light, each colour from violet, through blue, green, yellow, orange and red, has its own wavelength. When all these wavelengths are present together they produce a balanced mixture which we experience as 'white' light. If we shine white light through a glass prism, each of the different colours within the mixture is refracted (bent) at slightly different angles, due to the different wavelengths. The result is that the 'mixture' of colours is 'unscrambled': each of the individual colours becomes visible in the form of a spectrum of colours. The same process occurs when it rains on a sunny day. Sunlight is refracted through millions of raindrops, which separate out its con-stituent colours into a radiant spectrum, which we see as a rainbow. In the context of interiors, the same effect is sometimes observed in the glass droplets of a chandelier, which seem to glow with different colours as light from the lamps is refracted through them.

Although changing in quality, average midday sunlight is generally perceived to contain all the colours in the spectrum.

However, forms of artificial lighting can, at best, only approximate such a full spectrum of light. No commercially available artificial lighting source can completely mimic natural daylight, though several come very close. All visible light emitted by lamps falls within the spectrum range of violet to red, but different light sources concentrate their output in particular parts of the spectrum, in different combinations (ie they have different spectral compositions). A lamp's specific spectral composition gives its emitted light a characteristic colour appearance, and also determines its colour-rendering capability (see page 5). In some cases this light may appear unnatural or even uncomfortable to the viewer, precisely because no close corollary appears in nature.

Low-pressure sodium lamps *(ch 2)* are the most extreme example of lamps that concentrate their light in only one part of the spectrum (ie they are monochromatic). Virtually all of their light is emitted in a narrow range of the spectrum around 589nm, which gives it an intense yellow-orange cast. Therefore, our colour perception of non-yellow objects is totally distorted; this characteristic makes such lamps generally suitable only for night-time street lighting and other contexts where the perception of colours is not important.

The eye's response

Another important consideration is the eye's own response to light of different wavelengths. The nerve endings inside the eye are not equally responsive to all colours: in well-lit conditions they work most efficiently within the green-yellow areas of the spectrum and least efficiently at the extreme ends of the spectrum (ie with blue-violet light on the one hand, and red at the other) (Figure 2). In darker conditions, when eyes have become 'dark-adapted' (a process that can take up to an hour) their maximum responsiveness shifts

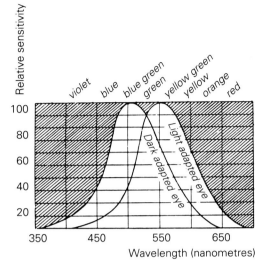

Figure 2 The eye's response to equal energy of radiation at different wavelengths

Courtesy: Electricity Association

towards the blue-green end of the spectrum, which is why, at night, green traffic lights seem to be much brighter than red ones.

This differential responsiveness is the main reason why low-pressure sodium lamps are the most efficient lighting sources available. All of the light they emit lies roughly at the middle of the visible spectrum, where the human eye is most responsive. At that wavelength eyes 'need' less light to make sense of the world, so light levels can be kept lower while still maintaining visibility and safety.

Although sunlight is often taken as the norm by which natural 'white' light is judged, it too can change its quality and composition, depending on the time of day, season and prevailing meteorological conditions. We discuss variations in natural daylight in the section on colour temperature (see pages 5 to 7).

So, if most original light is white and we are not viewing it through a prism, why do we experience objects as coloured? It seems to us that objects have an intrinsic colour quality and that light falling on them makes this colour visible, or that the colour is somehow emitted from their surface. To facilitate our understanding of lighting design, and to accord better with the findings of science, we have to turn this popular view on its head and consider all the colours in the world as being contained within the light rays, not within objects themselves.

Rather than things having a colour of their own which they emit, the colour-seeing process is more a case of subtraction. In other words, objects absorb from the light that falls on them (incident light) all its colours except the ones they give back (reflect). Put another way, the surfaces of objects have differential reflective characteristics. For example, a 'yellow' painted object will reflect back yellow light (comprising red and green) but will absorb

the blue; a 'green' object, on the other hand, will absorb all the wavelengths in white light except green, which is reflected back from its surface. With pigments in commercial materials, this process of absorption/reflection is not perfect, which is why, in practice, you never get 100 per cent colours.

Conversely, if we shine a purely green light onto a 'red' object, it will appear black (ie without colour). In this case the green light has been absorbed by the 'red' surface, but because there are no red wavelengths present in the incident light, there are none to reflect back to the viewer. Broadly speaking, a black surface is one that absorbs all the spectral colours; a white surface is one which reflects all of them back.

For anyone contemplating lighting design, this reversal of the conventional way of looking at the world is crucial: colours are not intrinsic qualities of objects, which light simply reveals; rather, colours are contained solely within light rays. Such a view has practical implications, in that it puts the emphasis firmly on getting the specific illumination right, rather than concentrating on colours and finishes in the first instance, and then adding light. When choosing materials, finishes and so on, samples or colour swatches should be viewed under the same type of lighting as the type that they will eventually be lit by when installed, otherwise the results will be misleading. This is one more reason for thinking about lighting design at an early stage in a project's evolution and not treating it as an afterthought.

Colour appearance and colour rendering

There are two distinct properties of light often confused in specifiers' minds.

Colour appearance

The colour appearance of light is most often expressed in terms of its particular colour temperature. This is an objective measurement rated in degrees kelvin (K). To convert Celsius temperatures to kelvin, add 273 (ie 100 degrees C = 373 degrees K). To understand the concept, think of an iron bar that is being slowly heated. It starts off black, and in the initial stages of heating, it radiates only invisible infra-red rays (ie heat); it then changes to dull red as it heats up; as it gets hotter, it appears more and more orange, then yellow, and at very high temperatures it is, as is commonly said, 'white hot'.

Each of these different colour appearances corresponds to the different temperature states of the bar (ie the bar's colour and its temperature are intimately related). The colour temperature of a light source rises with its thermal temperature: the higher the temperature, the more blue the light. This may seem a paradox, since the lowest colour temperatures achieve the 'warmest' lighting effects. For example, a candle burns at a 'cool' 2000 degrees K, but it offers a warm, yellow, comforting light; a 'cool' fluorescent lamp *(ch 2)* emits light at around 4000-5000 degrees K, which users often consider harsh and unfriendly; and daylight from a clear northern sky can be rated as high as 8500 degrees K, which we experience as very blue and cold (Figure 3).

Natural daylight is often seen as a norm, the natural benchmark against which other lighting can be judged. But the colour temperature (and hence appearance) of daylight varies widely. Summer midday sunlight lies roughly in the middle of the range between candlelight and a clear blue northern sky, at around 5500 degrees K. Incandescent lighting *(ch 2)*, which has a lower colour temperature than natural light, at between 2500 and 3000 degrees K, always appears warmer and more yellow, a difference revealed and even exaggerated by photographs of tungsten-lit rooms, taken with film intended for daylight use. (Film

emulsion does not respond to colour differences exactly like the human eye, which tends to compensate by 'averaging' them out.)

Colour rendering

Generally, while the direct colour appearance of light sources may be significant in determining a particular interior ambience, in most interior environments much of the light we see is reflected back off objects around us. In some cases, where light sources are concealed from direct view, we only perceive light reflected indirectly from objects, rather than directly from the sources. In these circumstances what is important is how particular light sources make objects appear, in other words their colour-rendering capabilities.

While the colour temperature of light can be measured objectively, assessment of a light source's colour-rendering capability is a much more subjective process. After all, as we have seen already, objects do not have a true colour in the way that they have a measurable temperature or a length (at least in normal earthly conditions).

However, the International Commission on Illumination (CIE) has developed a colour-rendering index (CRI) which, by averaging their spectral content, ranks different sources from 0 to 100; the higher the number, the truer the colour rendition at its colour temperature (Figure 4). It is important to remember that when it comes to comparing the colour-rendering capabilities of different lamps, this can be done only at the same colour temperature. So, fluorescent and incandescent lamps at, say, 3000 degrees K can be meaningfully compared for colour rendering, but an incandescent lamp of 3000 degrees K and a fluorescent of 4000 degrees K cannot.

The CIE table gives suggested recommendations of the suitability of different types of lamp for different locations. As we see in Figure 4, light

Figure 3 The different colour temperatures of selected light sources

Candle	*2000K*
High pressure sodium lamps	*1950–2250K*
GLS incandescent lamps (150W)	*2700K*
Tungsten halogen incandescent lamps	*3000K*
'Warm' fluorescent lamps	*2500–3000K*
Mercury discharge lamps	*3750–4500K*
'Cool' fluorescent lamps	*4000–5000K*
Late afternoon sunlight	*4000K*
Metal halide lamps	*4000–4600K*
Summer midday sunlight	*5500K*
Overcast sky	*6500–7500K*
North light/blue sky	*8000–8500K*

Figure 4 Correlated colour temperature classes and colour rendering groups used in the CIE Code

CORRELATED COLOUR TEMPERATURE (CCT)	CCT CLASS
$CCT \leq 3300K$	warm
$3300K < CCT \leq 5300K$	intermediate*
$5300K < CCT$	cold

COLOUR RENDERING GROUPS	CIE GENERAL COLOUR RENDERING INDEX (R_a)	TYPICAL APPLICATION
1A	$R_a \geq 90$	Wherever accurate colour matching is required, eg colour printing inspection
1B	$80 \leq R_a < 90$	Wherever accurate colour judgements are necessary and /or good colour rendering is required for reasons of appearance, eg shops and other commercial premises
2	$60 \leq R_a < 80$	Wherever moderate colour rendering is required
3	$40 \leq R_a < 60$	Wherever colour rendering is of little significance but marked distortion of colour is unacceptable
4	$20 \leq R_a < 40$	Wherever colour rendering is of no importance at all and marked distortion of colour is acceptable

*This class covers a large range of correlated colour temperatures. Experience in the UK suggests that light sources with correlated colour temperatures approaching the 5300°K end of the range will usually be considered to have a cool colour appearance

Courtesy: CIBSE

sources with a rating of 20-40 (rated 'poor') might be appropriate only for security lighting; while those rated in the range 80-90 ('excellent') are regarded as suitable for restaurants or shops, where accurate colour appearance is important. Efficient sources (fluorescents/HID) rated above 90 would generally be used only in specialist locations, where colour-matching operations (for example in the printing industry) are carried out. While the CIE table provides a useful starting point for designing with light, it should not be followed slavishly. In some cases, the penalty for better colour rendering is lower efficiency: the broader the colour spectrum a lamp has, the more energy it uses.

It is extremely important that those designing with light firmly grasp one simple fact, which may sound like a truism but is often ignored: things look different under different light sources (see page 7). It is these fundamental differences which can be exploited for effect. How lamps with different characteristics, with particular different colour-rendering capabilities, are employed is one of the crucial issues in interior design. While there is a great deal of technical data to help, which designers ought to understand, much of the designer's skill is intuitive (or based on previous experience). It cannot be based solely on tables or rigid guidelines.

In the final analysis there is no correct colour rendering which must be achieved under all circumstances; there are just conventional standards of what is acceptable, that designers cannot overstep with impunity. For example, 'cool' fluorescent lighting in a kitchen can change the appearance of most food, giving it a pale, green tinge and making it distinctly unappetizing (the exception is salads, which benefit visually from 'cool' fluorescent light). 'Warmer' or 'colour-corrected' fluorescents are likely to be much more aesthetically acceptable.

Colour rendering properties of different light sources with different colour temperatures. Clockwise from top left: 'warm' metal halide 3000˚K; 'cool' metal halide 5200˚K; 'cool' compact fluorescent 4000˚K; 'warm' compact fluorescent 2700˚K

Courtesy: Marlin

Incandescent tungsten filament lamps *(ch 2)* however, biased towards the red end of the spectrum, tend to bring out the red tones in objects, while dulling or flattening the blues and greens. As we have discussed already, low-pressure sodium lamps render everything yellow-orange. While that might be fine for functional street lighting, if there was an evening food or clothes market in the street, such an effect would be unacceptable.

How much light?

So far we have talked mainly about the colour aspects of light – how it appears, and how it renders colours. Equally important in determining an interior design's effect is the quantity of light used and the way it is distributed. It is no good choosing the correct type of source, with appropriate colour rendering and appearance, if the lamps are either not powerful enough to put sufficient light into the space to achieve the desired effect, or are too powerful and create glare.

Light has a number of measurable properties, all of them interrelated. We see an object because light flows from a source, hits the object's surface and some of it is reflected back to the eye. It is convenient to think of this process in four stages: (1) the actual source; (2) the flow of light from it; (3) its arrival at the object; and (4) its return from the object (Figure 5). Each stage has its own numerical measurement:

- The initial luminous intensity of a source is measured in candelas (cd). (This was based historically on the intensity of the standard candle, hence the name.) In analogous terms, luminous intensity can be compared with the pressure of water in a water pipe, which determines the rate of flow. In lighting design this unit is important when dealing with point source calculations.

- The flow of light from a source, or luminous flux, is measured in lumens (lm). This refers to the quantity of light emitted from a source (known erroneously as 'light output'). Again if we use the water analogy, luminous flux is equivalent to the volume of liquid that has come through a pipe. A theoretical point source with an intensity of 1 cd in all directions has a luminous flux of about 12.6 lm. A new 100W tungsten lamp produces a luminous flux output of 1200 lm. This unit is important for area lighting calculations (eg when determining the number and size of lamps to achieve a particular illuminance level).

- When light arrives at an object or surface, we talk about its illuminance (the quantity of light actually falling on it). This is measured in lux (lumens per square metre). In the USA the pre-metric unit, the foot-candle, is still used: one foot-candle (or lumen per square foot) is equal to 10.76 lux. Illuminance is an important determinant of the lighting level within a room, but it refers only to the light which falls upon particular surfaces, such as walls or worksurfaces; it does not give any indication of how bright the room will appear. That will depend on the reflective properties of the surfaces (see page 9).

- How we perceive the lit surface or object depends on how much light is reflected back off it. This observed brightness, an object's luminance, is measured in candelas per square metre (cd/m). As indicated, the reflectance properties of the surface play an important role here. Similar illuminances can result in widely differing luminances. For example, consider two rooms, one painted black and one painted white, both lit to the same illuminance level (ie the same lux). The luminance of the black room will be very low and it will

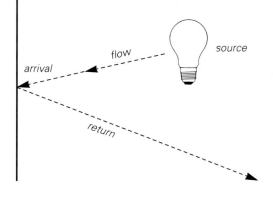

Figure 5 Schematic diagram of the four 'stages' of light, each of which has its own numerical measurement

appear dull; the luminance of the white room will be much higher and it will appear bright. This explains why it is difficult, if not impossible, to plan a lighting scheme without knowing the material finishes and colours which the room will contain, and why standard codes specifying only lux levels are of little use in practical lighting design situations. In Appendix 4 (see page 216) we include CIBSE's recommended standard service illuminance levels for different types of activity.

Reflectance

Reflectance relates to how much light is reflected by an object: for diffuse surfaces reflectance is a major determinant of luminance; for specular surfaces angle of incidence is important, too. Roughly speaking, for a matt surface luminance = illuminance x the reflectance factor divided by Π (Figure 6), although other factors, such as the angle of incidence, and surface texture (Figure 7) can all affect the calculation. A reflectance factor is expressed as a unitless figure between 1 and 100 (ie a percentage), or as a decimalized fraction (eg 0.8, 0.6).

Glare

Reflectance has an important bearing on certain types of glare, one of the most important yet often unconsidered defects in a lit environment. When light is emitted from a source, either directly or by reflection, in the direction of the eye, there is the potential for glare. In general we recognise only high levels of contrast or large luminance differences.

Glare occurs when the eye has to cope with a source of light which is much brighter than the average level of lighting which surrounds it. Such excessive contrast causes the muscles of the eye to adjust continually between the two levels of brightness, a process we find both tiring

and stressful. In physiological terms, lighting specialists often make the distinction between 'discomfort glare' and 'disability glare'. Discomfort glare is irritating but tolerable (ie we can still carry out tasks, but with increasing difficulty and discomfort). Eventually such glare can lead to eye strain, headaches and other symptoms. Disability glare is defined as glare which is so strong that it prevents specific tasks being carried out. A common example in the natural world is driving into a low sunset, where the road and other surroundings can't be seen. If we are subjected to disability levels of glare, even for short periods, without relief, damage to the eyes can easily occur.

Lighting specialists also make another practical distinction, which is important in lighting design terms. 'Direct glare' is caused by primary sources of illumination – the lamps and luminaires making up an installation (for example, a bright lamp which has been located against a dark background). 'Indirect glare' is due to secondary sources, such as light reflected off surfaces which are excessively bright. 'Veiling reflections' from the screens of visual display terminals are a common example. Indirect glare may depend on elements in the interior generally considered outside the scope of the lighting designer – wall or ceiling finishes, desktop materials, and so on.

The lighting specialist's comments on the decorative colours and finishes early in the origination of the scheme could help mitigate these problems. Even in existing installations there are several steps that can be taken to minimize glare – changing the colour finishes, increasing the area of the source, modifying the angles of incidence (Figure 8), or replacing the louvres or diffusers with more appropriate or efficient versions.

In certain situations designers have used glare deliberately to stop people

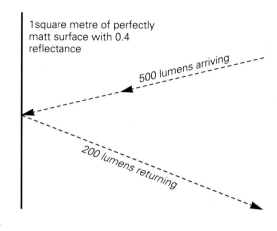

1 square metre of perfectly matt surface with 0.4 reflectance

500 lumens arriving

200 lumens returning

Figure 6 Basic calculation of luminance – illuminance x reflectance factor ÷ Π (3.142) expressed in cd/m². In the example above, 200 x 0.4 ÷ 3.142 = 64 cd/m².

Figure 7 Typical recommended reflectance figures for different building materials

White brick	*80 or 0.8*
White plaster	*0 or 0.7*
White marble	*60-65 or 0.6-0.65*
Portland stone	*60 or 0.6*
Middle stone or medium concrete	*40 or 0.4*
Yellow brick	*35 or 0.35*
Granite	*0-15 or 0.1-0.15*
Dark stone	*5-10 or 0.05-0.1*
Glazed windows	*0 (for practical purposes)*

External weathering or urban grime can reduce these figures still further

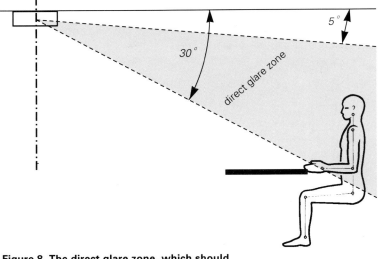

Figure 8 The direct glare zone, which should be avoided in designing office lighting. The luminance of luminaires should be restricted between 5° and 30°

The appearance of objects can be changed dramatically by using combinations of different beam angles and intensities

Courtesy: Concord Lighting

looking in a particular direction; for example, supermarket ceilings were often very brightly lit to subconsciously keep customers' eyes down to the goods on the shelves. Generally speaking, such a strategy would probably be regarded as unacceptable, or unethical, in environments where 'captive' users are forced to remain for prolonged periods of time.

Where is the light coming from?

Another issue for designers, alongside the qualitative and quantitative nature of the light itself, is where it is coming from, its direction. The direction of light within a scheme can be an important design variable. For example, if you want an object or an interior to look natural, broadly speaking you would mimic nature by creating an all-over effect, with most light projected from a high angle in the room (ie like sunlight). On the other hand, if you want an environment to look arresting or dramatic, you might use uplighting or a perpendicular, narrow-beam downlight, in a totally unnatural way.

As we discuss in chapter 7, flood-lighting a building, mostly from ground level, creates a distinct and unnatural effect, by reversing the normal daytime shadows. (We have all seen a similar effect when a face is lit by a torch shone from underneath the chin.) Mouldings that are not normally visible, for example under cornices, may thus be highlighted and featured for the first time – a classic example of 'seeing something in a new light'.

The combination of light type, strength and direction is the major determinant of what lighting designers call 'modelling' of an object or objects so that we can fully appreciate their form and texture. A fairly bright but diffuse light source, positioned above an object (for example an overcast sky) will produce very soft shadows and reveal a lot of detail. However, the exclusive use of such lighting tends to create a dull, flat, uninteresting effect.

An example of this from the interiors world is the once extremely common illuminated opal ceiling, using fluorescent battens, popular in the 1960s and 1970s. While this offered an overall, diffused light which was certainly logical and efficient in engineering terms, the design effect was dull and boring and offered no visual relief or contrast.

At the other extreme, bright, full sunlight, or narrowly concentrated spotlights emanating from single-point sources, can produce strong shadows and create zones of contrast within the object, which we tend to find more interesting. But here again harsh, one-directional shadows can be visually oppressive, as well as potentially misleading about an object's shape or texture.

Light angled obliquely at a wall or other object, so that it just grazes the surface, will reveal texture. Page 10 shows some of the comparative effects achieved with different combinations of beam intensities and angles.

In general, single types of source, emanating from one direction, create poor modelling, whereas a mix of sources, emanating from different directions, will tend to create the best effect. This has been common knowledge in the theatre for many years and it is at last being employed extensively in museums and art galleries where the perception of the objects on show is paramount. Exhibits are often spotlit from two or three directions, sometimes using more than one kind of lamp, for precisely this reason. Even in other lighting design contexts, we would generally recommend such combination lighting strategies for the best results, although budgetary constraints may militate against them.

An example of the 'unnatural' dramatic effect of lighting from below, reversing daytime modelling

Overall opalescent ceiling lit from above – an outdated lighting technique which produces a bland, undifferentiated effect

A good example of modelling, where a number of light sources at different angles have given the objects texture and depth

chapter 2

Light sources and how they work

In this chapter we survey the major types of artificial light sources currently available and briefly explain how they function, their capabilities, typical applications and their advantages and disadvantages for a lighting designer. There are many other lamps available for very specialist applications, such as photography and photo-printing, film projection, plant growth, and germicidal purposes which are not covered here.

New versions of the major lamp types are continually coming onto the market. While the prefix designations of the main groups of discharge lamps – for example, MBF, and SON – are explained, there are many variants with particular prefixes. Appendix 1 includes a recent compilation of these main prefix designations and what they mean. It should be remembered that different manufacturers often use different letters to denote broadly similar capabilities. The Lighting Industry Federation (LIF) publishes a regular *Lamp Guide* (see Bibliography) which should be consulted for more up-to-date information.

Luminous efficiency (efficacy)

As we explain in chapter 8, the efficiency (efficacy) of a lamp is generally measured in lumens per watt (lm/W), which refers to the units of light emitted per unit of energy consumed. In the case of a 100W tungsten lamp, if it emits 1200 lm that is equivalent to only 12 lm/W – 95 per cent of its energy is given off as heat (Figure 1). When this is compared with typical values of 70–80 lm/W for metal halide lamps and 55–120 lm/W for high-pressure sodium lamps, depending on wattage, control gear and so on, and 60–100 lm/W for fluorescent lamps, we can see how inefficient tungsten sources are. Compared with high-pressure sodium, tungsten lamps are somewhere between 4.5 and 10 times less efficient. Further, with tungsten lamps the luminous efficiency will simply be related to the nominal power; for discharge lamps there are energy losses associated with the control gear which have to be taken into account – these could be as high as 11–20 per cent. Moreover, manufacturers' methods of presenting performance data for their products are often inconsistent.

For example, some manufacturers calculate their figures on the basis of brand new lamps; others base it on what is

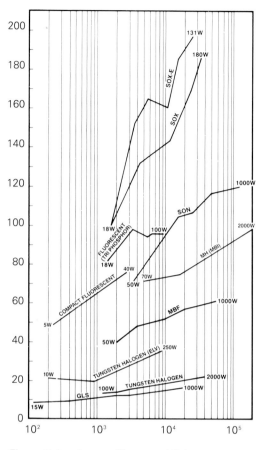

**Figure 1 Luminous efficacy and light output.
Demonstration of the comparative performance
of different types of lamp. Note how efficiency
increases in higher wattage lamps**

Courtesy: LIF

*A selection of some of
the more popular type
of mains incandescent
lamps – PAR lamps,
ISL lamps and GLS*

known in the trade as 'lighting design
lumen output' (ie output after 2000 hours'
use), which is conventionally regarded as
the average output through the lamp's life.
Designers' calculations are usually based
on this figure. In the case of fluorescent
lamps, for example, this could represent a
shortfall in luminous flux of 10–15 per cent
over the same lamp when new.

It is important then to make certain of
the basis on which lamp data have been
published before planning a scheme, and
always compare like with like. Because of
this problem we have tended to average
out figures, or to generalize, when quoting
figures in this book. We must stress that
figures which suffice to substantiate a
general argument are not intended for use
in calculating detailed loadings and outputs
for an actual lighting scheme.

Rated lamp-life

An even greater problem emerges with
different manufacturers' assessments of
lamp-life or rated lamp-life. Again there is
no common standard; some manufacturers
rate a lamp's life according to a 20 per cent
failure rate (ie when 80 per cent of lamps
are still operational); others take a 50 per
cent failure rate as the norm. Some lamps
are assessed on a period of continuous
use; others incorporate three or four
switching cyles a day (heating, cooling and
reheating tungsten filaments tends
to reduce their life considerably).

Under-running or over-running
at slightly lower voltages can
have a profound effect
(Figure 2).

With many types of
lamp the operating (burning)
position (horizontal, vertical,
and so on) can have a
considerable effect on its
operational life and/or efficacy.
Always check on any limitations on
operating position prior to specification.

Fluorescent and discharge lamps,
unlike incandescent sources, do not usually
suffer sudden failure while operating at
their optimum light output level. Instead,
their overall light output gradually declines
over time, to a point where their further
use is uneconomic. For commercial
purposes, manufacturers do not generally
give them a rated life; instead they publish
lamp and lumen mortality curves, on the
basis of which designers can work out
cleaning cycles and re-lamping periods.

Incandescent lighting

Incandescent lamps originated in the late
19th century and are the oldest existing
practical form of electric light. Their
principle is very simple: electric current is
passed through a filament (most often
coiled tungsten) inside a glass envelope
containing an inert gas or a vacuum. The
filament heats up rapidly and at around
900° C it starts to become incandescent.
At around its operating temperature of
2500–2700° C (2773–2973°K *(ch 1)*) it
produces its optimum luminous flux and
glows with its typical 'white' colour. The
designed operating temperature for
ordinary tungsten filaments is 3000°K,
hence the lamp is said to have a colour
temperature *(ch 1)* of about 2900–3000°K.
At such high temperatures, the tungsten in
the filament gradually evaporates. When so
much has evaporated that the filament
becomes too thin to carry the current, it
breaks – the main reason for tungsten
lamp failure.

Originally, all lamps were simple mains
voltage tungsten sources, such as the
common household GLS (general lighting
services) lamp still used today. Later
refinements, which considerably improved
performance, included tungsten halogen
sources (see page 17) and low-voltage
versions (see pages 19–20). For the
purposes of lighting design, incandescent
sources include mains voltage (240 volts)

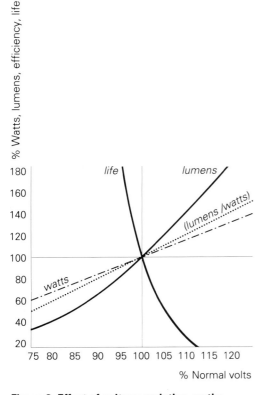

Figure 2 Effect of voltage variation on the performance characteristics of the incandescent lamp

GLS lamps, mains voltage tungsten halogen, reflector lamps, including sealed beam PAR (parabolic aluminized reflector – see page 17) lamps and low-voltage tungsten halogen lamps (see page 18).

Incandescent lamps come in a variety of shapes and forms, some with their own integral reflectors. Their versatility is extended by their availability in a range of wattages, from less than 5 watts to 2000 watts or more. They are relatively cheaply constructed, using mainly benign materials which do not present disposal problems. Except for the low-voltage versions (see page 19) incandescent lamps can be connected directly to the mains, without the need for control gear. They run on AC or DC current, which makes them suitable for many applications, including car headlights, battery-powered emergency lighting and lighting on board ships.

Tungsten and tungsten halogen offer remarkably good colour rendering at around 3000°K *(ch 1)* and are particularly flattering to skin-tones. Because incandescent light emanates from a relatively small point source, and because some lamps themselves are quite tiny, their light distribution can be controlled easily. They can be switched on instantaneously, with no perceptible warm-up time, and dimming can be achieved easily. The use of dimmers can markedly increase the operational life of incandescent lamps, but there is a price to pay in lost efficiency (see Figure 2).

All these positive features are achieved at a high price: incandescent tungsten lamps of all types are comparatively inefficient. Their instrinsically shorter lamp-life adds to maintenance and replacement costs and, more importantly, more than 90 per cent of all the energy they consume is emitted as heat (infra-red), rather than visible light. While occasionally this may be useful (eg in lamps over a long-hold hot food servery), generally it is wasteful of energy. Not only does it waste power

directly, it can also add to heat gain in buildings, so air-conditioning costs are higher. Except where colour rendering or precise control is vital (eg in retail display) tungsten lamps are not usually suitable for large-scale commercial applications.

Tungsten filaments are fragile and sensitive to vibration and shock, especially when hot. Even small increases in voltage can reduce lamp-life (though conversely small reductions in voltage, if achieved and maintained smoothly, can considerably increase lamp-life, with a reduced light output – Figure 2). Because of their relatively cheap, simple construction, Third World and eastern European versions are widely available, but these can be of inferior quality and may even be dangerous.

Tungsten lamps
Tungsten lamps are the most common and basic form of incandescent lighting. Mainly mains voltage (240V), with exceptions such as car lamps and shipboard lighting, they require no expensive control gear and are easily dimmed. Available in a wide range of shapes, wattages and types, tungsten sources include GLS, spherical globe lamps, linear models and reflector lamps, such as internally silvered lamps (ISL) and parabolic aluminized reflector (PAR) versions. The glass envelope of tungsten lamps can be treated in several ways, too – clear, pearl or colour tinted, for example.

The main quality of tungsten lamps, with their intrinsic red-yellow spectral tones, is their warmth. For example, low-wattage versions are close to candlelight and are ideal for recreating the low light levels of period interiors. In certain situations such light quality can be very flattering and reassuring. However, for most commercial applications, these benefits are greatly outweighed by tungsten lamps' shortcomings. Tungsten lamps are the least efficient of all light sources (even less efficient than tungsten halogen) and have a short lamp-life (typically 1000 hours). So, while they are cheap to make and buy, they are expensive to run. As they need to be replaced regularly, when used they must be located in accessible areas. In high-ceilinged spaces, for example, they should be re-lamped from above.

The fragile glass envelopes of most higher wattage tungsten lamps (with the exception of some PAR lamps – see below) are prone to thermal shock and are therefore unsuitable for unprotected outdoor use. The most practical commercial applications of tungsten lamps are temporary exhibitions, Christmas displays and events of that type. But because they get hot, they must be kept out of hands' reach.

PAR lamps

One of the most useful mains-operated tungsten filament lamps for the commercial designer or specifier is the PAR lamp. The parabolic aluminized reflector (PAR) lamp is a sealed beam source with, as its name implies, an integral aluminized reflector. Its robust pressed glass construction means that it is resistant to thermal shock, and can be used in outdoor environments.

The lamp is available in a wide range of sizes and wattages (typically 60W, 80W and 120W in the PAR 38 versions and 25W to 500W in PAR 36 to PAR 64 lamps). The number following the PAR refers to the diameter of the lamp in eighths of an inch, so a PAR 64 is eight inches wide. Rated lamp-life is typically around 2000 hours.

PAR lamps are popular with interior designers in the USA; readers will note the greater specification of such sources in several US schemes detailed in chapter 6. The reason for this is that standard mains voltage in the USA is 120V not the European 220/240V. At this lower voltage, the PAR lamp is a good compromise

between European mains-operated lamps and genuine low-voltage (12V or 24V) luminaires and gives some of the latter's advantages without the need of a transformer.

Tungsten halogen lamps

Tungsten halogen is a refinement of the tungsten lamp and gives slightly better performance and colour quality.

A small trace of halogen, often in the form of iodine, is added to the gaseous envelope surrounding the filament. This has three effects:

- by linking up with the evaporated tungsten to form tungsten halide, some of the tungsten vapour is recycled back onto the filament, thus prolonging its life

- the higher gas pressure and smaller sized envelope needed to facilitate this process mean that lamps can be run longer and hotter (quartz, rather than glass is used, to withstand higher temperatures closer to the filament)

- because the glass is free from blackening, there is virtually no deterioration in light output throughout its life.

The hotter the tungsten, the whiter the light, so tungsten halogen lamps are generally considered to offer a better quality of light than their tungsten counterparts, with a colour temperature of over 3000°K.

Colours can often appear 'crisper' and sharper. They can also achieve considerably longer lives, often lasting up to two or three times as long (2000–3000 hours compared with the 1000 hours of a normal GLS lamp). And, because light is emitted from a small point source, they can be controlled more easily than ordinary tungsten lamps.

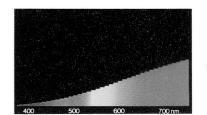

Typical spectral composition of an incandescent lamp showing its bias towards the red end of the spectrum
Courtesy: Osram

A selection of typical PAR lamps
Courtesy: Lampways

Tungsten lamps are often used in galleries and museums for their good colour-rendering capabilities
Courtesy: Marlin

Some of the wide variety of low-voltage tungsten halogen reflector lamps
Courtesy: Lampways

A selection of mains voltage tungsten halogen lamps
Courtesy: Lampways

Even tungsten halogen is relatively inefficient, compared with the proliferating range of discharge sources.

Tungsten halogen lamps come in two main forms: low-voltage versions, either capsules or reflector lamps (see page 23), and double-ended mains voltage lamps, typically in the 150–300W range. Recently, several companies have produced a tungsten halogen lamp with a standard GLS bayonet cap. A popular refinement of the low-voltage tungsten halogen lamp, introduced in about 1982, is the dichroic reflector. This has the advantage of reflecting light forward, while allowing heat to dissipate through the back of the reflector. Dichroic reflectors can come either as part of the luminaire, or as an integral part of the lamp, as in the MR 16, which has become ubiquitous in retail outlets since the mid-1980s.

Advantages

+ *wide range of forms, shapes and wattages*
+ *relatively cheap to produce*
+ *require no control gear*
+ *good colour rendering, particularly tungsten halogen*
+ *easily controlled in terms of distribution and quantity of light*
+ *instantaneous switching*
+ *ease of dimming, which can extend lamp-life*

Disadvantages

− *short lamp-life can entail high replacement and maintenance costs*
− *inefficient in energy terms (poor efficacy)*
− *high heat output increases air-conditioning costs and can be dangerous if not catered for*
− *fragile filaments which are sensitive to shock*
− *over-volting further reduces lamp-life*
− *dimming of lamps reduces their efficiency*

Low-voltage lighting

Low-voltage lighting has been one of the success stories of the lighting world since the late 1980s. Particularly in retailing, low-voltage tungsten halogen lamps (see page 18) were used in abundance to give brightness and sparkle to windows and interiors.

Low-voltage lighting became one of the clichés of high street display design and in the process was often specified in preference to other sources that might have been more appropriate.

It is easy to see why low-voltage tungsten and tungsten halogen sources have been so popular. The advantages they offer are considerable. They are compact, which facilitates optical control and offers the user relatively narrow beams of light for dramatic display purposes. Low-voltage lighting is also dimmable, which offers even more control. At the same time their colour rendering is very good, which is vital for displaying fabrics and other fashion artefacts where colour is important.

Low-voltage lighting rapidly became versatile, as the enthusiasm of specifiers and manufacturers led to the development of a huge range and variety of sizes, wattages, reflector types and beam angles.

Depending on the effect required, the hardware can be discrete or a prominent design feature. Because low voltages allow the use of two unsheathed wires, many systems have been developed where the power cables visibly support the fittings, in the form of a flexible, free-standing track *(ch 3)*, spanning the space.

Low-voltage lighting scores well on safety and efficiency. In the public context the use of a remote transformer hidden in a ceiling or floor, with all wires and fittings at non-life-threatening voltages of 12V or 24V, is attractive.

Used as a display source, low-voltage lighting is also generally more energy-efficient than mains voltage lamps. But

Ilustration of the brightness and high contrast that low-voltage tungsten halogen lighting (bottom) can offer compared with the more diffuse mains voltage tungsten (top) using the same power consumption

Courtesy: Thorn Lighting

A simple but more expensive option for low-voltage spotlights – the integral transformer with each luminaire. This system is the Concord Torch

low-voltage lighting has a downside, which most designers have chosen to ignore in their quest for the glitzy, glamorous effects that it can offer.

The need for a comparatively bulky transformer is the most obvious disadvantage. Although they are being made smaller, they still need to be hidden in a wall, cupboard, ceiling- or floor-void. In sleek, minimalist interiors this can sometimes be difficult. An additional complication is that future maintenance access to transformers should also be designed into the scheme. Impeded access can lead to ceiling panels becoming grubby or damaged through clumsy handling.

Attempts to reduce costs by using a large-capacity transformer controlling numerous lamps have often been counter-productive; under such conditions, poor-quality transformers can easily produce variations in voltage, particularly if one lamp fails. Even slight over-volting – five per cent (or 0.6V on a 12V lamp) – can halve the life of all the other lamps.

Running many lamps off one transformer also demands a high-capacity cable – only four 12V 50W lamps will require nearly 17 amps, and the specification of inadequate cable can run the risk of overheating.

There are many low-voltage luminaires with their own integral transformer. These obviate the need for a large remote transformer, giving each lamp its own dedicated mini-transformer, but they are expensive.

In many cases, too, integral transformer versions of slender, modern lamps, each incorporating their own box, are aesthetically unsatisfactory. Many of the problems associated with traditional wire-wound transformers can be overcome with the use of smaller, lightweight electronic versions. Many have built-in safety devices such as short-circuit protection and constant voltage regulators. Due to their

compact size they can be accessed through the ceiling cut-outs of the smallest downlighters.

Low-voltage lamps always need careful handling: touching the quartz envelopes with bare fingers, for example, can considerably reduce their life. Also, low voltages result in high currents which require additional attention.

When (ab)used in large numbers, to provide overall rather than feature or display lighting, low-voltage sources generate considerable amounts of heat. This can create local air-conditioning problems, as well as further reduce lamp-life. A combination of high density, long periods of use and poor handling, can massively increase maintenance and replacement costs. Replacement costs are even higher with the many low-voltage lamps that have their own integral reflector.

When it comes to re-fitting, the confusing variety of low-voltage lamp types, which initially was a boon to specifiers, can work against them. Sources which look the same but perform differently can often be retro-fitted incorrectly and a carefully designed effect can be ruined.

Advantages

+ *compact light source*
+ *easy optical control*
+ *good colour rendering*
+ *versatile; wide range of types to choose from*
+ *safe*
+ *energy-efficient, when used correctly*

Disadvantages

− *require a voltage transformer*
− *need delicate handling*
− *generate considerable heat when used in large numbers*
− *shorter lamp-life than discharge sources*
− *wide range of lamp types can lead to incorrect retro-fitting*

Fluorescent lamps

The modern fluorescent lamp is technically a low-pressure (approximately one-two-hundredth atmospheric pressure) discharge source but is normally regarded as a separate category of lamp, with its own special properties. As with other discharge lamps, the filament is not the major light emitter. Instead, an electrical discharge operates within a glass tube, filled with krypton or argon gas and coated internally with a phosphor powder mixture. The electrical charge flowing between the two electrodes excites the gas to create invisible ultraviolet and some visible blue-green light; this ultraviolet in turn excites the phosphor coating and causes it to glow. The exact mix of phosphors coating the tube determines the colour quality of the light created, from 'cool' to 'warm' and from poor to excellent colour rendering, and is kept a closely guarded secret by manufacturers.

The original fluorescent tubes were long, bulky and by today's standards relatively inefficient. Nowadays lamps come in a wide range of lengths, shapes and diameters – linear tubes from 150 mm up to 2400 mm long, circular tubes, short stubby compact versions, with one or two folds, and so on. They range from 4 watts to 125 watts and compact versions are available with or without integral starters and control gear.

The choice of shapes and colours of fluorescent lamps has proliferated in recent years and colour rendering has improved dramatically. However, as in all discharge lamps, radiation (colour) tends to be emitted in 'spikes' on the spectrum so it is truly never as good as daylight or, in the case of warmer lamps, their equivalent incandescent sources.

The advantage of modern fluorescent sources is their efficiency. Lamps have a very long life (typically 8000 hours) and light output typically ranges between 60 and 100

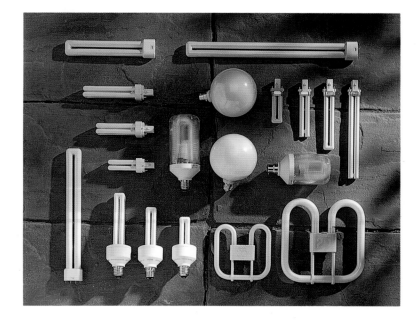

A selection from the wide variety of shapes and size of fluorescent lamps available, from the original linear and circular types (top) to the newer compact versions (bottom)

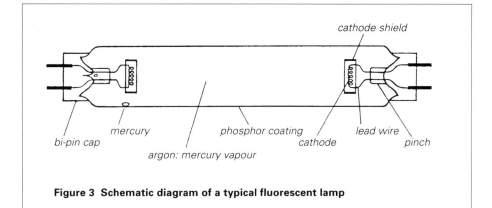

Figure 3 Schematic diagram of a typical fluorescent lamp

Typical spectral composition of a fluorescent lamp showing how its light is emitted in uneven spikes
Courtesy: Osram

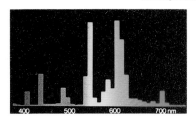

lumens per watt *(ch 1)*. However, the compact versions are less efficient than their larger counterparts. Particularly with the longer versions, relatively low wattages and light emissions from a large surface area of tube create fewer heat or glare problems.

Fluorescent lamps are relatively inexpensive to buy and their control gear is compact and cheap to make. Modern ballasts which permit dimming can further extend their application. For these reasons, fluorescent lamps have become a staple fixture in most workplaces, often regardless of their specific lighting effect or the needs of the workforce.

All this is achieved at some practical and aesthetic cost. Colour rendering *(ch 1)* is only average in cheaper lamps, and these are most often specified on false economic grounds. While fluorescent lamps are now offered in a wider range of colour temperatures, this proliferation can lead to retro-fitting problems, with different sorts of lamp being incorrectly mixed within the same space.

There are probably more than 25 different versions of 'white' fluorescent tubes in popular use. Although they may be given the same generic name – 'warm white' or 'cool white' – by manufacturers, different lamps will often have markedly different colour appearance *(ch 1)* or colour rendering *(ch 1)* properties. This mixing of lamp types is a common problem, especially in larger installations.

Proliferation of lamp types has also led to problems of incompatibility of control gear; the latest generation of energy-saving lamps, for example, is not suitable for switchless and quickstart circuits.

Some compact fluorescent lamps only achieve manufacturers' quoted efficiencies when operated in certain positions (such as horizontal, vertical) and all are susceptible to cold and heat. Their optimum ambient operating temperature is about 20°C –

outdoor temperatures can be much higher or lower than that for long periods. In outdoor winter locations compact fluorescent lamps will take longer to start and reach their optimum light output. These factors must be taken into account when designing a scheme.

For most people, the perceived effect of fluorescent lamps, when used on their own, is at best flat and bland, and at worst cold and unfriendly. This can best be alleviated by combining fluorescent lighting with other types of lamps, to create highlighting and produce a more interesting interior. Due to the size of most lamps, precise optical control is difficult, though compact versions are now being used in directional downlighters. For ceiling-mounted versions, low-brightness louvres are the most common form of control, but as well as reducing lighting efficiency, these are easily marked by careless handling (witness the fingerprints on many office ceilings).

Like all discharge lamps, fluorescent light is emitted in pulses which can produce visible flicker, particularly when seen in peripheral vision . According to mounting evidence, this is more than a mere irritation: it can contribute to user headaches and eye strain. In certain contexts it can even be dangerous, for example where a stroboscopic effect causes rapidly revolving machinery to appear stationary (see Jeavons 1975; Poulton 1966; Wilkins 1989).

To mitigate this, high-frequency versions are now available, with special ballasts which boost the operational frequency of the fluorescent cycle from the normal 50 per second to over 25,000 per second, well beyond the limits of human perception. High-frequency ballasts have other advantages, too: greater lamp efficiency and lower energy losses within the control gear; silent operation; dimmability; and longer lamp-life.

While fluorescent lamps can be an efficient form of lighting, when incorrectly applied the effects can be extremely bland

While high-frequency ballasts are currently both bulky and costly, a careful cost appraisal over the life of the scheme can show a relatively short payback period.

Even the longevity of fluorescent lamps has its downside. With extreme age, light output can fall well below economic levels, without the lamp failing. So in commercial contexts, lamps must be replaced *en masse* after reaching the end of their economic life.

Given the presence of mercury and phosphor, this can present disposal problems. Disposal instructions must be closely followed; dumping on a landfill site, for example, is illegal.

There are now various crushing and compacting machines on the market *(ch 8)* which can help make the disposal process simpler and safer.

Advantages

+ *long lamp-life*
+ *energy efficient*
+ *increasing range of shapes, sizes and colours*
+ *minimal heat problem, particularly with larger versions*
+ *relatively cheap to make and buy*
+ *can be re-lamped and maintained easily*
+ *can be dimmed*

Disadvantages

- *generally only average colour rendering is possible in low-cost versions*
- *large tube sizes limit optical control*
- *when used alone, can produce flat, bland effect*
- *visible flicker, unless costly high-frequency ballasts are used*
- *slow starting in cold weather*
- *positional limitations with some compact versions*
- *toxic materials present disposal difficulties*

Discharge lamps

In discharge lamps, as with fluorescent sources, there is no metal filament. Instead, light is produced by the excitation of a gas. Voltage is applied to two electrodes in a tube containing the gas. At a certain critical value, the current arcs between them and causes ionization of the gas atoms. In the process energy is given off (or discharged) which may be in the visible, ultraviolet or infra-red areas of the spectrum. However, the process is not instantaneous; striking-up and reaching the optimum level of ionization can take between less than a second and several minutes, depending on the type of lamp. To prevent the process accelerating indefinitely and hazardously, the current has to be carefully controlled.

All discharge lighting comprises three main elements: a gas which, when excited, emits light at the required wavelength; a means of initiating the discharge; and some form of control gear to limit the flow of energy. Most of the high-pressure discharge lamps also have a secondary glass envelope outside the gas envelope, to protect it from temperature change, moisture and mechanical damage. As a result, discharge lamps are bulkier, more complex, and more expensive than their incandescent equivalents. But with no fragile filament, they tend to be more robust.

The control of light with discharge lamps can present problems: dimming, for example, while not impossible, does demand specialist equipment. Discharge lamps cannot be dimmed to and from zero, which makes the imperceptible fade-in of lamps at sunset difficult to achieve. Similarly, with one or two specialist exceptions, discharge lamps, being either linear or large point sources, make precise optical control difficult.

Discharge lamps come in many forms and with a range of characteristics,

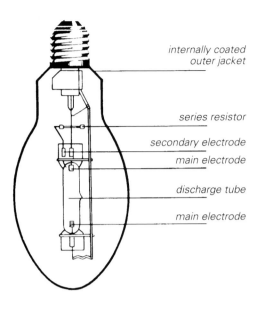

internally coated
outer jacket

series resistor

secondary electrode

main electrode

discharge tube

main electrode

Figure 4 Schematic diagram of a typical high-pressure mercury discharge lamp

Discharge lamps come in many different shapes and sizes – and can be high pressure (metal halide, mercury, sodium, etc) or low pressure (fluorescent)

Courtesy: Illuma

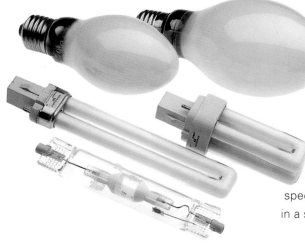

depending on the shape of the lamp, the type of gas used, the size of the discharge arc and so on. The two main groups are:

- low-pressure discharge lamps such as low-pressure sodium as well as fluorescents and cold cathode (including neon), which are treated separately (see pages 28 and 29)

- high-pressure discharge (or more commonly high-intensity discharge or HID), which includes metal halide, sodium and mercury lamps.

The main advantage of discharge lamps over incandescent lamps is their efficiency. The discharge process generally produces more lumens per watt *(ch 1)*; and with no single thin metal filament to burn out, the lamp itself lasts much longer. Because of their greater efficiency lower wattages are sufficient. Thus they run cooler than incandescent lamps with the same light output.

But, as with fluorescents, their longevity can be a disadvantage. While an ageing lamp may continue to emit light long after its useful life, energy efficiency and colour rendering will almost certainly have fallen to extremely poor levels. Therefore, for maximum efficiency, discharge lamps should be subject to a strictly observed replacement cycle, regardless of whether lamps have actually failed.

Discharge lamps are available in a wide range of wattages (from 4W to 2500W), efficiencies and colours, depending on type, and range from very poor through good to excellent colour rendering. In general, colour rendering is inferior to incandescent lamps. When you examine a typical discharge colour spectrum, light can be seen to be emitted in a series of spikes at different points on

the spectrum, rather than being distributed evenly across all the colours. There also tends to be a pronounced trade-off between efficiency and colour rendering: the more sophisticated, 'natural' looking discharge lamps, for example white SON, are less efficient than standard high-pressure sources; and the poorest colour rendering of all is offered by the most efficient type of lamp, low-pressure sodium.

Another important limitation with discharge lamps is burning position. Many sources only work at optimum efficiency when located in particular planes or positions (for example, horizontal, vertical – see Appendix 1 for code designations). Failure to take this into account can negate much of their efficiency advantage over incandescent sources. This can further restrict the applications of particular lamps.

Safety and disposal considerations are more critical, too. Gas at high pressure in a glass envelope is an intrinsically dangerous arrangement and demands additional user protection, such as safety glass shielding within the luminaire.

Some types of lamp emit harmful radiation; protective goggles may be required during the relamping process. When relamping extra care has to be taken to select the correct type of lamp from an often bewildering range of similar-looking sources.

Most discharge lamps use hazardous, toxic materials (for example mercury and sodium) in their construction, which makes disposal a critical process requiring strict procedures. It is illegal to dump old discharge lamps on a landfill site, for example. Manufacturers of these lamps, such as GE Lighting, issue detailed guidelines on the disposal of their products. Under the Environmental Protection Act 1991, specifiers who have not clearly briefed their clients on correct disposal could, in future, be liable to prosecution *(ch 8)*.

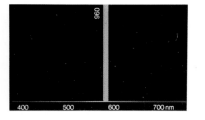

Spectral composition of a 'monochromatic' low-pressure sodium lamp showing how its light is concentrated in a very narrow band

Courtesy: Osram

Low-pressure sodium

Low-pressure sodium lamps (SOX) are the most efficient light sources available, offering up to 180 lumens per watt *(ch 1)*. However, all that light is in a very narrow orange-yellow range of the spectrum, around 589 nanometers and so very close to the eye's maximum response *(ch 1)*. The result is that SOX lamps offer an almost monochromatic light with no colour rendering. Because everything they illuminate appears bathed in orange light, they are not practical for interior use, except perhaps in service corridors or for security lighting. Even on most building exteriors, their colour rendering is likely to be unacceptable.

The main use of low-pressure sodium has traditionally been for street lighting and other large night-time outdoor areas, where colour is not a consideration. However, even here there has been a swing away from this form of lighting in many urban contexts *(ch 7)*, particularly because of the increased efficiency of other discharge lamps.

Low-pressure sodium lamps come in a range of wattages, from 18 watts to 200 watts. They require bulky control gear and their run-up time is ten minutes. However, when hot they can be re-struck within one minute.

Because of the sodium used in their construction, their disposal can be hazardous and needs to be carefully controlled.

Advantages

+ *long lamp-life*
+ *extremely efficient*
+ *almost instant re-strike*

Disadvantages

− *orange-yellow light quality makes them unsuitable for most interiors*
− *long warm-up time*
− *potentially hazardous in disposal*

High-intensity discharge lamps (HID)

HID covers a range of high-pressure discharge sources, which are either sodium or mercury based. The former is the most efficient (typically offering 60–120 lumens per watt) and tends to produce light which is orange-white; mercury-based sources are less efficient (around 70–80 lumens per watt) and emit a more blueish light. All these sources require control gear and, with special equipment, many of them can be dimmed to a limited extent. They are available in a wide range of shapes and wattages, typically from 35 watts (metal halide) up to 1500 watts.

High-pressure sodium (SON)

High-pressure sodium lamps, known by the generic acronym SON, work by striking an arc which excites sodium vapour at high pressure to emit light mainly in the orange-yellow area of the spectrum. The high pressure of the gas in the tube allows it to emit enough light from other parts of the spectrum to make colour discrimination possible. It is the most efficient white light source invented and has a long lamp-life. Its warm, orange-tinged light makes it suitable for closed, daylight-free environments such as swimming pools, gymnasia and civic centres. Regrettably, high-pressure sodium lamps have become ubiquitous in lighting exteriors *(ch 7)*.

Standard SON is not advisable in contexts where accurate colour rendering is important. More sophisticated variants are generally specified, which offer various qualities of 'whiteness' – for example Philips SONW, or white SON, which gives good colour rendering similar to a filament lamp. However, the 'whiter' the source, the less efficient it tends to be (for example, Philips SONW is only half as efficient as an ordinary high-pressure sodium lamp).

Midway between standard SON and SONW is the SONDL (high-pressure sodium deluxe) range of lamps. These have

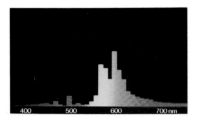

*Spectral composition of
a typical high-pressure
sodium lamp, showing
the distinct improve-
ment on its low-
pressure cousin*

Courtesy: Osram

a warm colour appearance and colour rendering roughly equivalent to a 'white' fluorescent lamp making them acceptable in commercial locations such as stationers, department stores and banks. They are easily interchangeable with standard SON, but with some loss of light output.

High-pressure mercury and metal halide lamps

High-pressure mercury lamps (designated by the letters MBF) work by striking an arc which excites mercury vapour to produce light mainly in the purple, green, yellow and ultraviolet parts of the spectrum. A further refinement has been the addition of a phosphorescent coating to the inside of the glass, which is excited by the otherwise redundant ultraviolet light.

MBF lamps are typically used to create a cool daylight effect and are often used in large-scale industrial interiors, such as warehouses and trading estates. However, in interior situations where colour rendering is important, ordinary mercury lamps with their blueish cast, are not appropriate. Neither are MBF lamps as efficient as SON sources, which is why they have fallen out of favour for many applications.

Attempts have been made to overcome these intrinsic problems by combining a mercury source with a built-in tungsten filament in the same glass envelope – the mercury blended lamp, as it is known. The filament acts as a ballast to the discharge tube and also increases emissions at the red end of the spectrum, to produce a more balanced light quality. However, they are little more efficient than incandescent sources though with a relatively long lamp-life.

One reason why standard MBF lamps have declined in popularity is the advent of the more sophisticated metal halide lamp, designated by the initials MBF(I). In these lamps, developed in the mid-1960s, metal halides have been added to the discharge

gas to widen the spectrum of emitted light, give the lamp better colour-rendering properties, and make it more efficient. However, metal halide lamps demand more complicated, expensive control gear both to ignite them and to maintain their stable operation. The double-ended versions are particularly intolerant of voltage variations, which can lead to intermittent operation and early lamp failure.

The halide additives are commercial secrets. In all cases amounts are so small and their effect so dramatic, that in mass production it is difficult to achieve identical colour temperatures, even from the same batch of lamps. Colour shifts of plus or minus ten per cent are accepted in commercial manufacture and these differences are noticeable in use.

Single-ended versions of the metal halide lamp are now available in wattages down to 35W. Because light is emitted only from the arc itself, rather than the entire fluorescent tube, they offer a concentrated point source . As a result, metal halide sources are smaller and optically more controllable than more diffuse mercury sources. They also offer a good substitute spectrum for daylight. Coupled with their efficiency and longevity, this generally makes them excellent for plant health lighting. In many atria and other indoor landscapes where natural light levels are low, metal halide downlighters will often be added to the lighting mix for this reason alone. Interiors lit by metal halide are effective when mixed with daylight, but can appear cold and sterile at night.

Ambient temperature variations have very little effect on HID sources, but they must be protected from rain, snow or other forms of moisture. They are generally of a robust construction and only severe vibration will effect them. In general they all suffer from the same drawbacks – some limitations on lamp orientation, more or less complex equipment for control and

*Spectral composition of
a typical high-pressure
mercury lamp, showing
its orange and blue bias*

Courtesy: Osram

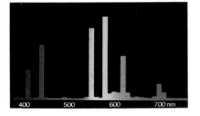

dimming, a lengthy strike-up period (three to seven minutes with metal halide) when first ignited from cold, and a delayed re-strike period after being turned off. Some modern HID sources allow instant re-strike, but at reduced levels of illumination.

One way to overcome this inconvenient time-lag is to combine a smaller incandescent source within the same fitting. Many luminaires on the market offer this option. The incandescent lamp gives a reduced level of illumination during the run-up or re-strike period, and then cuts out as the HID source comes into full operation. Many HID sources also exhibit visible flicker, so care should be taken when using them in workplaces where people may spend a long period in close proximity to such sources.

Finally, the materials on which HID lamps rely (sodium and mercury) are hazardous. So while they require less maintenance than incandescent sources, great care has to be taken in their disposal. The manufacturers' instructions should be followed carefully.

Metal halide lamps (above) require complex control gear. A typical control gear box (below) is often bulky and heavy
Courtesy: BLV and Hoffmeister

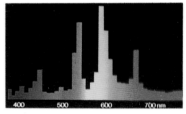

Spectral composition of a typical metal halide lamp. Note the more even balance of colours across the spectrum compared with standard high-pressure mercury or sodium
Courtesy: Osram

Advantages

+ *relatively energy efficient*
+ *long lamp-life*
+ *wide range of sizes, shapes and colours*
+ *fairly robust in operation*
+ *good daylight substitute (metal halide)*
+ *good to excellent colour rendering*

Disadvantages

- *higher capital investment cost*
- *bulky control gear*
- *warm-up and re-strike period required*
- *colour-rendering deficiencies with some types*
- *some limitations on dimming and precise optical control*
- *flicker, colour shift and considerable loss of efficiency with age*
- *toxic components demand high safety and disposal standards*

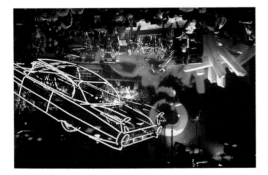

Cold cathode lamps can be custom-formed into many different expressive shapes and colours

Cold cathode

Cold cathode is a form of low-pressure lamp which relies on a high-voltage difference (typically 4000-5000V) between two electrodes to create the discharge, rather than heating them, hence the name. Two main types of ionizing gas can be used: argon, which produces light in the blue-green area of the spectrum, and neon gas, which produces red-orange light.

Available in a wide range of colours and diameters of tube (typically from 9 mm to 25 mm), cold cathode lighting is almost exclusively custom-made for use as feature and decorative lighting. Coloured versions can be bent into all kinds of shapes and are most often used as illuminated signage or as vivid display features to enhance retail or leisure environments. Other uses include edge lighting of buildings or interior architectural features, or hidden lighting behind coves. While the basic sources are relatively inexpensive to produce and do not involve large amounts of dangerous, toxic materials, the one-off nature of most installations makes for high initial investment costs. Cold cathode tubes are long-lasting, but require heavy, bulky control gear, and if a dimmer is used, this must be located close by.

There are two main drawbacks to cold cathode. First, light output is fairly low, with a pronounced degree of flicker at the cathodes, so they are not suitable as general ambient lighting sources. The white versions are only half as efficient as conventional fluorescent lamps. Second, because high voltages are involved, installation and safety demand special attention. Many safety officers require a dedicated firefighter's safety switch to be installed at the entrance to any premises where cold cathode is used.

However, a new addition to the market is a conventional wire-wound transformer designed to operate cold cathode tubes at less than 1000V. This could obviate the need for additional safety switches, but at the expense of 10 per cent loss in lamp performance.

This extreme disadvantage is gradually being overcome by the introduction of light-weight, electronic, high-frequency control gear. This innovative, expensive control equipment allows cold cathode to run at lower voltages (typically around 1000V) with much less flicker. However, to date they still have a number of limitations and do not have a proven track record for reliability.

Advantages

+   *wide range of colours and diameters*
+   *can be made up in virtually any shape or form*
+   *tubes are long-lasting*
+   *low surface temperatures*

Disadvantages

−   *custom-made systems involve high capital investment*
−   *careful planning required*
−   *high voltages require special installation and safety measures*
−   *heavy, bulky control gear*
−   *low light output*
−   *pronounced flicker*

A spectacular cold cathode installation, designed by artist Ron Haselden, which decorates the side wall of Nottingham Concert Hall (architects RHWL)

Courtesy: Ron Haselden

A typical large-scale exterior application of cold cathode – the Station Tower, Oslo

Luminaires and daylight
systems explained

In this chapter we look at the main types of luminaire available to the commercial specifier or designer and explain how they work, how they are commonly applied, and what their main advantages and disadvantages are. Within each section we showcase a representative selection of luminaires chosen for their historic importance or influence, their current popularity, their aesthetic appeal, or their innovative qualities.

Because of their limited suitability for the contract sector there are certain categories of luminaire which are deliberately under-represented (for example those utilizing simple GLS sources). For large-scale contract interiors most lighting has to be of a type that can be controlled. GLS tungsten sources are usually eschewed in the contract sector (except in some boardrooms, executive offices, and hotels) because of their relative inefficiency and short lamp-life. Consequently, several well-known, stylish luminaires have been omitted from our selection.

Downlighting

Ranks of fluorescent downlighters in the office (above) can produce a monotonous, bland effect. Directional downlighters, used as wallwashers, can create a dramatic and interesting interior with strong pools of light (above right), or illuminate walls unobtrusively and evenly (below right)

Downlighting is probably the most common form of lighting in commercial interiors. Despite its popularity, in many ways it is the one most fraught with problems. The principle is simple – the luminaire is located at a high point in a room, usually the ceiling, and light is directed down to the point where it is needed. What could be simpler and easier?

Without doubt direct downlighting can be the most efficient way of lighting a space, at least in terms of putting the maximum lumens per watt *(ch 1)* onto a horizontal surface, such as a desk or floor. As a result, crude cost-efficiency approaches to lighting, coupled with the long-established convention of wiring through a ceiling, have led to its widespread adoption in a range of lighting situations.

Ceiling-mounted downlighters (usually fluorescent) are popular in offices because they easily fit the customary modular grid of office designs. They can also be combined with air-conditioning systems.

Air-handling versions of downlighters have been developed, which obviate the need for separate grills or vents: recessed into the ceiling-void, lamp housings are connected directly to the air-conditioning ductwork. Warm air is taken out of the room through vents within the luminaire and in some versions fresh air is returned via an air-inlet slot around the reflector.

The popularity of downlighting has spun off a massive range of luminaires for the purpose: there is an almost infinite range of fittings available, in combination with every conceivable type of source.

Downlighters can be discreet or highly decorative; they can be suspended,

surface-mounted or recessed into the ceiling; and they can incorporate diffusers, reflectors colour effects, and so on. Downlighters can illuminate a large area or focus a narrow beam onto a small zone or even work indirectly, by gently washing side walls with light. Thanks to this adaptability, fixtures of the same standard appearance can be made to create a range of different effects.

Despite the many advantages of efficiency and flexibility which downlighters offer, by their very nature their use can easily result in one major

*Low-brightness
downlighters, heavily
louvred (above) have
often been the con-
ventional solution for
VDT-intense workplaces*
Courtesy: Zumtobel

problem – glare *(ch 1)*. Almost
inevitably, the light source is
going to be visible. Someone,
somewhere in the room will
be affected, if not directly, then
by reflection from one of the
glossy surfaces often used in
commercial interiors.

This unfortunate characteristic
has been doubly accentuated
with the arrival of VDT-based
office technology. Downlighting
can cause glare on computer
screens, particularly if the light
distribution is badly planned.
Attempts to obviate the
problem have spawned a
gamut of devices, such as
special reflectors, louvres and
diffusers to restrict both the
angle of incidence of light falling
on vertical surfaces and its
intensity.

There are recommended
restrictions on the angles of
light distribution to avoid glare
(ch 1). But such methods of
light control can negate the
original efficiency advantage of
downlighters, which is often the

main reason for their specification in the first place.

Uncontrolled overall downlighting can produce a very
flat, featureless, depressing
ambience. Also, if downlighters
are screened with louvres and
reflectors (to avoid screen glare,
for example) and used as the
sole source of illumination, a
'dark cave' effect may be
created. This involves dark
ceilings, over-lit horizontal
surfaces, poor lighting of
vertical surfaces and oppres-
sively heavy shadows on faces,
for example.

Grid-mounted downlighters
used *en masse* can lead to a
monotonous dotted ceiling
effect; while too widely spaced
downlighters (a common
mistake) can lead to patchy,
uneven light distribution.

The flexibility and versatility of
downlighters can have negative
consequences, too. With the
massive range of sources
available, it is easy to end up

*Two standard variants
of the fluorescent
downlighter: the
recessed luminaire
with a prismatic panel
(above left) and the
ceiling-mounted
luminaire with low-
brightness louvre (left)*
Courtesy: Philips Lighting

Recessed low-voltage downlighters (above) are increasingly popular in utility areas. However, ease of maintenance must be planned for

Courtesy: Marlin

Downlighting over pools, or other spaces which give problems of access, should be maintained and re-lamped from above

Courtesy: iGuzzini

with many different lamps in use, which can be difficult for the future maintenance of an installation. For example, low-energy compact fluorescent lamps *(ch 2)* are often retro-fitted in downlighters designed to take reflector lamps *(ch 2)*. Unless correctly applied, there can be a disproportionate loss in illumination.

The location of downlighters has to be carefully thought through. Ceiling-mounted downlighters located in inaccessibly high spaces or large interior volumes (for example over a swimming pool) are likely to lead to severe maintenance problems. A solution, if possible, would be an arrangement where the luminaires can be accessed for cleaning and re-lamping from above.

Advantages

+ *simplest, most efficient method of lighting a space*
+ *almost infinitely flexible range of luminaires and lamp combinations*
+ *standard versions can perform a range of effects*
+ *can easily fit the modern office ceiling-grid*

Disadvantages

− *glare on VDT screens and other shiny surfaces*
− *poor vertical illumination*
− *used exclusively, can contribute to bland, uninteresting interiors, or the 'dark cave' effect*
− *wide range of sources can lead to misapplication or maintenance problems*
− *monotonous effect when used in rows on ceilings*
− *potential maintenance problems if located in high spaces*

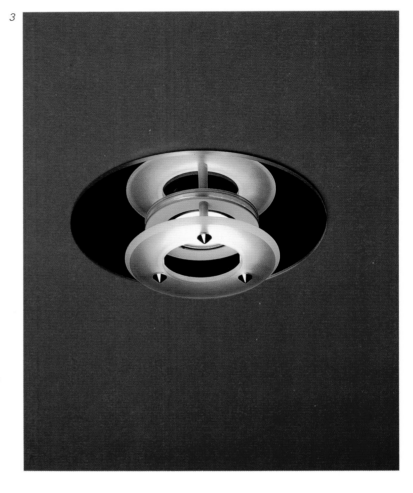

1

2

1 and 2: Illuma's D153X/C recessed, adjustable low-voltage downlighter incorporates a movable slot to give some directional capability, while the D111X makes a feature of its faceted dichroic reflector

3 and 5: Marlin's Matrix low-voltage downlighter range offers coloured diffusing bezels, or bold decorative trimmings

4: For different styles of interior, Artemide's Systema range of low-voltage downlighters offers mounting rings in various finishes

3

4

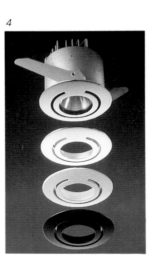

5

6

7

8

9

6 and 7: For spaces with high ceilings, suspended trough downlighters such as these two versions from Zon, distributed by Reggiani, may provide a solution

8: RZB's tiltable, semi-recessed metal halide projector, suitable for floodlighting or wall washing, distributed by BBI Lighting

9: Zon's wormlike Flex wall-mounted downlighter uses a tungsten halogen source and can be adjusted easily

10: The Laser series from iGuzzini offers a wide range of decorative or technical effects for low-voltage downlighters

11: The Downspot downlighter fitting from Reggiani offers a rotational capability for wallwashing or precise highlighting

10

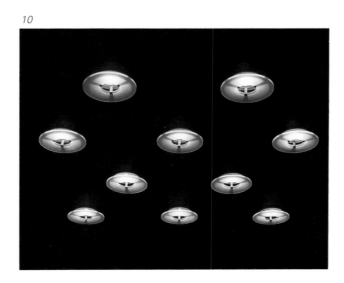

11

12

13

14

15

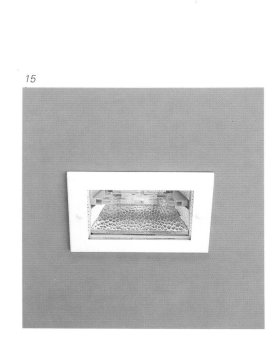

16

12: Erco's adjustable, recessed luminaires, showing the variable angles that can be achieved

13: Staff's fixed recessed range, with frosted glass diffusing rings

14: Semi-recessed RZB eyeball from BBI Lighting

15: Rectangular recessed flood, using an HID source, from Hitech

16: Wall-mounted tubular down-lighter/uplighter combination, with tungsten halogen sources; part of the Futimis Kingsprofile range

17: A simple recessed low-voltage down-lighter from Illuma showing the normally hidden housing

18: A ceiling-mounted fluorescent unit, with diffusing cover, from Philips

17

18

Uplighting

One of the best-known uplighting schemes, on London Underground, dates from the 1930s

The principle of uplighting is simple. Light is directed upwards onto walls and ceiling from a fitting, mounted above eye level, which conceals or screens the light source itself. Most uplighters give a wide symmetrical light distribution; the overall result is that light is softened and diffused, thus theoretically avoiding veiling reflections and glare often associated with many forms of downlighter (see pages 32–34).

Uplighters have been around since the 1920s and 1930s, when they were commonly used in hotels. Fitted with a concealed GLS tungsten source *(ch 2)* in a crude reflector, they provided an effective way of dramatically highlighting decorative interior features such as cornices or Art Deco murals. One of the best-known examples of uplighting from this period comes from London Underground, then at the forefront of corporate and interior design. Rows of distinctive brass fittings were mounted between the escalators to light the curved ceiling above. Updated with more modern sources, many of these are still in use. As new, more efficient light sources, such as fluorescent lamps *(ch 2)*, were developed they proved less appropriate for uplighter use. In addition, during the austere years during and after World War II, rooms ceased to be built on a grand scale where uplighting could be used to best effect. Hampered by their limited applications, uplighters fell out of favour for many years. For one thing, uplighting alone made it difficult to obtain the higher light levels that post-war workplaces and leisure facilities called for. Because they rely on reflected light, uplighters which used the obligatory GLS source were inevitably less efficient. Significant increases in light output demanded proportionately higher wattages, a trade-off which was unpopular with cost-sensitive managements. In workplaces such as

Uplighting in the workplace: free-standing uplighter (above) from Hitech Lighting; ceiling-suspended uplighters – a tailor-made SON and metal halide scheme for a dealing room (top left); iGuzzini's Lingotto range (below right); uplighters integrated into the furniture – a custom-made installation (top right) by Electrolite

offices the more efficient, if less aesthetically pleasing, option of rows of bare, ceiling-mounted fluorescent battens was normally preferred.

There has been a fresh burst of interest in re-applying the principle of uplighting to interior spaces. The office, in particular, has benefited; the anti-glare requirements of VDT-based technology have given this particular form of indirect lighting a new lease of life: The increased flexibility and versatility of uplighters, in terms of size, form and lamp type, have helped too. Today's models can incorporate several types of

lighting source in wattages from 100W to 2.5KW, but most commercial versions use HID high-pressure sodium *(ch 2)* or metal halide *(ch 2)*. These sources necessitate some form of control gear and are often prone to flicker, a distracting fault accentuated by large uplit ceilings. For reasons of efficiency and heat gain, halogen-sourced uplighting is not generally suitable for large-scale commercial interiors.

Uplighters can come in various forms: free-standing or wall-mounted versions are most common, but suspended pendants or troughs are also available. Free-standing versions have become popular because of their portability. They can be placed directly where they are needed, which is useful in rapidly changing office set-ups, and they combine well with task lighting (see pages 46-47). They involve no structural wiring via ceilings or walls, and so can be easily re-located to new offices when a company moves. There

may also be tax advantages: classed as furniture, any VAT paid on them is reclaimable.

Offset against this is the initial high purchase cost and the fact that they can be physically obtrusive if used as a major source of light in deep-plan spaces. They can also present a continuous wire-management problem where power outlets are poorly located.

On the other hand, fixed uplighting, concealed behind cornices, is an increasingly favoured and less obtrusive option, architecture permitting. The same discreet effect can be achieved by integrating

Hidden uplighting from behind a cornice (left) can be used to define a space or emphasize a ceiling. To minimize the dark silhouette of the uplighter body, some luminaires (eg from Targetti, below left) allow a small element of downlight

Uplighting a ceiling too closely (below) can result in ugly 'hot spots'

uplighters directly into tall pieces of furniture. Another option is the combination luminaire. This offers an uplit effect with a smaller percentage of downlight often from slots or a diffused panel on the underside of the reflector dish. As well as achieving an additional decorative effect, the downlighter element can help soften the dark shadowed outline of the luminaire body.

While the primary light source and type of luminaire reflector are important, the quality and intensity of the light obtained are dependent on the proximity, colour, material and texture of the surfaces off which the light is bounced. These reflectance *(ch 1)* properties are critical. White, non-absorbent surfaces maximize reflectance, while dark non-reflective surfaces minimize the effect of up-lighting. However, ceilings or walls which are highly specular (for example chromed finishes) will show ugly glare spots. Even an optimum ceiling finish will

produce hot spots if it is too close to the uplighter source. So uplighters are generally unsuitable for interiors with ceilings below 2.5 metres. The optimum floor-to-ceiling height is between 2.5 and 3.5 metres.

Problems of direct glare can also arise when uplighters are used in spaces comprising two levels (ie offices with mezzanine floors or open-plan stairs). While effective from ground level, there is nothing more ugly than a row of dazzling uplighter dishes seen from above.

In addition to its potential low-glare capability in VDT-dense workplaces, uplighting can be employed in other ways. Throwing light upwards can help 'raise' a ceiling or enhance the architectural structure or interior design features; or it may be used to boost local ambient light levels. Like all forms of lighting, it is rarely sufficient used in isolation and should be complemented by other forms of task lighting (see

At the Grand Theatre
in Clapham, London
(right) architects
Madigan & Donald
created a starkly
dramatic effect by
using uplighters
recessed into the floor.
Below, uplighting used
to emphasize the
architectural structure
of a church
Courtesy: Hitech Lighting

pages 46–47) or highlighting.
While uplighting can be used
as the principal overall lighting
component, an evenly uplit
space can be depressingly
bland, and at worst resemble
a flat, overcast sky.

Advantages

+ *produces little glare or veiling
  reflection, particularly in VDT-
  intense environments*
+ *wide range of luminaire types
  and styles*
+ *moderate range of light
  sources*
+ *can be integrated into the
  architecture or furniture*
+ *free-standing versions are
  highly portable and adjustable*
+ *good for creating soft ambient
  light or boosting local light
  levels*
+ *easy installation and
  maintenance*

Disadvantages

– *sources generally restricted
  to HID lamps in commercial
  luminaires, which can give
  flicker and colour-shift
  problems*
– *inefficient with unsuitable
  ceiling or wall finishes*
– *free-standing versions are
  expensive, potentially obtrusive and offer problematic
  wire management*
– *wrong applications can lead
  to 'hot spots' on ceilings*
– *can be unsuitable for split-
  level environments*
– *used on their own, can
  produce a flat, bland effect*

Throwing light up onto
fabric 'sails' at the
Greenpeace offices in
London (left) created a
soft, ambient lighting
effect
Photo: Michael Evans

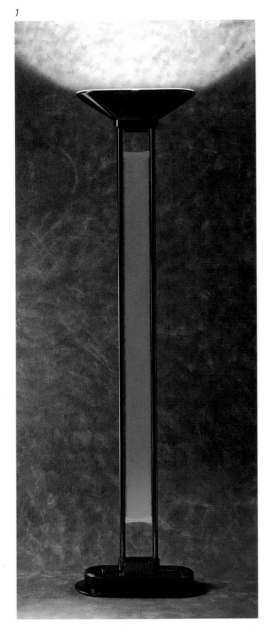

1

2

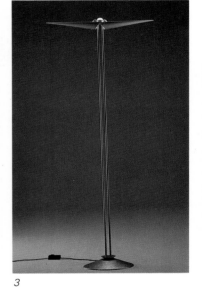

3

4

5

1: One of Orgatech's range from Hitech Lighting, the free-standing Antenna uplighter. The central panel can be used for graphics and signage

2 and 3: Two chic, free-standing models from Quattrifolio, designed by Guiseppe Linardi – Felux and Gabbiano – which use linear tungsten halogen sources

4: Thorn Lighting's Legato uplighter with either a compact fluorescent or metal halide source. The control gear is in the base

5: An ingenious solution for large-scale spaces, Concord's 2.5-metre high Hazel Duct, with its own reflector

6: Santiago Calatrava's expressive standard uplighter, Montjuic, by Artemide

7: Marlin's Capo uplighter has an adjustable head and variable height stem

8: Zon's Fata Morgana has two linear tungsten halogen sources; one uplights the integral reflector, the other illuminates the ceiling

9: King & Miranda's simple classic standard with sand-blasted glass diffusing head – Jill by Arteluce

10

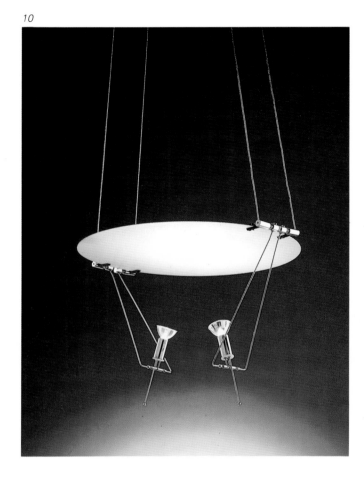

10: An integral reflector uplighter: Garcia Garay's Altair, distributed by Into Lighting

11: Concord's Quill uplighter by RSCG Conran Design, which uses a variety of discharge sources

12 and 13: Luxo's cornice uplighting strip system, with coloured trim, can be ordered to length

14: The Elliptipar, from Marlin, has an asymmetric reflector which allows even uplighting of a large ceiling or wall

15: Reggiani's wall-mounted Spacelight with HID source makes a powerful architectural statement

11

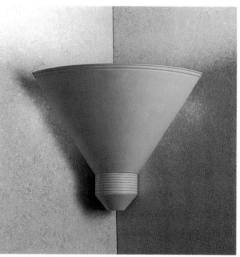

12

13

14

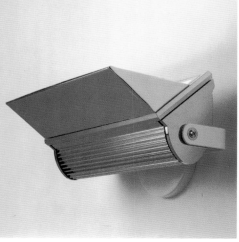

15

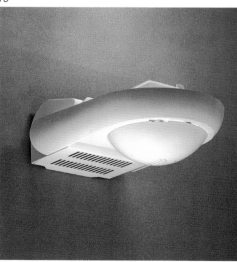

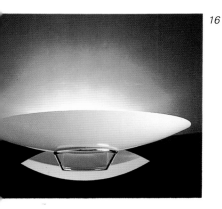

16

16: The elegant Gino model from Zon, with slender wall-mounted reflector bowl

17: An angular uplighter with fluorescent wall-strip detail, part of the Bofill range from Light, distributed by Futimis

18: The Kreon range is a series of recessed light boxes which can be used as uplighters or feature lighting

18

17

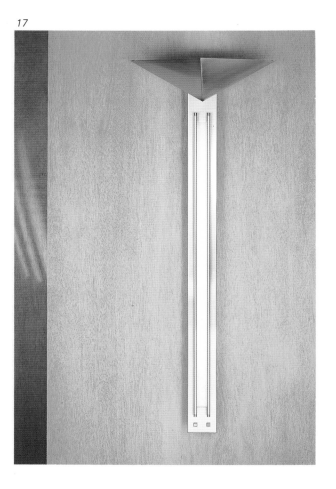

19: Garcia Garay's birdlike wall-mounted uplighter Fenix, distributed by Into Lighting

20: Cantilevered wall-mounted version of Artemide's Zen design with integral double reflector

20

19

Task lighting

Task lighting is local lighting providing illumination directly onto a working area or task. It is almost always used in conjunction with other forms of ambient lighting in the commercial working environment, although in small-scale or domestic workplaces some people prefer the cocoon-like concentration that dedicated task lights can offer.

Modern task lights come with a wide range of light sources, but most commonly they are low-voltage tungsten halogen *(ch 2)*, GLS *(ch 2)* or compact fluorescent *(ch 2)*. With the emphasis on personal controllability, they often incorporate local switches and in the case of low-voltage versions, dimmers. With this form of lighting the right quantity of light can be directed exactly where the user wants it. Task lighting is available in a variety of forms, ranging from free-standing versions to those that are desk- or wall-mounted, as well as those integrated into overhead

storage units. There is a very wide range of styles to fit any interior.

Because of their small scale and personal, user-friendly qualities, task lights, particularly desktop versions, have furnished several timeless design classics: the Anglepoise, for example, dating from the 1930s, and Richard Sapper's Tizio lamp for Artemide, designed in 1971.

Task lights can be fixed in terms of angle and position (for example small batten fluorescents mounted under the lip of a cupboard or bookshelf), but such an approach negates one of task lighting's most important features – personal controllability and adjustability. This degree of control offers considerable psychological benefits: complaints about lighting schemes tend to be rare in situations that permit personal control. Such control is particularly important for older staff who may require

Task lighting has produced several design classics, from the original Anglepoise (left), used by Lloyd George, to Artemide's 1971 Tizio (below), and King & Miranda's witty Donald for Arteluce (bottom)

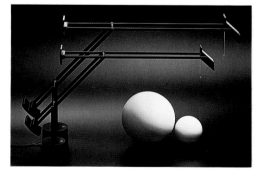

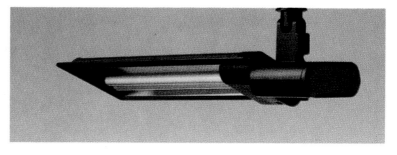

Task lighting used in conjunction with an uplighter (left) is an increasingly favoured solution, as is the use of the energy-saving compact fluorescent task light (below)

higher lux levels for efficient working than their younger colleagues. In exceptional working situations (for example lathe operation or intricate component assembly) task lights are the most practical way of boosting light locally to unusually high levels.

The widespread use of dedicated task lighting allows overall lower ambient light levels within a space, which can save energy. The portability of task lighting is also important; when desks are re-configured, the luminaires (either built-in or free-standing) can move too.

In general, task lighting should not be used on its own. A balanced combination of individual task lights with lower levels of ambient lighting (possibly from ceiling-mounted fluorescents) can be the most successful form of workplace lighting. This mix also helps to avoid the overall blandness that a single type of lighting produces.

There are disadvantages to task lighting. To equip a workplace with task lights, in addition to the general ambient lighting, requires additional capital investment. And, if task lights are added over a period of time, as they are needed, an office can end up with a plethora of models, which may be neither aesthetically appealing nor easy to maintain.

Task lighting entails a high number of individual power outlets or trailing leads, which can create a safety hazard. Another danger is the hot tungsten halogen lamp, which, although not in compliance with product safety standards, is often unprotected in many modern, stylish desklights. Such forms of lighting are definitely not recommended for environments where children may be present.

Task lights can be space hungry. Free-standing versions on desks, whilst convenient, occupy valuable working space.

And one person's well-positioned task light can be a source of glare or irritation for a colleague. In compact office environments, the controllability and user-friendliness of task lighting can be tested to its limits.

Advantages

+ highly controllable and user-friendly
+ energy-saving: can entail lower overall ambient light levels
+ a wide range of sources and models
+ highly portable and adjustable
+ can be used to create high local light levels, where necessary

Disadvantages

− expensive, in terms of capital investment
− requires multiple power outlets
− plethora of models can lead to problems of aesthetic coherence, and maintenance
− desk versions can be space hungry
− poor adjustment can lead to irritation for fellow workers

Free-standing desktop task lights (above) can be space hungry – the use of edge-mounted clamps (left) is more space efficient

Courtesy: Concord, Philips, Arteluce

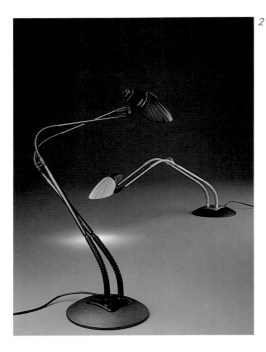

1: Flexible Pierino 'soft-stemmed' task lights from Quattrifolio

2: Quattrifolio's Tango range with sinuous twistable arms

3: iGuzzini's canti-levered model Ala

4: David Morgan's prize-winning Burlington, which uses a movable reflector in a 'bell jar' housing

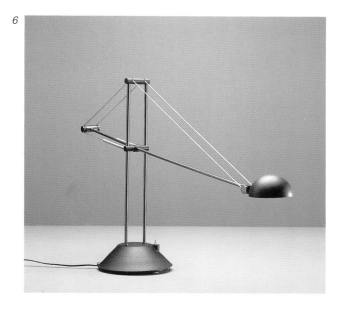

5: Hitech's Cone
task light

6: The unmistakable
crane-like form of Lev,
by Quattrifolio

7: Philippe Starck's Ara
lamp for Flos – already
a design icon

8: Luxo's Falcon
model, a simple
functional solution

9 and 10: Two variants
of the task light from
Arteluce – Ezio
Didone's Desk model
and the 612-613 with
elegant timber arms

Spotlighting

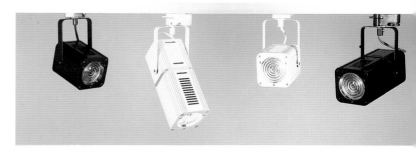

Spotlighting can be
used to create distinct
dramatic areas of
illumination as in the
SKA restaurant in
Zürich (above)

Courtesy: Erco

The spotlight is a form of
lighting where the light beam is
controlled in a precise manner,
often onto a relatively small
area. Spotlights have long been
used for dramatic effect in the
theatre to focus the audience's
attention. The same types of
technique are now commonly
applied in the commercial
sector; many of the spotlights in
use either copy the principles of
those found in the theatre, or
are standard theatre models
used without modification.

Spotlighting in commercial
interiors has only really
developed since the 1960s,
together with the rise in
popularity of track lighting
systems (see pages 56–58),
which gave designers the ability
to move spotlights around and

to reposition them easily.
Because of their narrow beams,
precise focusing is crucial when
using spotlighting.

There is a considerable range of
lamp types, lenses, filters and
reflectors available; gobos are
often used to create illuminated
shapes and images on floors
and walls. But for reasons of
precise optical control, most
spotlights still come with
incandescent (ch 2) sources,
which for commercial applications have a short lamp-life
and can be relatively inefficient
in energy terms.

As well as the common track-
mounted versions, spotlights
can also be mounted directly
onto walls, ceilings or floors.
In terms of power they range

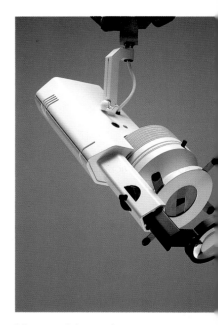

Many spotlights on the
market are derived
from theatre lighting
technology, as in these
luminaires by Micro-
lights (top). The range
of accessories for
spotlights is expanding;
the Concord Control
Spot (above) is a typical
example. It incorpor-
ates a framing head,
gobo holder, gel holder
and adjustable iris
head. Future
generations of
spotlights will offer
remote electronic
adjustability.
Hoffmeister's RC range
(below left) is one of
the first systems
available

Dramatic highlighting and good colour rendering (below left) are two advantages of tungsten halogen spotlights. Illuminated patterns or graphics can also be added (right) using gobo heads

from 20W to 1000W, although larger versions are available for specialized applications. The forms of luminaire vary. They are available in a variety of shapes, colours and sizes, from minimal bare lamp versions, through hi-tech to brass Victorian models. For situations where they are difficult to access, or where there are moving exhibits, motorized remote control versions can be used.

The most common interior applications for spotlighting are art galleries, museums, leisure complexes and retail environments. Spotlights are invaluable wherever the designer or architect wants to highlight features or focus a viewer's attention on an exhibit, a point-of-sale or product display, for example. Highlighting, the creation of localized, intense pools of bright light contrasting with darker surroundings, also helps create visual interest in a scheme. While highlights can be used on their own for dramatic effects in leisure environments (discos, for example), they are most often used in combination with ambient and area lighting.

One advantage of spotlighting is its flexibility. In retail interiors, for example, spotlights can be totally reconfigured with ease to create a new display effect. But this flexibility has its downside. Spotlights can easily become misaligned or go out of focus if they are not well maintained; and badly angled spots can

cause extreme glare, backlighting or unwelcome shadows. It is also very easy to retro-fit the wrong lamps, so any spotlighting scheme demands a high level of maintenance by a well-trained team. Without such service back-up, schemes using extensive spotlighting will soon deteriorate, an issue that designers should think seriously about before specifying such lighting.

Sparkle or glare? Narrow-beam spot- lights can be easily misaligned, leading to user glare and discomfort (above)

Advantages

+ *dramatic effects for highlighting or focusing attention*
+ *flexible and easy to reconfigure*
+ *high degree of control*
+ *wide range of fittings and accessories*
+ *choice of styles to suit all interiors*

Disadvantages

− *easily misaligned or put out of focus*
− *common incandescent versions are relatively expensive to run*
− *wide range of lamps often leads to incorrect retro-fitting*
− *demand high level of informed maintenance*

1

2

3

4

1: Microlights Microscoop range: theatre-type low-voltage spotlights with integral or remote transformers

2: Marlin Projex: its modular capability offers high flexibility

3: Dramatic and functional – Targetti's Toh spotlight with its distinctive dichroic reflector makes a strong design statement

4: The Futimis Strip low-voltage system makes a feature of the transformer and can take up to four 50W spotlights

5: Beating glare: the Franz Sill 710 projector spot with integral louvre to limit sideways spill light

6: Reggiani Lighting's Genesi spotlight offers a soft, rounded form to interior lighting

5

6

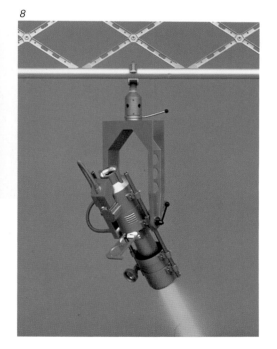

7: Track- or ceiling-mounted Thorn Lighting's Lightstream 50 low-voltage spotlights come with barn door or diffuser attachments

8: Erco's Emanon range of spotlights designed by Roy Fleetwood. This is one of the most sophisticated and expensive spotlights available

9: Staff's Solartron spotlight incorporates an integral transformer in a compact package

10: Hoffmeister's Spaceline luminaire showing the comprehensive range of lighting heads that can be clipped on to the standard base

11: Appropriate for close-up display spotlighting, Microlights Microscoop luminaire

14

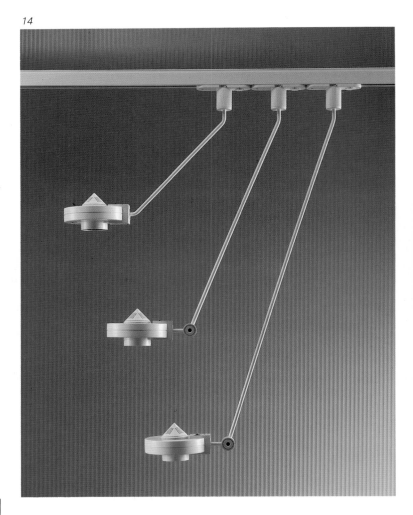

12: Light Project's Magnus spotlights, designed by Maurice Broughton with LDP, attach to metal surfaces with a magnetic base

13: PAR 38 lamps are still used for spotlighting, as in the Duo 140 model from Staff Lighting

14: The elegant form of the Discus spotlight family from Staff Lighting

15: With a prominent baffle to minimize glare, and a hinged body, Thorn Lighting's Lightstream Aria spotlight

16

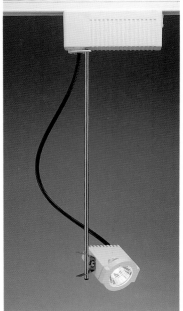

16: The Illuma THP443X rod-mounted low-voltage dichroic spotlight, powered through a box-like transformer on a 240V mains track

17: The Sunlight range of luminaires from Reggiani is an elegantly designed family for many spotlighting requirements

12

13

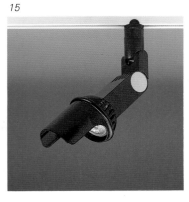

15

17

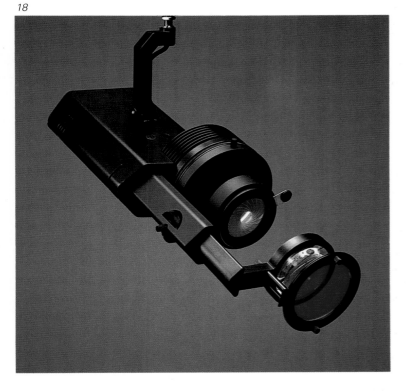

18

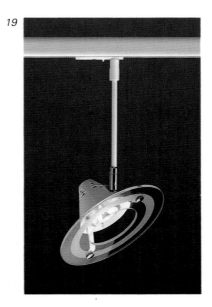

19

18: Robert Heritage's Control Spot range for Concord is the latest generation of highly adaptable accent and projection luminaires

19: Hitech Lighting's Cone spot low-voltage spotlight here fitted with a decorative diffuser ring

20: The Eclipse series designed by Mario Bellini for Erco has been hugely influential, spawning a host of low-cost alternatives

21: Solzi Luce's Sisterna range, distributed by GFC, includes stylish surface-mounted luminaires with a wide selection of form and detail

20

22

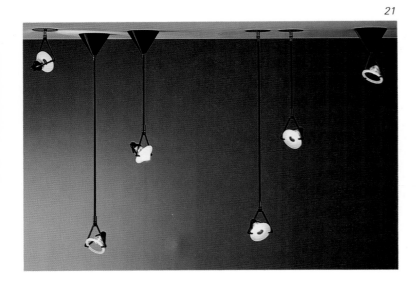

21

22: Packing more punch than low-voltage tungsten, Franz Sill's 700 projectors use a range of metal halide sources

23: Offering two sources on one extension, Hitech Lighting's bi-pendant Cone spot with its popular space-age details

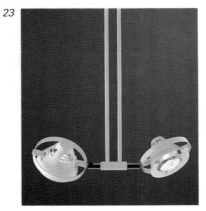

23

Track lighting systems

Track-mounted lighting is a popular and well-used lighting system with many models to choose from. In essence the track combines a convenient electrical distribution system, where the current, mains or low voltage, runs in an insulated metal sheath inside a supporting metal structure. Using a compatible lamp connector, the current is potentially accessible at any point on the track; lamps can be positioned where required. Safety devices ensure that the live track cannot be touched accidentally.

Track lighting is very flexible. As spotlights are not integral to the track, a combination of different types of lamp can be positioned on one track. Tracks are available in both mains and low-voltage *(ch 2)* versions. There are other advantages, too, such as ease of electrical installation. Because the circuit is completed within the track, power need be fed in at one end only; tracks are available

in single- or multi-circuited versions, so individual lamps or sets of lamps can be controlled independently. Ease of installation is ensured by the fact that most tracks can be cut to length on site. Most commonly, tracks are straight, but several companies produce curved or angled versions.

Tracks are most often installed directly onto ceilings or walls. Where this is too obtrusive, the track itself can be installed flush with the surface or recessed within the wall so only the lamps protrude. This can be an expensive and difficult procedure. Alternatively, where ceilings are too high or where the space requires uplighters (pages 38–41) or spotlights

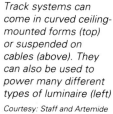

Track systems can come in curved ceiling-mounted forms (top) or suspended on cables (above). They can also be used to power many different types of luminaire (left)
Courtesy: Staff and Artemide

(pages 50–51) to be directed back at the ceiling, tracks may be suspended on rods or cables.

Sophisticated versions of the track system have taken this capability even further, so what was originally a functional lighting system can now be used to make a design statement. Track structures can be specified in different colours, to complement an interior or to highlight their presence. But over the lifespan of a lighting system, such colour choices can look dated, which is why neutral colours are usually chosen.

Alternatively, one or even two tiers of lighting can be hung off one track. Even more structural systems, such as Erco's Gantry and Axis, take the track system further into the realms of architecture. Here, luminaires are carried on an elaborate, modular lattice of steel members which can also serve as supports for canopies or exhibition stands. However, the cost of these heavyweight structural track systems, particularly if specified on a large scale, can be considerable. Simpler low-voltage rod or wire systems are becoming increasingly popular.

With the exception of recessed versions, most track systems are, by their nature, obtrusive, which is why in more bland, contemporary interiors, they can often be used to add design texture and focus to a space. Of course, track systems are not appropriate for all interiors. Their dominant linear quality is likely to conflict with certain types of decor – highly ornate historic interiors, for example.

Track lighting has been developed in a range of structural forms; for example Optelma's lightweight wall-mounted Mono (above left); Concord's Infinite (far left); Erco's Axis (above right) for exhibition use; and the same company's Gantry system (left)

Most track lighting systems are mounted horizontally; when suspended vertically (above) they can be used for sidelighting objects

Courtesy: GFC Lighting

Unless care is taken to calculate the total ampage track systems (especially low-voltage) are easy to overload, as more and more spotlights are added over time. Until recently, most companies' tracks and lamps were incompatible with each other, so commitment to a system meant tying into one particular manufacturer. Now, several leading European manufacturers, including Erco, iGuzzini, Hoffmeister, and Staff, have reached agreement on a standard 'Euro-track', which means their tracks and fittings ought to be interchangeable. Finally, the very flexibility of the track system can lead to problems. With masses of spotlights or small floodlights overhead, all of them able to swivel and turn at virtually any angle, it is difficult to avoid some glare at ground level. With units mounted high up on a wall or ceiling, adjustment and maintenance can pose a logistical problem.

Advantages

+ *relatively easy to install*
+ *wide range of track forms and fittings*
+ *flexible: allows for the combination of lamps of different types*
+ *high design capability, particularly modern versions*
+ *safe*

Disadvantages

− *incompatible with some interior styles*
− *large degree of incompatibility between systems*
− *misaligned lamps can cause glare*
− *initial equipment costs can be high*

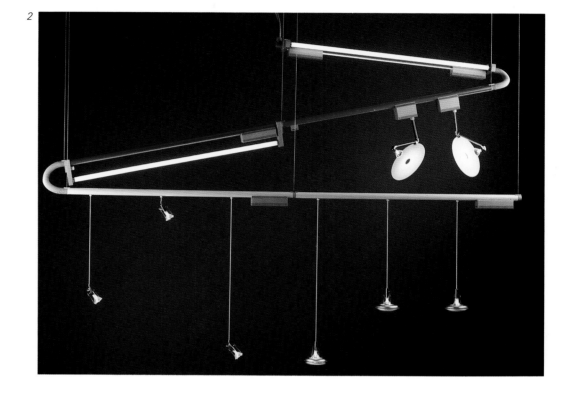

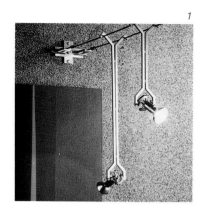

1: Angular, informal struts on wires mark out the Light Cable system from Futimis

2: Low-voltage track lighting systems usually aim for a minimal, hi-tech presence as in the Flos Flight range

3: The Trolli wire system from Reggiani, with distinctive flying-saucer accessory

4: Geometric Krokomobil system from Bruck, distributed by BBI

5

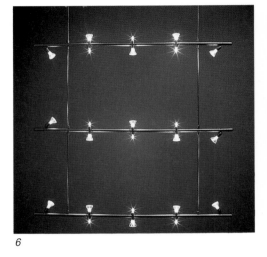

6

7

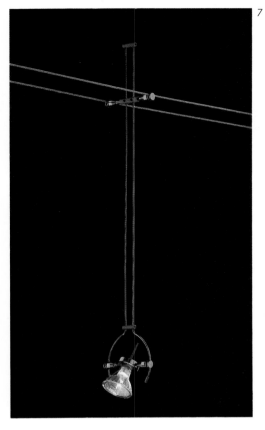

8

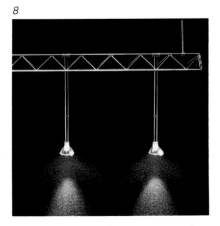

9

*5: The free-floating
Filigrano range from
Staff*

*6: The Axis Euclid
system allows the
mixing of spots and
decorative lighting*

*7 and 13: Hitech's Hi-
wire, one of the most
stripped-down versions
of low-voltage systems*

*8: Track lighting
systems can be used
to make an architec-
tural statement, as in
Targetti's semi-gantry
system*

*9: Optelma's Yuma
range – a popular
model which has now
made its appearance
in domestic lighting*

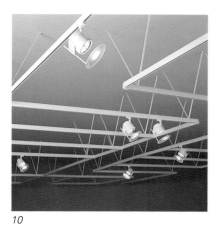

10

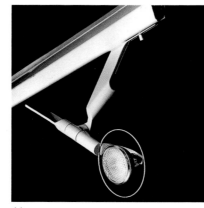

11

*10: iGuzzini's Lighting
Tracks used here to
form a strong ceiling
grid*

*11: Richard Sapper's
Argo system for
Artemide combines a
streamlined, modernist
form with a more con-
ventional, solid track*

*12: Concord's Infinite,
designed by Terence
Woodgate, can be built
up in structural layers*

12

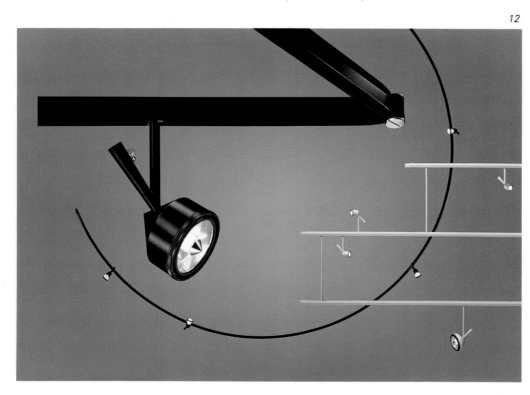

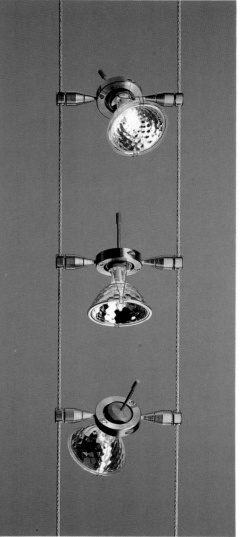

13

Linear lighting systems

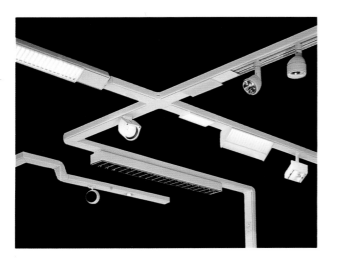

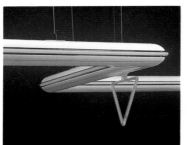

Zumtobel linear lighting (top) showing the variety of possible sources. By adding cold cathode (eg Concord's system, above), linear lighting can be used decoratively or functionally. Minimal fixings are required in a period interior (right)

Linear lighting systems were developed by European lighting companies in the 1960s and 1970s. Many offer considerable versatility and even today several companies are investing heavily in new versions.

Linear lighting systems are recognizable by their continuous tubular form (most often an aluminium extrusion) which is usually suspended from the ceiling (though it can be surface-mounted or recessed).

The linear structure carries the necessary electrical and lighting components – wiring, lamps, control gear, louvres, reflectors even illuminated signage and alarm systems – either within the body, or housed on the outside. With some versions it is possible to incorporate ambient fluorescent *(ch 2)* downlights (see pages 32–34), tungsten halogen *(ch 2)* spotlights, and even metal halide *(ch 2)* uplights (see pages 38–41), within the same structure. More recently,

systems have been adapted to carry both communications and data cables.

Linear systems come in myriad shapes and sizes. While most original versions had a circular profile, square, oblong and wing-like, aerofoil versions are now available. Linear systems are extremely adaptable; many tubes can be cut to length on site and can be made to change direction, using flexible rubber, plastic or mitred joints. Because they are self-contained, linear systems can negate the need for a suspended ceiling and therefore may be used in most types of building. They are a particularly effective way of incorporating modern lighting into a period building. Since they usually require only one power feed and a limited number of suspension fixings, there is minimal interference with the building fabric.

The essential linear quality of this form of lighting can also serve as an effective directional

device to channel people down particular routes. The addition of colour can turn them into a decorative feature, while they can also be used to delineate interior spaces, such as display areas on exhibition stands.

Linear lighting has several disadvantages which must be considered. Initial equipment costs can be high and installation can be complicated. In design terms their strong linear statement is inevitably obtrusive, even overwhelming, while coloured versions can date rapidly. In addition, if specifiers rely on standard modular components, this can be limiting. The more flexible, fully comprehensive ranges are commensurately more expensive. Tubular systems, especially the small discreet versions, can also be inefficient in terms of light output, due to their limited reflector sizes.

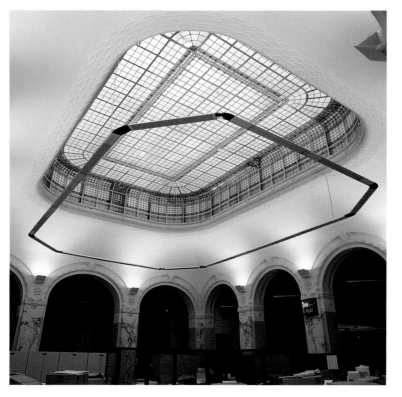

Three distinct strategies for linear lighting which show its adaptability: a closed 'loop' delineating the space and echoing the form of the laylight (above); a centrally located strip used as indirect lighting from a vaulted ceiling (top); and a zigzag formation used as an ambient light source (right)

Advantages

+ *versatile, self-contained and multi-purpose*
+ *many components and forms available*
+ *require single power feed and few fixings*
+ *linear structure makes a strong design statement*
+ *can serve as a directional device or as a boundary feature*

Disadvantages

– *complicated to install*
– *strong linear form can be obtrusive*
– *standard components can be limited*
– *limited reflector sizes can make them inefficient*
– *can be expensive*

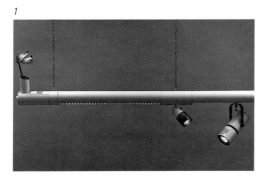

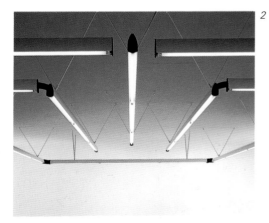

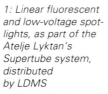

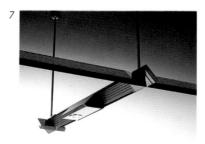

1: Linear fluorescent and low-voltage spot-lights, as part of the Atelje Lyktan's Supertube system, distributed by LDMS

2: iGuzzini's simple, low-profile XO system

3: For high ceilings, linear systems such as Artemide Litech's Aton Barra can be used for general ambient lighting

4: A triangular profile system that can be wall-mounted or suspended – Light's TG range, distributed by Futimis

5: Concord's Lytetube system incorporates a baffled uplighter and can change direction with a flexible concertina joint

6: iGuzzini's Prisma luminaires incorporating signage

7: Complex geometry in an angular extruded form – Hoffmeister's R&R range

8: A Staff Orion
installation combining
fluorescent and low-
voltage downlights and
an uplighting element
in a sculputural
arrangement

9: Atelje Lyktan
Supertube used as
downlighting and
wallwashing in an
office interior

10: Linear system
used for counter area
delineation – the BPS
system, distributed
by LDMS

11: Highly structural in
style – the appropriately
named Structura from
Targetti

12: Lecture-room
lighting using iGuzzini's
Prisma linear system

Fibre optic lighting

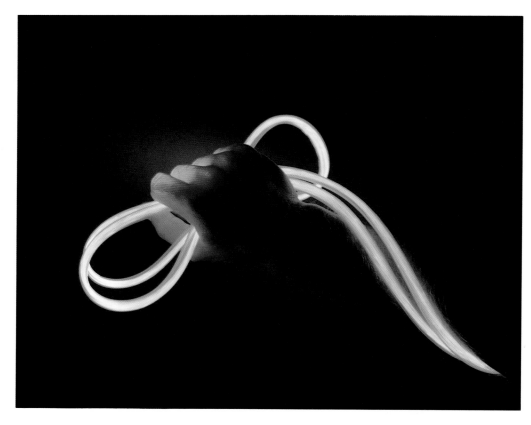

Fibre optics first arrived on the lighting scene in the form of garish domestic tabletop gizmos; later, when fibre optics became applicable to the contract sector, the system was consistently touted as a major breakthrough in lighting technology. Fibre optic lighting systems, while having a place in the lighting designer's repertoire, have several limitations which must be understood.

Fibre optics, specialized versions of which are also widely in use in communications systems, are either solid or, more commonly, consist of thousands of minute, specially coated strands of glass or Teflon-based acrylic. These strands are bunched together into a flexible cable or 'tail', which generally varies between 3 and 7 mm in diameter. Tails can be harnessed together into bundles of different sizes, depending on the intensity of the light emission required. Light is shone down one end, using a low-voltage quartz

There are two main forms of fibre optic lighting: end-emitting fibres (left); and side-emitting fibres, which glow along their whole length (above)

halogen dichroic *(ch 2)* or metal halide *(ch 2)* lamp housed in a light-box with a special lens, filters and reflector.

Due to the different refractive indices of the coating and the core material, light travels down the tail by internal reflection, to be emitted in the form of a small beam at the far end. In other side-emitting versions (for example, the US-originated Fiberstars), the outer refractive coating is omitted – the fibres glow along their whole length.

The effective length of the tail depends on the function. Used as a small spotlight, 3 to 5 metres is the general maximum; side-emitting versions or those used to provide small, sparkly points of light, can be longer, sometimes up to 15 metres. Attempts to exceed these lengths lead to light loss and a pronounced green colour shift.

Currently there are four main types of application of the system. The thinnest tails can be used as an alternative to low-voltage halogen for decorative ceiling lighting in night clubs and retail environments. Thicker tails bundled together to provide a more substantial beam can substitute for low-voltage down-lighters, as at Bentalls store in Kingston-on-Thames.

In its Fiberstars version, fibre optics can also be used as an alternative to cold cathode – often referred to as neon *(ch 2)* – to provide coloured decorative outlines to rooms, bars or passage-ways, or as illuminated signage. Alternatively, it has been used increasingly in museums, galleries and up-market retail establishments, often integrated into display cabinets, where it is useful for illuminating delicate or temperature-sensitive exhibits. Because objects are illuminated at very short distances and only light, not heat, is transmitted down the tails, fibre optics provide an ideal cool mini-spotlight for such locations. It is probably in this area, the

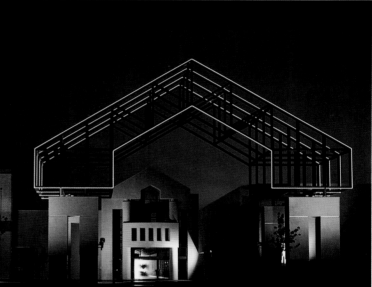

Lateral or side-emitting systems are often used to emphasize the edges of rooms or buildings, as in this Crescent Fiberstar installation (above), while end-emitting systems are increasingly used as substitutes for small low-voltage downlights, illustrated here (right) in a supermarket project by Absolute Action

The cool beam of fibre optic lighting is ideal for close-up display spotlighting of fragile or heat-sensitive objects

development of unobtrusive, miniaturized lighting, that fibre optics show greatest potential.

The main advantage of the system is the remote nature of the primary light source, which can service dozens of fibre optic tails. Thus the hot lamp and all the potentially dangerous electrics can be kept isolated; ambient temperatures at the point of application are also kept down. While this can put less load on the air-conditioning system locally, because of losses inherent within the

system more light (and heat) is produced at the light-box than would be necessary with alternative direct light sources. So this substantial component requires adequate ventilation to prevent over-heating. In general, heat gain and energy consumption within the building could be higher as a result.

When it comes to maintenance, only the single unit has to be cleaned and re-lamped, compared with possibly hundreds of individual lamps, which might be mounted inaccessibly.

When re-lamping there are no refocusing problems. The tails can be immersed in water or touched with complete safety; they are flexible, and can easily be bent round corners, or in the case of side-emitting versions, into complex shapes.

The colour and quality of light can be controlled. Infrared and ultraviolet filters in front of the light source can screen out harmful rays; and the addition

of a colour filter or colour wheel means that light colour can be changed easily, for additional decorative effect.

The downside to all this is that fibre optics are only applicable where low levels of illumination are required. To date, lux levels *(ch 1)* achievable with fibre optics are relatively low. The initial process of reflecting usable light down the fibres is inefficient and technically exacting. As yet, fibre optics are most successful in environments with low ambient light levels, where the delicate light has little competition.

Relative costs are a moot point; while installation is relatively cheap and easy, the capital equipment is expensive; one light-box with twelve outlets can cost upwards of £2000. This has to be set against lower maintenance costs for a large number of individual lamps. One 150W single-ended metal halide lamp can generate sufficient light for up to 85

sparkly 3.1 mm light tails;
replacing an equivalent number
of halogen starlights, this makes
fibre optics more viable. For
such applications, provided the
user is happy with the
alternative effect, overall costs
could be reduced considerably.

It is important to remember that
the technology is in a constant
state of evolution, with new
light heads and better reflectors
coming on stream all the time.
What is state of the art now
may be obsolete next year.

Advantages

+ *remote light source means*
  greater comfort and safety
+ *tails safe to touch and*
  impervious to water
+ *flexible tails allow complex*
  configurations
+ *can reduce maintenance and*
  re-lamping costs
+ *simple control of colour and*
  light quality
+ *cool light emitters for lighting*
  delicate objects

Disadvantages

− *inefficient*
− *low overall lux levels*
− *colour shifts*
− *high initial capital costs*
− *different qualities of glass*
  supplied by different
  manufacturers
− *limited cable lengths for*
  maximum efficiency

At Warwick Castle
Eurotec used fibre
optics within the
handrail to light the
steps below, an
interesting application
of the system's small
point sources

Decorative lighting

To enhance the ambience of particular types of room or interior environment, decorative forms of lighting may be required in place of, or in addition to, the types of lighting already discussed. Virtually any luminaire may be considered decorative within a chosen design scheme, although many are custom-designed specifically for an interior. While decorative lighting can be functional, as a general rule in commercial interiors it is preferable to see it used in combination with more conventional forms of ambient lighting fixture.

Decorative lighting can be classified into two groups. First there are those instances where the lighting effect itself is used as the decorative element, to add colour, glamour or dramatic effect to an interior. Examples might include the use of fibre optic star-effect ceilings, or coloured cold cathode tubes around bars in clubs. The other form of decorative lighting is where the fixture itself is strongly featured as an interior design element, to fit in with and enhance the ambience of a space. One example is the use of a crystal chandelier in a period building; or the incorporation of ultra-modern, high-profile designer lamps in a retail interior to establish its up-market design credentials. While both types of luminaire can offer a degree of functional illumination, their main purpose is stylistic or decorative.

There are several problems associated with such lighting design techniques. Most commonly these arise where specifiers or designers select fittings based on appearance, with little or no regard for their optical function. While decorative lighting can have a functional role of its own, it can also be highly unpredictable in its effects, particularly if it has been custom-designed for the space and is untested in terms of efficiency or light distribution *(ch 9)*.

Decorative lighting need not be traditional or conventional: a star-effect ceiling for a hotel bar (top) and a pendant uplight and freestanding light boxes for a company headquarters (above)

The chandelier is a good example. A centrally hung unit is a poor form of overall ambient lighting in a large space. It can produce glare from exposed or reflective sources, and like all pendant downlighters generally produces a bland, unflattering effect when used on its own. It is much better to reduce the brightness of the chandelier itself, either by incorporating a dimmer unit *(ch 5)* or by using low-wattage lamps, and supplementing discreet or hidden forms of ambient lighting which do not detract from it.

A problem often associated with custom-designed decorative lighting is that little or no thought has been given to the question of safety, maintenance or re-lamping. Cleaning and re-lamping, particularly if relatively short-life tungsten sources are used, can be logistically difficult.

Lastly, the unobtrusive and sympathetic incorporation of the light source into a decorative

fitting is crucial. It is remarkable how often the effect of an authentic-looking period lantern fitting, for example, is negated by the use of inappropriate energy-saving compact fluorescents *(ch 2)*.

Classic forms of decorative lighting: the chandelier (left) and the column-mounted lantern (above), both recreated for use with modern sources

1

2

1: A modern reworking
of the chandelier
from Arteluce, the
2097, designed by
G Sarfatti

2: A new twist on
the Tiffany lamp by
Christopher Wray

3: Lombardy pendant
from Chelsom

4: Andy Thornton's
solid brass Art Deco
standard lamp with
marbled globes

5: Lightwork's SPS55
1000 mm-square
pendant uplighter
with coloured diffusing
panels

4

5

6

8

9

7

6: Adelphi table lamp
from Christopher Wray
– a touch of Art Deco
glamour

7: Andy Thornton's
Derby collection in
brass – a postlight
and pendant

8: The Tuscany triple
wall light, from
Chelsom, in beaten
wrought iron

9: Luceplan's
suspension luminaire
Trama

10

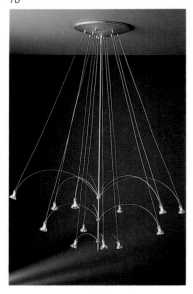

11

13

10: Solzi Luce's Orione
hi-tech chandelier,
distributed by GFC

11: Arteluce's Murana
wall light by King &
Miranda

12: Marlin Lighting's
double luminaire from
the Accent Café range

13: Christopher Wray's
faceted opalescent
pendant, Durand

14: Atelier Sedap
decorative wall and
ceiling panels from
the Normandie range,
distributed by Optelma

14

12

*15, 16, 17, 18: Marlin
Lighting's Opaline
range of contemporary
wall lights for the
contract market
illustrated here in
a variety of decorative
trims*

15

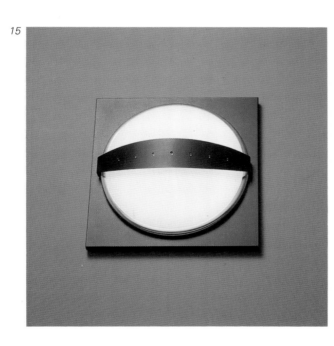

16

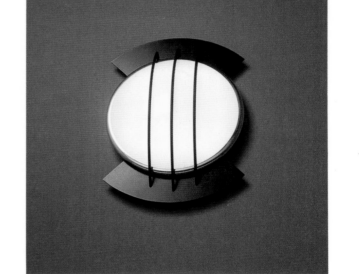

17

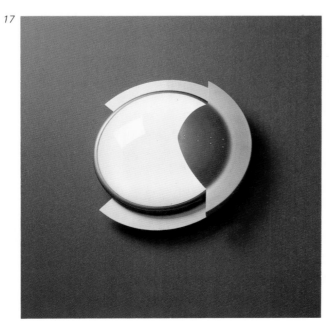

18

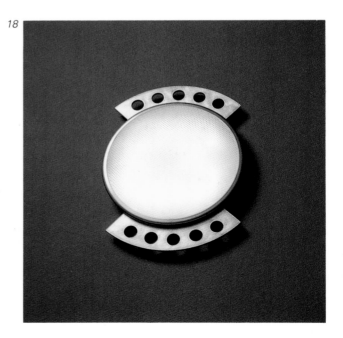

Emergency lighting

Emergency lighting is a necessary safety requirement for commercial and public buildings. There are, broadly speaking, two types: stand-by and escape lighting. Stand-by lighting is a back-up system, normally involving a separate generator, designed to maintain overall, but reduced, lighting levels so that essential work can continue if the mains supply fails. Escape lighting, often powered by batteries, ensures a low level of lighting, sufficient to allow safe exit from a building via defined escape routes, in a fire or other emergency. For the purposes of most designers and architects, escape lighting is often a statutory requirement and therefore function is the main consideration.

The fundamental point about emergency lighting is that, although essential, it should be as unobtrusive as possible and should not be allowed to interfere with the overall interior design of a building. However, emergency lighting should not

be compromised for aesthetic reasons. Emergency lighting should be carefully planned by the designer and architect from the beginning of the scheme, in accordance with statutory regulations; it should never be left to the client or to a third party to add anomalous fittings at a later stage.

Because instant illumination is required, tungsten *(ch 2)* and fluorescent *(ch 2)* sources are almost always used in emergency lighting, even if the main lighting is a form of discharge lamp *(ch 2)*. Power for the system is usually a battery which may be part of the luminaire, mounted remotely or located within a central battery room. There are different economic arguments for all three systems, depending on the size of the project. Given the relatively high costs of battery-powered lighting, it should always be carefully planned to eliminate wastage and duplication. Local regulations usually require a

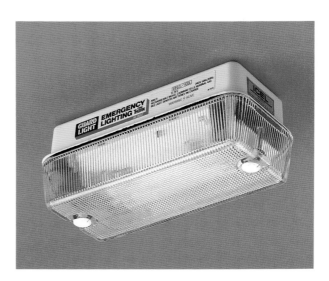

Typical low-cost, self-contained bulkhead emergency lighting fixtures, from Thorn Lighting (above) and JSB (right). Emergency lighting is often specified without consideration of the interior design scheme. Unobtrusive, sympathetically designed luminaires are readily available

running time of a minimum of three hours for any battery-operated emergency system, ensuring a minimum pre-specified lamp performance at this duration.

There are three types of emergency luminaire:

- non-maintained versions housing dedicated lamps, which are used only for emergency illumination

- maintained luminaires, which utilize a lamp which can be used for general lighting, but can be switched over to emergency mode, often at a lower level of illumination

- combined systems (also known as sustained), where a single housing incorporates two lamps, one for standard illumination, the other for emergency situations.

The ideal solution is usually the combined (sustained) system, with the emergency lamp invisibly integrated into the

Exit signage must be lit by emergency lighting. Luminaires which incorporate light source and sign, such as the JSB Royalux system (above) are a useful option. Standard ceiling or wall fittings, such as the Chelsom decorative downlight (right) can be fitted with an invisible emergency unit – such as this pack from Concord (top right) whose batteries can provide emergency power for up to three hours

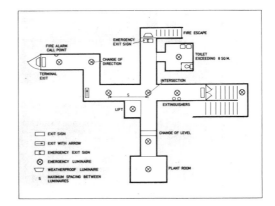

regular lighting. A wide range of emergency versions of standard luminaires is now available. Standard fixtures can often be easily modified for emergency requirements. Nevertheless, unsightly non-maintained bulkheads are often specified for interiors, when in the majority of cases they are not necessary.

As well as national standards, many licensing and local authorities have their own requirements for emergency lighting in buildings and these bodies must be consulted at an early stage of design and planning. Where explicit guidelines are unavailable, designers should follow the current national standards (eg the BS 5266 Code of Practice and CIBSE TM12), which offer recognized minimum standards. They are a good basis for submissions to the local authority and fire officer who can then advise on modifications necessary to meet local requirements. When designing

emergency lighting there are particular areas and/or features that must be illuminated: fire alarms, fire-fighting equipment storage points, changes in escape route direction and floor levels, and final exit and directional signage.

Because all batteries degrade over time, with life expectancies of between five and ten years, a regular servicing routine must be specified with every scheme. This must be kept up to date in a log book available for inspection by visiting fire officers.

Typical office floor plan (above) showing points where emergency lighting is needed
Courtesy: JSB

Existalite's low-voltage lighting strips which can be used to emphasize doorways (above) or to show direction at ground level (right)

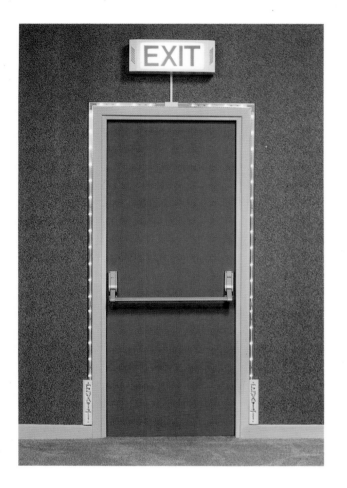

In a matter of a few minutes smoke will drastically reduce visibility at normal standing height. Existalite's system helps to keep exits illuminated

Daylight control systems

Daylight is natural, free and plentiful and is generally regarded as the purest form of light. On economic, comfort and environmental grounds, it ought to be a major interior lighting option during daytime hours. Paradoxically, for the purpose of controlled interior lighting it can often be more of a problem than a help.

Particularly in northern latitudes, daylight is variable and un-predictable – there is often either too much or not enough of it. So control systems are needed, either to limit light coming into the building or, more unusually, to boost or redirect daylight into darker interior areas. Whilst fashion-able, this latter technique is not new. A 19th-century example can be seen at Soane House in London, where mirrors in the basement were installed to re-direct daylight onto the ceiling above. More recently, sophisticated versions of the same technique were employed by Norman Foster Associates in

the Hong Kong and Shanghai Bank, and by Freidrich Wagner at the BMW pavilion in Munich.

The most common forms of daylight control are curtains and blinds, mounted inside the windows and operated manually or automatically. Blinds come in many forms – adjustable vertical or horizontal slats, or solid roller versions, for example. As well as reducing or totally eliminating daylight, blinds also ensure

Daylight control systems can range from the simplest blinds and drapes (right) to hi-tech heliostats, by Siemens for the BMW building in Munich (above)
Courtesy: Technical Blinds and Siemens

In a VDT-intense office (above left), excessive daylight must be controlled by blinds (left) or other systems to reduce veiling reflections and glare

privacy, cut out unattractive exterior aspects, and can act as an interior design element to add colour or pattern to a room. However, left to individual manual control, blinds often look untidy. They also prevent visual access to the outside world, a limitation which many workers find oppressive. When mounted inside the window on sunny days they can heat up and act as radiators, thus contributing to heat gain (rather than, as may be expected, reducing it). The lighter (more reflective) the exterior finish of the blind, the greater the degree of thermal rejection.

For this reason exterior blinds mounted outside the window are often a better solution for solar control. But the necessary automatic mechanical control systems can be prone to break-down and therefore require a high degree of maintenance.

There are other forms of adjustable and non-adjustable screening systems which can

As these three installations by Technical Blinds demonstrate, louvred blinds can be applied inside toplit spaces (top), above the glazing itself (middle), or in the case of wall windows at the new British Library, mounted on the outside in the form of an architectural canopy (bottom)

be used to control daylight and prevent heat gain. Non-adjustable systems include different glazing treatments – silk-screened dot matrix patterns, tinted glass and stick-on reflective film, and so on. Louvres and awnings can be fixed to the outside of the building. While requiring little or no maintenance, these might be aesthetically, structurally or architecturally unacceptable.

The main problem with all fixed, non-adjustable systems is that they are generally set up for the worst-case scenario, so that for 80 per cent of the year they are excluding more light than they need to. They might actually entail the use of more artificial interior lighting.

Ideally, then, daylight control systems should be adjustable, so that they can be modified easily or taken away entirely on gloomy days. Well-planned systems can be electronically integrated with the building's artificial lighting and energy

Glazed office buildings (above) can be treated by using inconspicuous stick-on film, to reduce solar gain

Courtesy: Banafix

Another solution to daylight glare is the permanent exterior louvre (right) which is effective but can be architecturally obtrusive

Courtesy: Technical Blinds

control systems. One promising solution is electronic tinting, which uses light-sensitive liquid crystals within the glass. These either darken or lighten automatically as the light changes, or can be switched on to order. Currently under development, the system is as yet both expensive and unproven on a large scale.

Other forms of hi-tech daylight control system developed recently are not designed to exclude light entirely. These either screen out certain types of natural light and/or redirect it within the building where it is required. Siemens has developed a light-management system, which consists of acrylic prismatic panels, combining angled prisms and partly silvered surfaces. These reflect away harsh sunlight, which often both creates solar gain and produces glare (particularly in VDT-intense environments), while allowing in softer vertical (zenith) light. The panels, used on Richard Rogers

Partnership's conversion of Billingsgate for Citicorp *(ch 6)*, come in four versions, depending on the side of the building where they are located, in relation to local sunlight conditions.

As well as allowing in only useful light these panels also refract it so that it is thrown into the spaces where it is required. Another version of a sunlight redirection system employs the heliostat (as used by Norman Foster Associates on the Hong Kong and Shanghai Bank), a reflective mirror that follows the line of the sun. Such costly systems for channelling light into atria or basements can demand high levels of maintenance so they are not practical as a primary interior lighting source in inclement, unpredictable climates, such as the UK's. They can, however, be a worthwhile option in sunnier regions of the world.

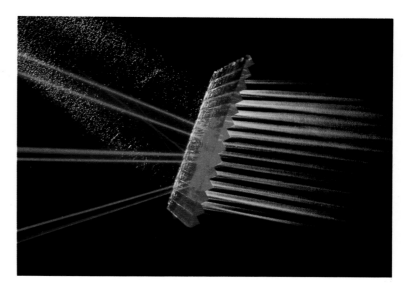

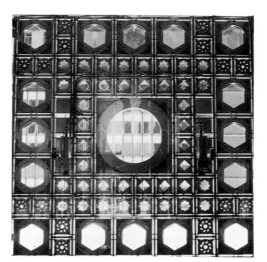

At the leading edge of light-management systems: Siemens' acrylic prismatic panels (above) which reflect away intrusive sunlight while letting in softer, zenith light; and the custom-made electronic iris system (right) which opens and closes in response to light, as used by Jean Nouvel on the Institute of the Arab World in Paris

Variants and 'specials' versus standard products

Today's market offers a wide range of lighting products for lighting designers and other design specifiers. Occasionally, specific needs or requirements come along that cannot be satisfied by existing luminaires, and designers either have to adapt existing models (variants) or create entirely new ones (specials or one-offs). All cold cathode and neon types of lamp are specials, custom-made for every new application. Several of the projects featured in chapter 6 involve variants or specials.

The 1980s saw a huge growth in the market for custom-made lighting products. This was particularly evident in the retail sector, with its short refurbishment cycles and retailers' growing demand for uniquely distinctive in-store identities. It also applied to leisure environments, offices, hotels and exterior applications of all kinds. As functional and aesthetic requirements accelerated and diversified, many lighting manufacturers were unable to keep step. Variants or specials filled the gap. Their scale of use is considerable, ranging from single bedside lighting units for affluent residential clients, to enormous projects such as Erco's lighting for Stansted Airport *(ch 6)*.

However, one-off products earned a poor reputation in many sectors during the same period. Badly designed specials created a series of problems – such as control gear *(ch 2)* failure, premature lamp failure, overheating, and discolouration of

ceilings and walls. Even now there are a lot of specials around, and still being made, that would not pass safety and/or performance standards.

Such failures and the early 1990s' recession have made designers and their clients cautious about the added cost and uncertainty of specifying non-standard products.

The recession has led to less attention to detail and a greater emphasis on meeting project budgets and completion dates. Time-consuming, expensive specials do not fit that mood.

Specifying non-standard lighting products

The first rule about specifying non-standard lighting products is 'think again'. Are they absolutely necessary and have you explored all the possible options? A great deal of the specials' mania of the late 1980s was as much a function of product

Custom-made luminaire, based on a Mackintosh design, where the decorative motif matches the wall detail

An example of a 'special' that entered the mainstream: the Alexandra period pendant designed by LDP for Designed Architectural Lighting

ignorance as innovative spirit. Systematic research may throw up an off-the-shelf product which looks just right or has the technical capabilities you require. For example, if you're simply seeking a particular performance standard, there's very likely a product somewhere to meet it.

Specifying adapted (variant) products or specials usually has a downside; in most cases, unless a large number of luminaires is specified, it will be more expensive. Supply problems should be considered: how long will they take to make? Will the client be able to get compatible spares or replacements at a later date? Will the standard of finish be comparable with standard mass produced items? Equally important, newly designed or modifed luminaires will not automatically comply with existing standards, which could lead to problems in the future.

Taking specialist advice

The second rule for architects and interior designers is 'don't do it on your own'.

Collaboration with a specialist is essential to ensure a safe and effective result. In most cases adapting an existing product or inventing a new one will probably involve expertise in thermal control, photometry or mechanical/ electrical engineering.

Non-specialist specifiers or manufacturers may automatically assume that a luminaire will work in its new form, without sufficiently evaluating or testing the modifications.

There may be little understanding of electrical requirements and regulations. For example, a common problem, when re-fashioning low-voltage lighting *(ch 2)* in a new way, is to locate the remote transformer too far from the lamps, without allowing for the considerable drop in voltage this involves. 'Playing safe' or over-specifying can be an equally common mistake, since judgements of anticipated

The range of specials
is enormous – from
futuristic floor-lights by
Electrolite for a car
showroom (left), to the
same company's
suspended brushed
metal downlight rafts
for the Institution of
Structural Engineers
(below right), and
sculptural exterior
standards by Fisher-
Marantz at Broadgate
(below left)

performance are made without reference to photometric data. This can result in too high a level of illumination from the new, innovative fitting or lamp configuration.

The main lesson here is that a close collaboration with either a sympathetic, knowledgeable lighting manufacturer and/or a lighting design consultant is a prerequisite for the creation of successful variants or specials. We discuss the manufacturer's contribution below, and the role of the lighting consultant in chapter 9.

Advantages of variants and one-offs

There are two main motives for designers to specify variant or one-off products: (1) technical and (2) aesthetic. On the technical front, there are dozens of reasons for adapting existing products: a product may not be exactly the right dimensions for the space, or the reflector may not provide the right beam angle , or it may not be able to house a lamp source of the right type for the installation. For example, at BT's (British Telecom's) offices in Oswestry the lamp holders and control gear of a standard compact fluorescent *(ch 2)* downlighter *(ch 3)* range were adapted to make them dimmable.

Sometimes modifications of this sort will prove so successful that companies include the improvement as a standard feature of their range. In this way lighting variants and specials, when well conceived and executed, have become one of the major forces behind lighting innovation and development.

One of the most common adaptations is the incorporation of emergency lighting *(ch 3)* within the luminaire. Another, when sourcing from European companies, is the simple change of a European adaptor plate to suit the British BESA box ; or with US products, changing the 120V standard to the British 240V.

If the modification is minor or simply the specification of a different coloured

Two versions of the wall torchère: Electrolite's over-sized versions designed by Peter Leonard Associates for the Virgin Megastore in Paris (above); and the SOM-designed models with translucent bowl (left) for the Broadgate Centre, manufactured by Designed Architectural Lighting

paint finish, many manufacturers will be willing to carry out the change at little extra cost, particularly if the project is a large one. Where the modification involves cutting and re-assembling products, in many cases you may have to buy the standard product and get the work done elsewhere.

Manufacturers' policies vary widely; some far-sighted companies offer 'special' work as part of their service. But it can still be difficult to clarify exactly what the client wants and communicate that down an extended production chain. Administratively, many companies are not able to deal with non-standard demands, and long delays can result. It is advisable to establish a company's track record in this area, before placing an order.

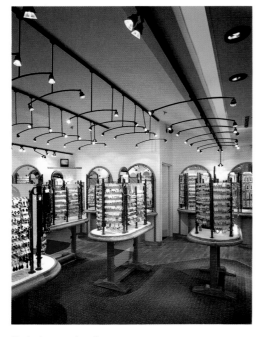

*Period or modern?
'Traditional' chandelier
for the EuroDisney
Newport Hotel (top)
and Microlights' sleek
low-voltage downlight
system for a jewellery
shop (bottom)*

Achieving a distinctive look

Aesthetic reasons for modifications, or more commonly brand-new products, vary. The designer may be seeking a particular lighting effect or luminaire appearance, possibly to match an existing style or finish. The specification of one-off products for period interiors is common – chandeliers are a case in point. The client may be looking for a corporate style which is distinctive, involving unique light fittings. Such demands as these have helped to spawn the growth in the 1980s of a series of specialist companies such as Electrolite and Designed Architectural Lighting (DAL), originally dedicated to the production of 'one-off' lighting products.

Where a specific aesthetic appearance is required, it can often be more practical to design a new product from scratch, rather than attempting to adapt an existing model. With low-volume runs, often hand-constructed, labour costs will be higher than those from a mass manufacturer. In the case of unique, often elaborate one-off products the choice of, and collaboration with the right manufacturer are essential.

LDP designed this hi-tech, bowlike lighting system for the Friary Centre, Guildford

Not all manufacturers will specialize in what you require; for example, the company may be excellent metalworkers, but have no experience of working with glass. Others may not know how to design and manufacture a reflector to suit a particular need. Few of the small-scale craft companies that may seem appropriate, in terms of dealing with the exterior style of the luminaire, are likely to be experienced in all aspects, including basic electrical engineering.

These failings are accentuated by the fact that many designers pay more attention to the outward appearance of a luminaire than to its performance. While successful one-off designs, such as DAL's decorative opal pendant uplighter, Alexandra, have become standard volume products, one-off luminaires designed by specifiers more often resemble artistic light sculptures than functioning light fittings. As a result, they will have a limited, short-life application for the manufacturer.

Often basic functional criteria are neglected. All lighting equipment, even specials, must be fit for purpose and may have to comply with relevant standards. Specifiers may not know how to get luminaires tested and the budget or timescale may not allow for it. Whilst a lighting consultant usually cannot make time for such approvals testing, they should ensure that all the components employed are appropriate and that the new luminaire will be capable of satisfying such requirements.

Advantages

+ *can be made to satisfy a new technical need or requirement precisely*
+ *can be made to match exactly the style of a particular environment*
+ *can help create a unique identity*
+ *on large-volume projects, custom-made lamps may be comparable in cost terms*

Disadvantages

− *small-scale, hand-crafted production runs can be expensive*
− *lighting performance may be untested*
− *technical standards and/or finishes may be inferior to mass-manufactured products*
− *manufacturers may be unable to meet production requirements or timescale*
− *non-standard products may increase designer's legal liability*
− *may increase potential maintenance and replacement (spares) problems*
− *time-consuming in design and development*

The capsule lamp by Box Products – a semi-bespoke model that can be used in a wide range of contexts

chapter 5

Lighting controls

For many years, the only way of controlling and changing the levels of illumination within an artificial lighting design scheme was the switch. A switch controlling a circuit only has two states – on or off – which can be inflexible and hardly makes for a subtle shift in lighting effects. Manual switches have distinct disadvantages; where, for example, do you locate them and who does the switching? In large installations, a proliferation of localized switches can lead to chaos and conflict, whereas the more centralized the switching operation, the less personal control of the lit environment is given to the individual.

An example of early, state-of-the-art lighting control

Developments in dimming, rather than switching, came from the theatre, where for dramatic enhancement, subtle, almost imperceptible changes in lighting effects from one scene to another were essential. Dimming racks, used with incandescent lamps *(ch 2)* for which they are particularly suitable, were manual devices which allowed gradual fading in or out of particular lamps, simply by stepping the voltage up or down in stages, via an electromagnetic coil. Simple, manually operated dimmers were then developed to replace the single switch and were introduced into commercial interiors. As well as being able to turn an incandescent lamp off, dimmers could be set for different degrees of brightness between fully on and fully off. If installed locally, this gave users added personal control of their own light levels.

Single dimmers can work only on one lamp or on one circuit; in the theatre manual setting of different combinations of dimmers to create a desired scene relied on long rehearsal and precise memory cues, controlled by experts, a situation that is hardly practicable in non-theatrical locations. When controlled centrally, a simple combination of switches and dimmers did enable the first rudimentary attempts at scene-setting in commercial interiors, but constant manual adjustment was necessary if the space was to respond appropriately to changing needs and/or light levels.

For a long time, the only types of lamp to which dimmers could be applied were mains voltage, incandescent, tungsten filament sources. More efficient fluorescent lamps (ch 2), invented in the 1930s and popularly used in offices since the 1950s, could not easily be dimmed.

The microchip
The breakthrough in this technological stalemate came in the 1970s with the development of the microprocessor. This led in turn to the evolution of a generation of electronic ballasts and dimmers which could be applied to a wider range of lamp types, such as fluorescent and some other discharge sources (ch 2).

Second, and again following their pioneering use in the theatre, the 1980s saw the proliferation of more sophisticated automated, programmable control systems, which did not rely on manual intervention or human memory.

This rapid expansion in lamps and lighting technology was stimulated by new demands and applications in the commercial sector, requiring greater individual control and high flexibility: in the retail area an emphasis on style-conscious, constantly changing visual merchandising; the move to the automated office, with different lighting requirements for different tasks; the need for highly flexible lighting in multi-purpose leisure installations; and, more recently, the growing desire to create

different moods and environments at home. Every one of these new contexts inevitably meant that electric lighting and lighting control, as they had been understood and practised for almost a hundred years, had to be radically changed.

Today, a wide range of electronic lighting controls has been devised to enhance both the creativity of interior designers and architects, and to improve a building's use at different times and for different functions.

The main advantage of any control system, using automated switches and/or dimmers, is that it gives the designer, manager or user the chance to control an interior ambience over time, while more closely matching lighting levels to the needs of the space. This may also have the advantage of saving energy, by reducing the wasteful use of lamps when not needed (ch 8).

While automated controls have become relatively commonplace, the rapid sophistication in their development and reductions in size and cost will probably lead to new applications in coming years. Increasingly, many of these systems will interface with other building management control systems, such as air-conditioning and security, leading to the so-called 'smart building' scenario.

Many systems still have to be tailored or custom-designed and manufactured for particularly complex, large-scale applications. However, for less complex purposes, ready-made lighting control packages, such as the Electrosonic systems, are available to serve the needs of many lighting schemes relatively inexpensively.

It is worth reviewing the precise benefits of such devices, as well as pointing out some of their pitfalls. These have often been ignored in the stampede to fully automated control.

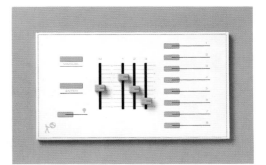

Two typical forms of control panel. Electrosonic's four-scene version (top) and Strand Lighting's Premiere, offering eight scenes, with slider dimmers (above)

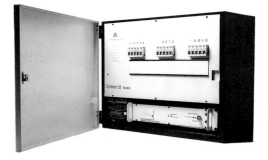

A self-contained lighting control system incorporating dimmers and programme controller
Courtesy: Electrosonic

Setting the scenes

There are two broad contexts in which the issue of controls needs to be considered, each with almost diametrically opposed requirements. On the one hand there are large, commercial, public environments such as shopping centres, hotels or leisure complexes, with a largely transient clientele and little or no end-user control. Increasingly, many of these may also be daylight lit, via atria or other forms of extensive glazing. While this will mean that artificial lighting may not be needed for much of the time, the issue of smooth transition between the two forms of illumination should not be ignored.

Rooms within a hotel or leisure facility may have several changing functions, with radically different lighting requirements, over the course of a day. For example, a conference suite may be used as a boardroom, a seminar room, an exhibition space or an audio-visual presentation facility; a restaurant may have to change its atmosphere over 15 or 16 hours from a bright and cheerful ambience at breakfast, through a functional business lunch, to a more subdued, romantic ambience for dinner in the evening.

For retail or hotel complexes probably the greatest potential benefit is this ability to constantly and imperceptibly modify the interior mood, using lighting, to make it dynamic and fresh. In this way customers don't get jaded and can be encouraged to return again and again.

Where spaces are daylit, the transition to night-time use can be achieved automatically by photocell-controlled dimming systems which gradually bring in, or reduce, the artificial lighting. In addition, discrete, dedicated sub-systems ought to be able to offer maximum flexibility for different rooms within the facility, to make them even more marketable. A conference room could perhaps have three or four clearly signed function buttons, enabling quick and easy transformation of the space, for different activities.

In the public spaces, the main need is for a centralized electronically controlled programme, possibly linked to a timeclock, offering a predetermined series of shifting lighting scenes over the course of 24 hours, plus perhaps one or two unique lighting effect set-ups for special events. Microprocessor controlled systems allow each scene to be memorized so that they can be played in sequence, or specifically called up using a single button. In many cases, as scenes change, the same luminaires can be used for different effects. Many of the projects featured in chapter 6 employ automated control systems with great success.

However, there can be some disadvantages, which need to considered at an early stage. The first is cost: sophisticated control systems involve greater initial capital investment. More lighting equipment might also have to be specified, to allow for overlap of lighting effects, as scenes change. All this should be offset against potential energy savings *(ch 8)*, reduced maintenance from extended lamp-life *(ch 1)* due to dimming, and increased custom and revenue, as a result of using such a system.

More difficult are the logistics. The electrical circuitry involved can be complicated and needs to be considered at the outset; utilizing sophisticated controls with existing installations can be extremely limiting. In chapter 10 we discuss imminent developments which may ameliorate this problem, such as individually addressable luminaires feeding off one single mains cable.

Meanwhile, with current software, programming time can be lengthy and difficult; and post-completion snagging needs to be thorough. With custom-made systems, briefing the manufacturer is critical and often prone to error, so you may

In a restaurant or café, lighting controls can be used to create different 'moods' – bright and businesslike for breakfast, subdued and romantic for dinner

*The Rica Hotel, Oslo –
a sophisticated control
system can be used to
create a changing
series of lighting
'scenes' throughout
the day and night*

*Dimming racks can
occupy a considerable
amount of space within
a building. Pictured
here, a single rack
which may be one of
many in a large
commercial installation*

Courtesy: Electrosonic

find that the system doesn't do exactly what you want, once it is installed.

With full automation additional considerations – the imponderable 'what ifs?' – need to be taken on board. What if there's a fire? What if the cleaners come in at a different time? What if the restaurant needs to open later one evening? Without considerable knowledge and experience, the biggest drawback with current technologies is designing an inflexible system, or one that is over-complicated and difficult for the user to operate.

Ironically, the more automated a system is, the more inflexible it can become and so there is a greater requirement for a manual over-ride capability. Not everyone should be allowed access to the over-ride facility, otherwise it is liable to be abused. Even where a manual over-ride is accessible only to trained, responsible personnel, if the system is unresponsive or over-complicated, they may simply decide to switch off the automatic system and leave it on manual and the scheme could be wrecked. Improved hardware, combined with better software, will overcome many of these problems; systems are becoming more user-friendly and reasonably easy to re-programme by trained lay people, rather than having to call specialists back on site to make simple adjustments.

Lighting control in the workplace

Workplace locations, particularly offices and home environments, where users tend to spend long periods of time, possibly undertaking a precise and/or changing regime of tasks, pose a different set of issues. Here, the promise of new technology is more the maximization of personal end-user control of lighting, to enable, say, office workers to tailor local lighting more closely to their individual needs, capabilities, or even mood. Demographic changes and the re-entry of

Scene selection panels can come in myriad shapes, sizes and finishes to suit an interior's needs

older women into the workforce have particular implications. Older people may need considerably higher light levels for efficient working than younger staff, so unless set at the upper limits, uniform, overall lighting levels will be unsuitable for a mixed-age workforce. Lower ambient lighting supplemented with local, adjustable task lighting *(ch 3)* may be the preferred solution.

There will still be need for an overall pre-programmed building lighting programme; for example, a timeclock to turn the lights off and on at predetermined times of the day (with a seven-day facility, if required, so it doesn't operate at the weekends). If the ambient lighting is required only after dark, a solar timeclock may be used, programmed to adjust the on and off times to take account of changing seasonal day-lengths. A combination of photocell, responsive to light levels, in conjunction with a timeclock, can be an ideal way to control floodlighting *(ch 7)* or any other part of night-time lighting.

Automated programmes should be capable of being over-ridden or supplemented manually by staff, within their location, where necessary. In some cases, where lighting is linked into the overall building control system, this might be done simply by dialling a number on the telephone.

Unfortunately, practical experience shows that staff are unwilling to respond to exhortations to switch lights off, no matter how large the lettering on the notices. The initiative should lie with staff to turn systems on for their own use, while relying on devices such as proximity detectors, timers or photocell controls to ensure that general lighting is switched off when not required.

One device that is sometimes used is a re-set switch, which may be fitted in conjunction with any of the above technologies; each luminaire or group of luminaires is switched off at periodic, predetermined intervals during the day. If the lighting is still required, the user has to operate the re-set switch; if sufficient daylight is available or staff are absent, energy can thus be saved.

Photocells in use

Individual proximity detectors and photocells, to monitor both lighting levels or room occupancy, are available as part of a standard luminaire (GE Lighting markets a unit incorporating both).

The use of photocells is now widespread and may seem the obvious solution in many installations. But photocells aren't totally free from problems. For example, someone has to choose the level at which they are set. If the chosen task illuminance is, say, 500 lux *(ch 1)*, the answer may seem to be to set the photocell to turn off the lamps when 500 lux of daylight is available. This would, in fact, mean that at the moment of switch-off, there will be 1000 lux in the space – 500 lux from daylight and 500 lux from the electric light. A sudden 50 per cent reduction in light levels from 1000 lux to 500 lux can be very noticeable, even distracting. A solution could be to select a higher light level as the switch-off point – say 1000 lux – so that the sudden reduction, from 1500 to 1000, lux won't be as noticeable. However, less energy saving will be realized by maintaining light levels beyond what is strictly necessary.

This solution is frequently applied to installations using fluorescent lamps, probably the commonest form of workplace lighting. With the advent of improved electronics such as high-frequency, dimmable ballasts *(ch 2)*, this problem can be eliminated, so that lamps can be dimmed down correspondingly, as soon as daylight is available. In this way the process will take place over an extended period of time, for a gradual effect.

Making the right choice

The choice of lamp is crucial, in both public and workplace environments, whenever automated control and dimming systems are being considered. Tungsten halogen and low-voltage *(ch 2)* sources are still the most flexible for imperceptible dimming to very low levels, for example, but they involve additional energy and maintenance costs. HID sources *(ch 2)* are the most unresponsive, with their slow warm-up time, limited dimming and considerable colour shift when dimmed. There are also potential incompatibility problems between dimmers and control gear and transformers – these should always be checked.

Specifiers should be careful to avoid embarrassing scenarios like that experienced by a London-based design consultancy whose new offices, including the client conference room, were lit primarily by metal halide *(ch 2)* uplighters *(ch 3)*. This resulted in clients sitting in the dark for several minutes, following audio-visual presentations, waiting for the lamps to re-strike.

Advantages

+ *enable precise control of changing effects over time*
+ *eliminate problem of haphazard manual switching*
+ *can extend range of functions in specific rooms*
+ *can save energy by tailoring lighting to occupancy and use*
+ *allow imperceptible transition between daytime and night-time conditions*
+ *dimming of incandescent lamps can extend lamp-life*

Disadvantages

− *relatively expensive to buy and install*
− *circuit wiring can be complex and costly*
− *extended period needed for installation, programming and snagging*
− *limited range of lamp types when using dimmers*
− *systems can be inflexible*
− *detailed planning required*

The 'intelligent' luminaire? This incorporates light and presence sensors at the centre of the louvre

Courtesy: Thorn Lighting

chapter 6

Lighting design case studies

In this section we illustrate and analyse lighting design projects chosen from around the world in most of the main commercial categories. These projects have been chosen for their innovative qualities, for their influence on lighting design, or as exemplary illustrations of a particular lighting design technique. In most cases the textual descriptions are based on interviews with the designers and/or written project notes provided by them. All the case studies are cross-referenced where possible to other sections of the book where particular terms or techniques are explained more fully.

Citicorp Dealing Room, Billingsgate, London

Lighting: Lighting Design Partnership
Architects: Richard Rogers Partnership
Engineers: Ove Arup & Partners

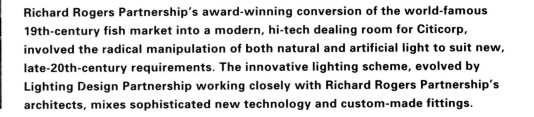

Richard Rogers Partnership's award-winning conversion of the world-famous 19th-century fish market into a modern, hi-tech dealing room for Citicorp, involved the radical manipulation of both natural and artificial light to suit new, late-20th-century requirements. The innovative lighting scheme, evolved by Lighting Design Partnership working closely with Richard Rogers Partnership's architects, mixes sophisticated new technology and custom-made fittings.

Day and night views of the main dealing floor (top and above). This is lit by dual-function dimmable fluorescent luminaires around the skylights which downlight the space by day and, in addition, uplight the structure after dark

Given the unavoidably strong natural light, and the sensitivity of VDT screens to reflection and glare *(ch 1)*, the design of the lighting system was critical. The principal space at Billingsgate is the main trading hall, 16 metres high and 45 metres wide. Here, a dealing deck is suspended across the space, in the form of an H-shaped bridge. The space is lit largely by daylight, via glazed double-height galleries on two sides and rows of skylight windows around the timbered roof vaults.

To avoid excessive glare, all the upper windows were replaced with a unique prismatic light-management system *(ch 3)*, by Siemens, in its first use in Britain. These complex acrylic panels, combining angled prisms and partly silvered surfaces, reflect back harsh beams of sunlight, while allowing in softer, more diffuse zenith (vertical) light from the sky above. The panels are made in four reflector strengths, depending on which side of the building they are located. The new panels allow in 30 per cent more light of the right type than other daylight management systems, such as sunscreens *(ch 3)*. The light is also better distributed – the prisms 'bend' the light, throwing it deep into the room.

In addition to daylight, the main trading hall is lit by dual-function high-frequency dimmable fluorescent lamp *(ch 2)* fittings, high up around the perimeter and below the skylights. During the day, two rows of fittings on a central spine point downwards, while at night another row uplights *(ch 3)* the glorious structure of the building.

All the lighting is controlled automatically by photo-cells *(ch 5)*, maintaining an overall level of 500 lux *(ch 1)*. This automatic system is less an energy-saving requirement than a way of dramatically extending maintenance periods, to minimize disruption of the dealing room.

The spectacular central bridge floor presented particular problems. It has no natural light overhead, and the deck inevitably throws shadows below. Rows of high-frequency fluorescent lamps are set into its underside, and specially louvred in order to light only the furniture, not the white-painted structure. The area above the bridge deck is lit by a series of specially designed metal halide *(ch 2)* uplighters *(ch 3)* containing 2 x 250W lamps, which float on thin wires between the bridge spars.

There were two other areas where lighting was critical. One is the historic Haddock Gallery, above the main hall, where fish were once smoked. This long, narrow office back-up area is lit on both sides by tall windows (again with prismatic panels). A continuous trough of metal halide uplighters is hidden in the curved roof beams so that during the day the sides are light and the ceiling dark; the effect is reversed after dark.

Below the main hall is the deep basement area, formerly used as the refrigerated fish store and now completely restored as plant rooms, offices and a café area. Lighting is used here to moderate the claustrophobic effect of the closed, brick-piered space. The main illumination is provided by visually striking custom-made *(ch 4)* metal halide uplighters, with an integral white reflector and a suspended lower translucent disc and bowl. These units, and their control gear *(ch 2)* are cleverly located below the access holes where the fish and ice used to pour into the cold store from above.

The rooflights of the main dealing floor (above) were fitted with Siemens prismatic panels (right) to screen out excessive daylight. Downstairs in the basement, a custom-made metal halide uplighter (opposite page, bottom) adds texture and interest to the windowless space

Hasbro Building, London

Lighting design: DPA (UK) Lighting Consultants
Architects: Arup Associates
Interior design: Sussman Prejza

Located at a focal site on the Stockley Business Park near Heathrow Airport, the British headquarters of the US toy manufacturer, Hasbro Bradley, is an unashamedly modern, two-storey building, arranged around two glazed atria. A central component of the interior decor is an extensive, award-winning art collection.

The lighting design scheme had to highlight the quality interior details and show off the artworks to good but not over-stated effect. Given the extensive glazing of the building and the absence of exterior lighting, the external appearance of the interior spaces at night was an important consideration.

The three areas that DPA addressed were the double-height entrance hall, the two central atria spaces, and the restaurant/snack bar. The entrance hall, a double-height void with the staircase wrapping around the reception desk to the rear, is lit by a mix of uplighting *(ch 3)* and downlighting *(ch 3)*. The revolving entrance doors have four low-voltage tungsten halogen *(ch 2)* downlights recessed within the circular door head. Mounted above it 250W HID metal halide *(ch 2)* uplighters floodlight the space and the external glass canopy. A carefully calculated cut-off angle ensures that the lamp is not seen from the first-floor landing.

Four HID downlights, mounted on a central structural member, cast bright circles of cooler light onto the geometric patterned floor. Ambient lighting under the balconies is supplemented by low-brightness recessed units. Linear tungsten halogen wallwashers , recessed into the soffits, give even illumination to the artworks mounted on side and rear walls. Here, as elsewhere, non-reliance on emphatic, exhibition-type display lighting underscores the integration of the artworks into the working environment, typical of Arup's signature.

The two atria, with a coffee shop at each end, are heavily toplit spaces during the day, due to the glazed skylights, but with darker areas under balconies and solid ceiling areas. At those points on the upper level, pairs of simple recessed low-brightness downlights echo the circulation corridor lighting pattern; while on the ground floor, decorative wall fixtures cast gentle upward illumination onto the undersides of the upper balconies. Four decorative floor standards frame the coffee area and give an additional bright focus to the space.

The restaurant/snack bar, housed on two levels within a prominent glazed conservatory, is a major architectural feature, so its internal and external appearance had great importance. It was intended that it would have a warm, attractive feel, in contrast to the cooler tones of the office spaces around it. For

The conservatory restaurant (opposite page) is lit primarily with tungsten halogen sources to give a 'warm' feeling. The central atrium spaces (left and below) have strong daylighting, supplemented by low-voltage downlights and wallwashers, particularly in the darker exhibition spaces under the galleries (bottom)

this reason, tungsten halogen sources were specified, in a range of luminaires. These included a series of pedestal-mounted decorative fixtures, matching the handrail design, mounted at each angle of the octagon and uplighting the sloping ceiling structure.

The pools-of-light effect specified by the interior designers for the dining areas was created by narrow-beam, low-voltage tungsten halogen spotlights *(ch 3)*;

24 of these were mounted at high level within the conservatory apex, with less powerful versions under the lowered ceiling soffit. Because of the difficulty of re-adjustment, a symmetrical arrangement of pools serves the centre of the space, within which tables can be adjusted to suit different layouts. The spandrel wall is floodlit, using the same sources, located at the junction of glass wall and sloping roof, and angled back into the space.

In the principal central space leading from the front door (left and below), with its recurring steel arches, hidden uplighting silhouettes the structure. Discreet downlights both pick out the furniture and provide direct task lighting in the work areas (opposite page, bottom). The huge granite portals (opposite page, top) are washed by ceiling-recessed PAR 56 fixtures

Photos: Jaime Ardiles-Arce

Union Bank of Switzerland, New York

Lighting design: Cline, Bettridge Bernstein
Architects and designers: Gensler and Associates

This project is a classic example of where the early involvement of a lighting designer in the project team led to a totally integrated result which creatively enhances the architecture. The client wanted a strong street-level presence at its new Park Avenue offices. The existing space, 38 metres long, 8 metres wide, and 7.5 metres high, was awkward, with an elaborate coffered ceiling lit by chandeliers.

To create a more contemporary image, Gensler swept all this away and divided the space into four distinct areas, according to different functions, using glass and steel substructures within the old shell. The lighting scheme had to accentuate these divisions, while pulling visitors through the spaces. At the same time the stainless steel roof structure and gateway arches were to be highlighted, while providing sufficient, but understated, ambient light for staff and customers to transact their business.

The chosen strategy was a direct/indirect system: indirect lighting for the reflective white ceiling, which would in turn silhouette the steel arches, supplemented by direct downlighting *(ch 3)* for task illumination and to pick out the texture and colour of the furnishings. The steel arch system was the natural place in which to hide the fixtures. Uplights *(ch 3)* could be integrated into the beam far enough from the ceiling to light it evenly, while the downlights could be placed high enough not to shine into users' eyes at normal viewing angles. Mains powered incandescent *(ch 2)* sources were chosen, in preference to low-voltage lamps *(ch 2)*, to avoid the need for a transformer and to cut installation costs. The uplights consist of 150W quartz halogen *(ch 2)* sources mounted in a custom-designed reflector; the downlights incorporate 50W reflector lamps *(ch 2)*.

The granite portals are monumental; the formal progression of the spaces was enhanced by creating a repeating rhythm of light at these gateways, using concealed, ceiling-recessed PAR 56 *(ch 2)* fixtures. These are focused through the ceiling structure, in an asymmetric pattern, so that light slips between the steel arches below without spilling onto them.

Part of the banking hall was set aside for a gallery, showing a constantly changing art pro-gramme. The vertical plane of the exhibition wall is evenly lit by 500W PAR 56 quartz halogen wallwashers which, by choice of beam angle, allow easy illumination of different-sized pictures or objects. The light reflected back into the room balances the brightness from the daylit exterior wall.

In order to create distinct moods for varying uses of the facility, the lighting designers specified a four-scene automatic pre-set dimming system *(ch 5)*: daytime and night-time use, plus a scene for general reception events and another for gallery openings.

Saint Mary Axe, London

Lighting design: Lighting Design Partnership

In this office refurbishment in the City of London, Lighting Design Partnership (LDP) had to achieve modern ambient light levels whilst respecting the historic turn-of-the-century interior. After research into other buildings of the period, LDP's main solution was the development of a range of fittings in an appropriate period style, all fitted with modern sources, principally metal halide *(ch 2)* and compact fluorescent *(ch 2)*. The luminaires were custom-made by Architectural Metalworkers, with an antique brass finish and grill detail chosen to match those of the existing interior doors and windows.

For a number of the office spaces, pendant and bracket versions of a special period luminaire (opposite page, left) were designed with a range of sources. In the entrance hall, with its small rotunda (opposite page, right), tungsten halogen is used exclusively to pick up the gold-leaf detail. On the upper floors, which have low ceilings, specially designed surface-mounted glazed opalescent fixtures (above) help to create interest

Due to the building's limited floor-to-ceiling heights, the creation of usable ceiling or floor voids was not possible. All the fittings had to be surface-mounted, with the control gear *(ch 2)* integrated into the antique brass ceiling rose of the pendants and the brackets of the wall-mounted versions.

Various rooms in the building had their own particular problems and were treated in different ways. In the main banking floor, with its high ceiling, 250W metal halide sources were used. In the entrance hall, with its small rotunda, 300W double-ended tungsten halogen lamps *(ch 2)* were preferred, to add warmth to the reception area and also to emphasize the gold-leaf detail in the wall and ceiling decoration. In the smaller cellular offices on the first and second floors, the metal halide luminaires were installed on shorter pendants. The HID *(ch 2)* versions were fitted with an opalescent glass liner to diffuse the light, plus a sandblasted sheet of safety glass which softened the shadows on the ceiling.

The long corridor on the ground floor was originally lit by natural light through a series of lay-lights, which have since been covered by the new office extension above. Fluorescent battens behind the opalescent glass now provide apparent daylight. In the other corridors, a smaller version of the pendant luminaire was fitted with compact fluorescent sources for maximum efficiency and minimum maintenance.

The three upper floors of the building have low ceiling heights, so pendants were ruled out. Conventional ceiling-mounted fluorescent downlighters *(ch 3)* were also vetoed by the planning authorities.

A decorative but functional office luminaire was custom-designed, comprising a frame structure with opalescent panels, housing three louvred compact fluorescent lamps, which achieves adequate office lighting levels while avoiding the appearance of a typical bland office refurbishment.

22-23 Austin Friars, London

Lighting design: Lighting Design Ltd
Architects: Rolfe Judd

This five-storey listed Victorian building was designed by Aston Webb in 1888. Rolfe Judd refurbished and re-fitted the building for speculative office rental. The interior design follows Webb's historical precedents, with extensive use of terracotta and faience to accentuate the structure. Lighting Design Ltd was responsible for lighting the public areas of the entrance and the small central atrium; the treatment had to be sensitive to the historic materials and textures of Rolfe Judd's scheme.

The atrium lighting scheme was designed to avoid heavy downward glare when viewed from the ground floor (left). At the upper level of the atrium (below) custom-made torchères conceal standard tungsten halogen floodlights

The circular staircase (left) is emphasized by a ring of six narrow-beam reflector lamps recessed into the mosaic base. In the atrium, a single hidden spotlight gives added focus to the keystone above the lifts (below)

The small entrance lobby focuses on an impressive spiral staircase, rising up through the five floors of the building, beyond which the visitor can see the covered courtyard. To give maximum emphasis to the staircase's form, a ring of six narrow-beam, 20W 12V metal reflector lamps *(ch 2)* was recessed into a circular plinth of original Roman mosaics below the stairs. These uplight the staircase, picking up the outer edge of the steps and throwing shadows of the balustrade onto the underside of the spiral soffit. Additional ambient light is provided by custom-designed compact fluorescent *(ch 2)* wall lights, painted grey to match the metal balustrade.

Beyond the stairs is the covered, ten-metre-square atrium, with lifts and balconies arranged along one side. The walls are opulently clad in banded faience and terracotta, rising up from a floor comprising fan-pattern granite sets. The lighting strategy was to layer the lighting from the bottom to the top of the space, and to avoid powerful downlighting *(ch 3)* glaring down from high level.

On the ground floor, narrow-beam, tungsten halogen *(ch 2)* uplighters *(ch 3)* were recessed into the granite sets around the perimeter of the space. These cast fingers of light up the walls, between the custom-designed wall lights, with their gridded, Rennie Mackintosh-style detail. In addition, the light beams also catch the edge of the balcony cornice at first-floor level.

An additional shielded spotlight *(ch 3)*, recessed under the first-floor balcony, gives added visual focus to the keystone above the lifts. On each level, ceiling-recessed, low-voltage dichroic *(ch 2)* downlights *(ch 3)* create additional illumination in the lift lobbies. From higher floors these appear as warm, pleasant pools of light punctuating the balcony spaces.

To give the atrium a crowning emphasis, a third layer of lighting was created at the very top of the space. A row of custom-made torchères was designed, comprising a metal bracket, which neatly hides a standard tungsten halogen floodlight *(ch 7)* behind it. The bracket is the same width as the balustrade, and its curvature echoes the form of the bronze-coloured wall panels. Ranged around the upper walls, and controlled via a photocell *(ch 5)*, the torchères illuminate the rendered finish wall surfaces below the glazed ceiling and provide a changing ambience throughout the day.

In keeping with the subtle, classic design of the space, overall ambient light levels on the ground floor are very low – 20 lux *(ch 1)*. Yet all the main architectural features are well emphasized and the relatively low-powered 20W spotlights provide bright, sparkly details when seen from below.

Jaeger factory, Campbeltown

Lighting design: Lighting Design Partnership

The lighting of factories and other large non-office workplaces is often regarded as a functional matter and is rarely given design attention. The usual principle seems to be to put the required level of illumination (lux) into the space, using the minimum number of the most efficient light sources, such as fluorescent battens or SON lamps, spaced uniformly across the ceiling. The demands of the work being undertaken and the potential psychological effects of lighting on workers are rarely considered.

The lighting scheme for the Jaeger factory uses high-frequency fluorescent trough luminaires, each chosen specifically to suit the functions of the different work zones

An exception is the Campbeltown factory of Jaeger, the up-market clothing manufacturer. When the production facility was upgraded in the mid-1980s, this enlightened client, aware of the importance of lighting for staff morale and efficiency, commissioned Lighting Design Partnership (LDP) to devise a scheme geared specifically to their needs.

The first decision was the selection of main light sources and luminaires. Ideally, one lamp type was to be used throughout, for ease of maintenance, so the choice had to be correct. Jaeger agreed to the use of

more expensive high-frequency fluorescent *(ch 2)* trough reflector luminaires throughout the scheme, to avoid flicker *(ch 2)*, all fitted with tri-phosphor lamps *(ch 2)*. This gave good colour rendering *(ch 1)* in areas where there was no daylight, as well as offering high efficiency *(ch 1)* and long lamp-life *(ch 1)*. At that time it was an innovative step for a factory management.

The luminaires weren't just installed uniformly. The various parts of the plant had specific requirements. In the general production area, luminaires were mounted on continuous trunking to give even downlighting *(ch 3)* to the working plane. But unusually for a factory, additional fittings were also installed above them, to give some diffuse uplighting *(ch 3)* to the ceiling and to improve the ambience of the space.

In the cloth-cutting area the same high-frequency fluorescent sources were specified, but as light levels on the working plane had to be higher, a greater density of luminaires was fitted, each louvred to prevent glare. The final inspection area presented the biggest challenge, in that a series of fixed workbenches each had a specific task – steam-pressing, sewing, visual inspection, and so on – with different lighting requirements. For example, the pressing benches needed cross-lighting from two sides to eliminate shadows, whereas the visual inspection workstations needed strong, vertical illumination.

The solution was to mount two rows of luminaires above the workstations, each with a specific light beam distribution. The exact configuration and combination of fixtures changed according to the requirements of the area being lit. Some had mirrored louvres, to provide uniform, even illumination. Over the steam-pressing area, both rows were employed together, to give the necessary cross-lighting. The fitting chosen for the vertical inspection areas was one normally specified for high bay lighting in warehouses, providing a very strong vertical beam. All the luminaires had to be mounted in dust-proof housings, to prevent the lamps and louvres getting clogged up, for example with dust and lint.

The Jaeger scheme is a rare example of a complex, non-uniform industrial lighting problem solved with lighting design.

Due to the irregular ceiling (below) uplighting was not possible. Zumtobel therefore developed a custom-made direct/indirect luminaire (right) with its own reflector and louvred down light

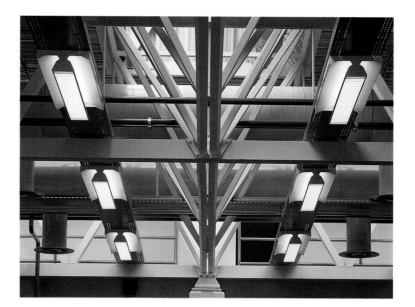

Neue Züricher Zeitung, Zürich

Lighting design: Zumtobel Lighting

An interesting custom-designed lighting solution for an industrial workplace can be seen at the printing plant of *Neue Züricher Zeitung*, one of Europe's leading newspapers. During the planning stage of the plant, a key consideration was how to create optimum lighting conditions for staff. Most of the work is done during the hours of darkness and twilight, so natural daylight is rarely enjoyed. The strategy was to provide the nightshift workers with at least the illusion of daylight.

Industrial safety was a prime consideration. Working on the sorting machine, for example, requires good light and shadow distribution. Operators must be able to see the task and equipment clearly, to avoid the risk of accident, particularly in the early morning hours when concentration may start to fail.

These combined requirements of an attractive visual ambience and industrial safety pointed towards a dual, direct/indirect lighting system. However, the irregular steel girder structure of the building meant that this could not be achieved in a conventional manner (ie where the ceiling is used as the reflector). To get around the problem, Zumtobel developed a customized *(ch 4)* direct/indirect luminaire to meet the plant's requirements, which incorporated its own diffusing reflector and which could be installed on the standard cable ducting.

The luminaire houses two 50W daylight fluorescent lamps *(ch 2)* located one above the other. A curved reflector spanning the upper surface of the luminaire generates indirect, diffuse illumination from the upper lamp, to produce a daylight ambience. A louvre underside to the housing provides good glare control for the direct downward lighting onto the work surface. The combination of the two guarantees the necessary level of illumination for the working plane, plus good shadow conditions required for effective three-dimensional perception.

In the lobby (above) and reception areas (opposite page, far right) warm incandescent lighting contrasts with the cooler sources outside to invite customers in

The SAS Royal Hotel, Brussels

Lighting design: Lighting Design Partnership with Atelier d'Art Urbain, Christian Lundwaal and Nicolas Lecompte

The SAS Royal Hotel in Brussels, designed to fit its Art Deco context by architect Michael Jaspers, is the Belgian capital's most prestigious hotel. Appropriately, the latest control systems *(ch 5)* were used to produce an infinitely flexible and subtly nuanced lighting scheme. The hotel's night-time profile is crucial to its commercial success: it operates around the clock and the way it is perceived both by day and night is important for business.

The exterior lighting *(ch 7)* is used to express the building's verticality and to emphasize the architecture. It deliberately gives the hotel a dramatic, eye-catching night-time profile, with fingers of light grazing the building's façades. Light beacons on the roof of the hotel were designed by Lighting Design Partnership (LDP) using standard street lamps enclosed in specially constructed cages.

To prevent light shining in through the bedroom windows, the light sources were located very close to the building's façade, to wash light up the exterior walls, a technique already used successfully at London's Savoy Hotel *(ch 7)*.

Contrasting colour temperatures *(ch 2)* of different light sources were used to draw guests inside. The visually cool lighting directly outside the main entrance contrasts with the more warmly lit façade and the warmer reception and atrium areas. The hotel's main atrium is intended to feel like an exterior space, so fittings were used which look the same as the bracket fixtures on the exterior walls.

The hotel is built over the remains of an old Roman wall which was retained and integrated into the atrium space. Theatrical gobo projectors were

The lighting in the main public spaces, such as the atrium (top) and the restaurant (bottom) is controlled by photocell and computer so that different 'scenes' can be selected automatically throughout the day

used to throw leaf patterns and shadows onto the Roman wall, giving it extra texture at night. The light also falls on guests sitting in the bar areas; the shifting light patterns soften the appearance of the atrium space and respond to the presence of the trees and plants within it. The Roman wall sits in a pool of water. Spotlights *(ch 3)* under the water shine upwards, casting shimmering ripple patterns across the surface of the stones.

An important feature of any hotel lighting scheme, for psychological comfort, is the creation of a sense of change over time *(ch 5)*. This strategy is particularly important in the hotel atrium. Here the entire lighting installation is controlled by photocell *(ch 5)* and timeclock, interfaced with a central computer. The system can be programmed to take account of every combination of weather condition, as well as seasonal, diurnal and functional variations.

The computer-regulated system installed at the SAS Royal Hotel is one of the most technically refined. As well as ensuring ideal lighting conditions, the system also acts as a combined building management and energy conservation system. This simplifies maintenance.

For example, LDP wanted to use effective, but relatively inefficient, tungsten halogen *(ch 2)* lamps. By dimming them down, using control systems, their lamp-life *(ch 1)* was increased by up to ten times, thus offering optimum visual effect with maximum energy efficiency.

This use of purpose-selected light sources is particularly noticeable in the public areas where tungsten and tungsten halogen lamps ensure enhanced flesh-tones to make guests feel good. Within the bar and restaurant areas, lighting is pre-programmed for different times of the day – breakfast, lunch, dinner, late dinner, and so on. There is an up/down adjustment facility for fine tuning and, as in other public areas under automatic control, a manual override facility.

The stage-like central lobby (left) is lit by theatrical profile projectors, low-voltage tungsten halogen spotlights and downlights. Each table on the balcony carries a Starck-designed coloured glass lamp

Courtesy: Morgans Hotel Group

Paramount Hotel, New York

Lighting design: Jules Fisher & Paul Marantz Inc
Architects: Haigh Space
Interior design: Philippe Starck

Following the success of the Royalton Hotel in the late 1980s, the Paramount Hotel was Philippe Starck's second Manhattan hotel for style entrepreneur, Ian Schrager. The Fisher-Marantz team was responsible for the lighting in both establishments. Schrager's intention was to transform the seedy, run-down hostel into a modestly priced, but sophisticated hotel, which would attract the young, design- and fashion-conscious traveller.

The compact bedrooms (above) are mainly illuminated by an incandescent uplighter, switched alternately with a pattern projector. In the tiny bathroom (right) a conical glass lamp provides intriguing illumination

Courtesy: Morgans Hotel Group

The lighting had to play its part in this market re-positioning, while at the same time accentuating the always provocative, unorthodox design details of Starck's interior. To reduce costs, Starck suggested paring down the design details to a refined collage of furnishing and lighting elements, with minimal alteration to the architectural structure of the building.

The lobby was envisioned as a large living/dining room, providing a central social focus, a stage for the extrovert target guests. The central area is furnished with a collection of designer chairs and a Starck table/lamp combination, set on a skewed chessboard carpet, in front of an updated version of the Ziegfeld Follies stairs. A café runs round the mezzanine balcony.

The lighting of the space is similarly collage-like. The perimeter of the larger space, the encircling mezzanine, is washed with neodymium-filtered tungsten *(ch 2)* sources to establish a neutral, cool colour baseline. Each café table on the balcony carries a tiny Starck-designed coloured glass lamp to anchor the ring of diners overlooking the scene below.

Over the main area, the ceiling houses four discrete lighting elements, including a grid of concealed theatrical profile projectors, to frame the chessboard seating group. In addition, a large eyelid droops down to reveal a line of low-voltage, narrow-beam tungsten halogen *(ch 2)* lamps positioned to reflect a platinum glow from the gold-leaf wall behind the grand stair; while an arc of low-voltage tungsten halogen downlighters *(ch 3)* frames the service desks. Finally, a line of eyeballs, fitted with neodymium reflector lamps *(ch 2)*, illuminates the 'quiet' side of the room.

The guest rooms are tiny compared with most commercial hotels in the USA, so furniture and fittings had to be compact and multifunctional. The rotating armoire contains room for storage of personal items, the TV set and VCR, and concealed on top, the main room lighting, an incandescent *(ch 2)* uplighter *(ch 3)* switched alternately with a simple uplight pattern projector, when less light and a more restful ambience are required.

The headboard to the bed (in some cases bearing a huge computer-printed reproduction of Vermeer's 'The Lacemaker') has a picture light mounted over the frame. Fitted with two low-voltage, tungsten halogen reflector lamps, this also doubles as the bed reading light. An elongated, Starck-designed pendant downlight, in cast aluminium, hangs over the table and, to save extensive re-wiring, is connected to the original central ceiling rose by a custom-made, purple braid-covered cable. In the bathroom a backlit mirror detail, topped by a conical glass lamp, completes the intriguing guest bedroom lighting.

Sterling Hotel, Heathrow Airport, London

Lighting design: DPA (UK) Lighting Consultants
Architects: Manser Associates
Interior design: Peter Glynn Smith Associates

The 400-room Sterling Hotel at Heathrow Airport's Terminal 4, which opened in 1990, is BAA's (British Airport Authority) flagship hotel. The radical design by Manser Associates has an essentially hi-tech airport aesthetic. In form it has been likened to a giant hangar, with two accommodation wings ranged down opposite sides of a 30-metre-high covered atrium with huge glazed walls at each end. All the public activities of the hotel – reception, restaurant, bars, and so on – are centred here and can be directly overlooked from the guest room windows.

The interior designers wanted the lighting to create the effect of a gently-lit, enclosed street, with a warm and intimate environment at ground level. During the day the space is lit from the massive glazed openings at either end. This is insufficient for the tropical palm-tree planting, so for

12 hours a day they are given additional growth light from critically focused metal halide *(ch 2)* spotlights located in the roof. At night these are turned off and low-voltage uplighters *(ch 3)* mounted in the planting boxes bathe the underside of the leaves, for decorative effect.

On dull days and after dark, light levels are controlled by photocells *(ch 5)* linked to a pro-grammable Lutron dimming system *(ch 5)*. Over the course of 24 hours, this sophisticated system sets various 'scenes', so the lit ambience is constantly changing. The most dramatic effect takes place at sunset, when the daytime lighting pattern is reversed and an ethereal blue/green wash illuminates the atrium ceiling like a flood of moonlight. This is created by wide-beam metal halide luminaires with blue glass filters installed below the ceiling between structural columns. Barn door screens mask possible glare for viewers on the high-level walkways.

Most of the ambient lighting is provided from banks of US 120V 500W PAR 56 *(ch 2)* lamps, set in long-nosed PAR cans and mounted on ceiling-mounted tracks *(ch 3)*. These offer a warm light and a narrow, easily controlled beam; they are also easily dimmed and have a 4000-hours rated lamp-life *(ch 1)*.

In addition, there is some low-level decorative lighting *(ch 3)* to help define the various spaces – café, brasserie, cocktail lounge and reception are all identified by a different style luminaire.

Computer-controlled switching cycles correspond to their function and opening hours. For example, tall mushroom-like stretch fabric table lights adorn the lounge, the limits of which are defined by four tall illuminated fabric corner columns. In the brasserie, canopies conceal track-mounted low-voltage *(ch 2)* spotlights to light the table tops. While such fittings make interesting visual foci for visitors, their purpose is mainly psychological; they make little contribution to the overall ambient light at floor level.

On either side of the free-standing glazed lifts are two sets of elegant walkways, giving access to the bedroom wings. To maintain the effect of lightness and to keep the ceiling uncluttered, these are lit by recessed uplights set in the floor, a technique vaguely reminiscent of runway lighting. Pools of light thrown onto the underside of the walkways give added dramatic effect to the atrium.

By day the massive glazed walls (opposite page, right) provide daylight to the atrium. At night various computer-controlled scenes take over, such as the 'moonlight' wash at high level (below). On the walkways recessed uplighters cast pools of light on to the ceiling (right), while individual public areas (opposite page, left) are designated by their own style of local luminaire

Taj Bengal Hotel, Calcutta

Lighting design: Lighting Design Ltd

The Taj Bengal Hotel in Calcutta is an opulent, five-star hotel, with a strongly indigenous Indian interior design. Lighting Design's (LDL) brief was to produce a lighting scheme for the lobby and the eight-storey interior atrium which would enhance the regional design theme, using lighting sources and equipment which would not present local maintenance and replacement problems. Simple, widely available tungsten sources, of various kinds, were mainly specified; these had the added advantage of complementing the warm stone finishes of the walls.

The lobby area is punctuated by huge octagonal stone columns, around which are arranged the seating areas. Alternate faces of the columns are uplit, using PAR 56 lamps *(ch 2)* hidden behind the stone bulkhead that runs around the base of the columns. The textured banded stone facets are further emphasized by a series of low-voltage tungsten lamps *(ch 2)* around the top of the columns. Their crisp white colour appearance *(ch 1)* was chosen to contrast with the hidden mains voltage tungsten lamps lighting the adjacent ceiling coffers. More decorative lighting *(ch 3)* elements were provided by local table lamps around the seating area, which give a sense of human scale, and a series of flamboyant pendant chandeliers, incorporating clear-glass tungsten lamps (for added sparkle) mounted in glass shades. To focus attention on the reception desk, low-voltage downlighters *(ch 3)* are used, and, so as not to create a blank, dark background, the same sources are used as wallwashers behind the desk.

Above the atrium, an extensive glazed ceiling comprises two distinct elements, both of which required lighting after dark. A starlight effect is provided around the ceiling by tiny long-life incandescent lamps *(ch 2)* mounted in disco-type panels. These are under-run to extend their lamp-life *(ch 1)* in this fairly inaccessible location. In addition, a series of decorative stained glass ceiling panels are backlit at night by fluorescent battens *(ch 2)* mounted behind an acrylic diffuser, to soften the effect.

For the main ambient lighting LDL didn't want powerful sources glaring down into the space from high level. So it opted for a layered series of relatively small, low-voltage 50W downlighters (using capsule lamps mounted in reflectors because of their relative availability).

Photocell-dimmer controls *(ch 5)* further extend their lamp-life. Around the top of the space the lamps can be serviced from above, while on the lower façades they can be re-lamped directly from the balconies, where they create an interesting scalloped effect.

One side of the atrium comprises an imposing, full-height granite wall. This is given some relief illumination, using two linear tungsten halogen sources, directed up and down the wall. These are cleverly shielded from view by a block of apparently dislodged stone protruding from the wall's surface.

Other lighting elements within the space include a series of low-level tungsten spotlights *(ch 2)* uplighting *(ch 3)* the trees, and table lamps in the seating areas. Indian statues are dramatically uplit, using low-voltage lamps recessed into the plinths.

The large atrium space (left and opposite page) is lit by fluorescent battens mounted behind decorative stained glass ceiling panels plus a series of low-voltage downlighters around the balconies. Alternate facets of the octagonal stone columns in the lobby area (below) are uplit by PAR 56 spotlamps, with smaller low-voltage fittings ringing the column heads

Casual Quilted Giraffe, New York

Lighting design: Jerry Kugler Associates
Interior architecture/design: J Woodson Rainey

When the Casual Quilted Giraffe (now the Quilted Giraffe) opened in the shadow of Philip Johnson's AT&T building in 1987, it was hailed as one of Manhattan's best-designed, most stylish eating places. Without doubt a large part of its success is due to early collaboration between lighting designer and architect, and the resulting close integration of lighting and interior design.

The lighting fixtures themselves had to form part of the restaurant's architectural vocabulary, while the lighting effects play off and accentuate the strongly textured, but largely colourless materials which dress the space – terrazzo, inlaid stainless steel, brushed metals, etched glass, and grey granite.

All the sources are incandescent *(ch 2)*, to give consistent coloured lighting throughout and not to detract from the subtle gradations of interior finish.

The restaurant comprises a single rectangular dining room, flanked by a tall window behind the bar, with a U-shaped court of tables in the centre and an L-shaped dining balcony, with banquettes, on two sides.

Two custom-made torchères, acting as visual anchors and functional light sources, mark the four corners of the central space. These are cast in aluminium, with hemispherical martelé reflectors. Their 75W incandescent T-lamps give off a soft, but powerful glow, and uplighting *(ch 3)* onto the hammered bowl adds a complementary sparkle.

These complex fixtures contain three lighting components, all controlled independently – the glass cylinders, uplighters directed onto the hammered urn, and a cluster of tiny wheat grain lamps inside the urn, which merely reflect dots of light onto the ceiling.

The entire room is controlled by a Lutron 11-zone, four-scene pre-set control system *(ch 5)*, which balances the lighting levels for daytime, evening and night-time conditions.

Within the same family of fixtures, custom-made, stainless steel wall sconces run the entire length of the upper tier; light from their 75W T-lamps washes the twin layers of finely perforated steel which form

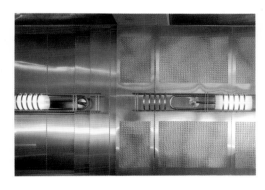

The view of the restaurant (opposite page) shows the play of light on the perforated steel walls. One of the custom-made, incandescent wall-sconces is shown in close-up (above). The central space is marked out by a series of giant torchères (right) with hammered bowls and martelé reflectors

Photos: Nathaniel Lieberman

the wall. The subtlety of light playing on materials is explored most fully here – a moiré pattern of shadows is set up, accentuated by the curvature of the wall, while the gently brushed surface catches the light, creating a swirling, diaphanous effect. This textural treatment produces a far livelier result than the usual flat, perfectly reflective metal.

As well as creating these innovative, textural effects, both these fixtures offer a soft sphere of downward illumination which is essential for the appropriate modelling *(ch 2)* of customers' faces at table level.

Within the split metallic barrel-vault ceiling are track-mounted *(ch 3)* and recessed low-voltage *(ch 2)* accent lights. These punch light down onto the bar and the perimeter tables, to create a sense of intimacy, as well as picking out strategically placed flowers, to give occasional flashes of high colour contrast. Larger tables in the centre court also have accent lights focused on them.

Dress Circle, Harrods, London

Lighting design: Lighting Design Partnership
Interior design: Maurice Broughton Associates

The Dress Circle comprises an elongated circle, which wraps around the double-height void of the Harrods Food Hall below. The brief was to provide a lighting scheme which creates an airy, light ambience, to compensate for the lack of natural daylight, as well as accentuating Maurice Broughton Associates' (MBA) cool, modernist interior design details. The solutions are simple but effective and rely almost entirely on diffuse light reflected from wall and ceiling surfaces. The scheme won a citation in the 1987 International Association of Lighting Designers' Awards.

There are two main, contrasting ambient light sources. Running around the space is a trough detail, which appears as an extension of an encircling, curved ceiling bulkhead. Within this, a cool daylight linear cold cathode *(ch 2)* source is concealed, to wash the adjacent ceilings with fresh, white light. Some light also percolates down through the slot between the trough and the bulkhead. The cold cathode source contrasts well with the warmer tungsten halogen *(ch 2)* used elsewhere. Around the outer edge of the ceiling, below the bulkhead, are a number of evenly spaced, semi-recessed low-voltage *(ch 3)* dichroic *(ch 2)* sources. Angled close to the high-gloss wall, their double scallop effect down the wall surface echoes the three-sided lozenge form of the laminate-topped tables.

These two ambient sources are supplemented by a series of decorative, custom-made *(ch 4)* fixtures. Cantilevered off the wall on slender brackets, these comprise large discs of pale green-tinted glass, concealing a mains voltage linear tungsten halogen source which is used as an uplighter *(ch 3)*. The delicate form and tones of the glass are gently lit from behind by reflected downlight. A smaller, modified version of the same luminaire, using the same green glass detail, is used as a downlight *(ch 3)* over the food servery area; a centrally mounted low-voltage tungsten halogen capsule lamp provides the illuminations.

Lighting control is by simple switching; there are no dimmers or control systems. Dress Circle, Harrods, is a good example of how simplicity of sources and technique can be equally effective, for its purpose, as something far more ambitious and complex.

Totally lit with artificial light, the café's modernist style is emphasized by three main light sources: cold cathode around the ceiling bulkhead, supplemented by low-voltage dichroic lamps casting scallop shapes down the wall (opposite page and above left). In addition, custom-made uplighters (above right and left), using mains voltage tungsten halogen lamps, uplight the space and add a subtle decorative detail

Courtesy: Maurice Broughton Associates

Princes Square Shopping Centre, Glasgow

Lighting design: Lighting Design Partnership
Architects: Hugh Martin Partnership

Princes Square in Glasgow is a prize-winning speciality shopping centre, created by glazing over the inner courtyard of a group of existing 18th-century buildings and excavating a lower ground floor. Its four-storey interior is in the turn-of-the-century Arts and Crafts style. The lighting scheme had to both echo that style, and enhance the impressive vertical structural ironwork and original stone walls.

Incandescent sources are used throughout. This accentuates the warm tones of the stone and timber (right and opposite page, bottom). Special theatre projectors, mounted in custom-designed wrought-iron orbs (above) throw gobo patterns onto the ground floor, while the vertical steel structure (opposite page, top) is picked out with tungsten halogen floodlights mounted at the head of each column

On the whole, fairly diffuse ambient lighting , supplemented by more intense pools of warm, soft light, was preferred, rather than strongly accented directional display and feature lighting which might have been used in a more modern retail environment. Almost all the light sources in the centre are tungsten *(ch 1)*. This relatively energy-hungry solution was chosen for two reasons: first, tungsten's good colour rendering *(ch 1)* and warm appearance were seen as appropriate to enhance the natural stone walls and timbered balconies. Equally important, given the high level of natural lighting, was the transition from daytime to night-time use. A photocell-controlled dimming system *(ch 5)* was installed, which, as daylight fades, brings up the artificial lighting almost imperceptibly. Incandescent *(ch 1)* sources are ideal for such dimming control.

Much of the direct downlighting *(ch 3)* onto the ground floor is provided by 1KW and 2KW tungsten halogen *(ch 1)* theatre projectors . These are mounted in a series of large, decorative orbs, custom-made in filigree wrought iron, hanging within the glazed ceiling. To create more varied, less uniform illumination, some of these projectors throw abstract gobo patterns onto the central lily pond mosaic floor below. Two further projectors mounted under the upper-level soffits give a similar treatment to the main interior façade, while four others highlight the grand staircase below.

To emphasize the vertical steel structure, tungsten halogen floodlights were positioned at the head of the tall columns, just where they branch out to support the glazed roof. These were disguised by painting them the same colour as the ironwork. More diffuse ambient lighting is provided by a series of handcrafted, wrought-iron period globes, with tungsten sources. Located along the balustrades, on the stairs and high on the rear wall of the upper-floor food court, these fixtures also help break down the strong horizontal lines of the three balconies.

Fixtures on the three levels are differentiated by enamelled surface finishes – light blue, rose pink and green. The two middle levels of the centre contain the bulk of the retail outlets. So as not to detract from the shop frontages, the only lighting here is furnished by recessed low-voltage *(ch 2)* downlights under the balconies.

Safeway Superstore, Coventry

Lighting and interior design: Addison Design

Until recently, lighting in many British supermarkets has been functional and unexciting. Symmetrical rows of ceiling-mounted fluorescent battens (ch 2), with or without diffusers , were the main order of the day. By the end of the 1980s, superstore design shifted in an attempt to make supermarket shopping more pleasantly leisure-oriented.

Part of this change included restructuring traditional in-store logistics, and segmenting the store into different departments, each with its own distinct ambience. More sophisticated lighting design had an important part to play in this process, as can be seen from Addison's design treatment of the 3,850-square-metre Safeway superstore in Coventry, which opened in 1990.

The store is divided into a central core area for functional everyday goods, with a practical race-track layout, and, wrapped around it, against the perimeter walls, a series of luxury departments, such as wine, bakery, dairy, and delicatessen. Each of these areas has been given a distinctive feel, using co-ordinated floor finishes, ceiling heights and forms, and lighting. Different sources and colour temperatures *(ch 1)* have been well employed to create character and contrast.

For example, the functional race-track area had to be fast, efficient and bright. Metal halide discharge lamps *(ch 2)* with panel diffusers, were set into the four-metre high, 600 mm grid ceiling, giving 1200 lux *(ch 1)* of evenly distributed illumination at the floor. Only the occasional hot-spot feature – special product lines, displayed in ash-veneered cabinets – are highlit with low-voltage *(ch 2)* accent lighting to punctuate the long gondola runs. At the centre, six skylights bring natural daylight into the store, an increasingly important requirement of modern supermarket design.

Around the perimeter, over the bakery and delicatessen areas, the ceiling drops to three metres, to give a more intimate feel. The lighting, too, shifts gear, with a mix of white SON *(ch 2)* and warm compact fluorescents *(ch 2)* to give a warmer, less utilitarian feel. Here, customers are encouraged to linger as they purchase more luxurious, higher margin goods. Occasional recessed low-voltage halogen *(ch 2)* downlighters *(ch 3)* throw added light onto the high-level departmental signage, creating a subtle shadow behind the free-standing lettering.

The boundary between these two areas is defined by a bulkhead, decorated with white-lettered signage. Concealed fluorescent battens, overlapped in a herring-bone layout to avoid dark spots, make this ceiling feature glow overhead. Hidden fluorescent lamps are also used around the perimeter of the dropped ceiling, as gentle wallwashers . The tile-clad walls, with their rippled finish and subtle dado line, provide a bright visual focus, rather than the usual dark void.

Like many modern superstores, Safeway in Coventry includes a café/patisserie area for customer convenience, and to increase dwell-time. Attractively furnished in timber and glass, it is lit by a range of sources. Ceiling-mounted white SON and compact fluorescent lamps provide the general ambient lighting while an inner ring of recessed low-voltage dichroic *(ch 2)* downlights gives added punch to the children's play area. Plaster ceramic dish uplighters, housing tungsten sources and mounted on the ash partitions, add more intimate customer lighting over the tables.

The central 'race-track' for everyday goods (below), brightly lit with 'cool' functional metal halide sources, is surrounded by fresh food, bakery and deli-catessen departments (above and opposite page). These are given a more intimate feel with white SON and warm compact fluorescent lamps, interspersed with low-voltage downlights. The café area (top) also uses wall-mounted, ceramic dish uplighters to create warmth over the eating areas

Bulgari, New York

Lighting: H M Brandston & Partners

The lighting scheme for this exclusive Manhattan store received a 1991 Award
of Excellence from the International Association of Lighting Designers (IALD).
The brief was a lighting scheme which focused attention on the jewellery,
while softly highlighting the store's geometric interior form and rich, classic
materials. The luminaires themselves had to be as unobtrusive as possible,
to encourage a direct relationship between customer and product.

*Light from the
intensely lit vitrines
provides much of the
ambient illumination
(opposite page, left).
In addition, miniature
low-voltage strips
embedded in the
beams emphasize the
wall and ceiling forms
(above). In the sales
rooms (opposite page,
right) table lamps are
supplemented by
ceiling-mounted 50W
dichroic spotlights
directed onto the
fitting-tables*

Photos: Norman McGrath

Entering the store from busy Fifth Avenue, a long, curved central gallery provides a contrastingly quiet, opulent atmosphere. The tall, elegantly proportioned space is punctuated by a series of vitrine showcases which echo details on the store frontage. The sweep of the space is reinforced by the lighting which is soft, diffused and indirect, punctuated by points of brilliance in the vitrines. These are lit by multiple 12V 50W dichroic lamps *(ch 2)* on tracks *(ch 3)* hidden above, a row of fixed floodlights with tempered glass spread lenses, plus rows of adjustable spotlights directed at individual pieces of jewellery, which ensures that the jewellery sparkles, even at midday. The intense 'light windows' indirectly provide much of the floor-level illumination as well as eliminating veiling reflections outside.

The ambient lighting reveals and accentuates the geometry of the shop's interlocking vault forms, finished in hand-rubbed plaster. The illumination is smooth and even but not uniform, allowing the profiles of the ceiling and walls to be read clearly. It is furnished by miniature low-voltage strips, embedded into the free-floating beams which traverse the space. In addition, square diffused apertures cut into the vertical fascia of the vaults wash light out and down the opposing ceiling forms.

Off the central gallery spine is a series of comfortably furnished sales rooms, where customers can examine jewellery pieces on leather-topped tables and then try them on in front of bevel-edged mirrors. The lighting strategy here is two-fold: to display the jewellery with the same sparkle as in the showcases, which requires a powerful, highly directed light beam. At the same time it has to offer a flattering image of the customer in the mirrors – this demands softer, more diffuse illumination.

The solution was a custom-made *(ch 4)* luminaire using the 50W dichroic *(ch 2)* lamp, which incorporates a special adjustable lens. A clear central section offers a glittery, intense beam onto the table, while around it a diffused perimeter ring softens the light falling on the customer. The overhead lighting is reinforced by theatrical fill-in lighting provided by diffuse light from table-top lamps. Located at seated customers' head height, they obviate any harsh facial shadows.

Tallaght Square Shopping Centre, Dublin

Lighting design: Lighting Design Ltd
Architects: Burke, Kennedy & Doyle

This award-winning shopping centre in the Tallaght suburb of Dublin, comprises three malls which converge at different levels onto the central Square – an atrium 60 metres across, with a 40-metre-high pyramid-shaped glazed ceiling. Lighting Design's (LDL) brief was to provide a functional, secure ambience in the malls, while creating a dynamic, theatrical atmosphere in the central square, both by day and night.

At night, the strategy in the main square was to keep overall ambient levels low – around 15-20 lux *(ch 2)* – to emphasize both the brightly lit entrances to the malls and a series of dramatically lit features within the space. The traditional use of local street-lamp-type lighting in the square was eschewed, in favour of a series of 150W metal halide *(ch 2)* projectors mounted at high level, on the atrium structure. Using gobo projectors and colour filters these throw random leaf patterns onto the floor and planting. Elements such as the travelator and scenic lifts are similarly framed in light from high level. As daylight fades, pre-set photocell control *(ch 5)* of all the luminaires ensures a gradual stepped introduction of effects.

Within the square, the main visual foci are an old ruined stone wall and water fountain, which act as a backdrop for a performance stage, and a separate fountain and watercourse feature. A special miniature theatre rig, on its own control circuit *(ch 5)*, was mounted above this, to light stage acts, promotional events, and so on. A number of waterproof PAR 36 lamps *(ch 2)* at low level behind the stage, linked in to the fountain's own computer programme, uplight the display of water.

Overhead, the larger elements of the roof structure are also emphasized at night, using narrow-beam metal halide lamps with a blue filter, which shine up the glazing structure. Around the base of the pyramidal structure is a continuous Magnagrid louvred ceiling concealing the smoke extractors. Alongside each extractor is a metal halide light-box supplying illumination to a series of fibre-optic *(ch 3)* starlights which shine out through the grid – a revolving wheel-shutter creates the effect. Fibre optics also frame the outline of the crow's nest radio station.

The malls have their own distinctive treatment. The entrances are illuminated brightly, using a mix of metal halide downlighters and low-voltage, bare capsule, tungsten halogen *(ch 2)* starlights. A softer, more diffuse ambience is provided in the malls by fluorescent battens *(ch 2)* mounted behind the Magnagrid ceiling panels. For security reasons, light levels in the malls are fairly high – around 200 lux – but light intensity is reduced close to the shopfronts so as not to distract from window displays.

The malls are punctuated by a series of coffered ceiling features, usually at turning points, where additional interest had to be created. Here, light levels are increased to around 500 lux, using additional metal halide downlights *(ch 3)* and low-voltage capsule lamps. The coffers themselves are uplit with hidden cold cathode *(ch 2)* sources.

In the main square, with its 40-metre-high pyramid roof (opposite page), low ambient light levels are maintained. The roof structure is emphasized using narrow-beam metal halide lamps (above). Within the space, the old wall and fountain (left) are specially lit using a theatre-style rig and waterproof PAR 36 lamps

For maximum
promotional impact,
the glazed entrance
and staircase (left and
below) are lit by lines
of blue cold cathode
around the stairs and
PAR 36 spotlights
which create a sunray
effect on the back
walls. Different bars
and catering areas
(opposite page) have
their own distinctive
treatment, often using
hidden cold cathode
and localized low-
voltage downlights
to minimize general,
direct lighting

The Atrium Leisure Centre, East Grinstead

Lighting design: Maurice Brill Lighting Design
Architects: Pavardin Associates
Interior design: Pavardin Associates, Raylian
London Ltd and Khuan Chew & Associates

**The Atrium is a multi-purpose leisure centre comprising two floors of ten-
pin bowling, two cinemas, a nightclub, restaurants, bars, and an exhibition
space. Maurice Brill Lighting Design had to light the building in a colourful,
entertaining fashion, appropriate to a leisure destination, while giving
each of the facilities its own thematic identity.**

The entrance and staircase, enclosed in a full-height, glazed corner section of the building, had to make maximum impact. The helical staircase, rising up through three storeys, was dramatically lit with two lines of blue cold cathode *(ch 2)* mounted on the underside, which echo the form of the stairs in vibrant, swirling curves. Unusually, the tubes themselves had to be twisted and bent in two directions; and to minimize vibrations, due to footfall on the stairs, they were fixed on special spring-loaded mounts.

Additional lighting was built into the landing edges, using PAR 36 *(ch 2)* Thomas cans to create a set of asymmetric sunrays on the rich orange back wall of the stairwell. A four-metre lighting boom was also mounted down the inside of the front walls, where they meet the glazing. Long-nosed PAR 36 Thomas Cans throw pools of light onto the front entrance way and landings; in addition, mounted at ceiling level, 500W PAR 56 cans cast perpendicular beams down onto the stair sides and create ambient light at floor level.

A more decorative effect was provided by custom-designed *(ch 4)* metal, barred wall lights by Box Products, located between the lift doors on each level. Maurice Brill also developed a series of ceiling-mounted light-rafts, housing cold cathode *(ch 2)* sources to uplight *(ch 3)* the dark blue ceiling, and dichroic *(ch 2)* downlights *(ch 3)* to boost ambient levels outside the bars and bowling-alley doors.

The family (as opposed to club) bowling lanes had a distinctive and unusual treatment: a range of sources mounted over the lanes, including ultraviolet lamps, low-voltage PAR 36 *(ch 2)* pin spotlights with five-colour filters , plus standard fluorescent battens *(ch 2)* offer for the possibility of changing lighting effects.

Lighting within the catering areas – the food servery in the Rock'n'Roll Bowl and the two bars, the Harley Bar and the Club Bowl – have strategic similarities but are differentiated by colour and detail. There is little direct lighting . For example, dropped ceilings or raft features around structural columns provide concealed locations for continuous tubes of cold cathode (white in the two bars, aquamarine blue in the servery), which give a soft glow on the ceilings. Low-voltage tungsten halogen *(ch 2)*

sources, usually hidden, give a more natural light over the food and drink areas – the low-voltage dichroic lamps, which are recessed within the back bar of the Harley, give added sparkle to the glasses and optics.

Each bar has its own decorative features: in the Harley, three rings of yellow cold cathode around some of the columns; and in the Club Bowl a circle of low-voltage downlights recessed around the satin metal, pear-shaped columns, whose light grazes the metal and shines down through three protruding glass fins. Here, too, hidden fluorescent lamps give a 3-D effect to the barrel-like details on the back bar.

Trondheim Concert Hall, Norway

Lighting design: Lighting Design Partnership
Architects: Arkitektgruppa/Jakobsen & Holter Arkitektkontor/KS Per Knudsen Arkitektkontor

The concert hall at Trondheim is a new building inserted into the fabric of the old town. The lighting brief encompassed the concert hall auditorium and the public circulation areas outside in the glazed gap between the hall itself, a new hotel and the surrounding two-storey, timber-built townscape. Norway's cool climate and abundance of hydroelectric power meant that neither lighting heat gain nor energy conservation were major issues.

In the main auditorium (right) the dual lighting system is mounted on motorized overhead gantries. For the glazed foyer/circulation spaces (below and opposite page) with its walkway/balconies, a low-voltage wire system is used extensively to emphasize the interior structure

While the performance area of the 1200-seat concert hall is lit with a conventional theatre lighting rig, the auditorium seating areas demanded special attention, to cater for the building's dual function as a performance venue and conference facility. Performance use requires lower lighting levels, here provided by 300W incandescent *(ch 2)* downlights *(ch 3)* fitted with dimmers enabling them to be gently faded down. Supplementary illumination comes from 250W metal halide *(ch 2)* floods , giving 500-750 lux

(ch 1) for conference functions. All the luminaires are mounted on motorized overhead access gantries, for easy maintenance.

The main public circulation and foyer area is contained within a glazed infill and consists of a series of balcony/walkways connecting the hall with the hotel opposite. The lighting strategy here was to emphasize the internal massing of these structures, while putting the steel glazing bars into silhouette against the lit interior, when viewed from outside. As the balcony-walkway structures are exposed, with little or no recess depth, an extensive surface-mounted, low-voltage wire system had to be employed. Tungsten halogen *(ch 2)* was favoured, both for its warmth and to enable slow, imperceptible dimming from daylight to artificial lighting, using photocell controls *(ch 5)*.

With this system the undersides of all the walkways are uplit; the walls of the concert hall block are gently washed using the same method. To further highlight the circulation routes, the connecting staircases are given their own lighting treatment. Concealed, indirect lighting, in the form of a fluorescent batten *(ch 2)* fitted with a prismatic cover, was fitted at the back of each stair tread. By this method, the treads above appear bathed in a gentle glowing light when viewed from below, while indirect illumination provides necessary, safe definition to the circulation routes. The effect of this is most spectacular on the large semi-circular staircase, where the enclosing lattice steelwork is strongly silhouetted.

For the main public retail floor, Lighting Design Partnership created a special decorative *(ch 3)* pendant luminaire, consisting of glass panels and a conical louvred refractor . Fitted with a single-ended tungsten halogen Halostar lamp, these general ambient lighting fixtures are also used in the main foyer seating areas.

These simple lighting devices are supplemented here and there by special effects. For example, the inner atrium between the hotel and the public circulation area proper is lit from high level by theatre projectors . Gobos add colour and pattern to the floor surfaces and create incidental interest for users, as they move through the constantly changing light and shade.

Daylight illumination provides dramatic shadows and silhouettes in the glazed lobbies (opposite page, bottom). As darkness falls, the entire building begins to glow from the inside like a lantern (left). Ground-level lighting is provided by a series of custom-designed standards which mark the stairway in the lobby (below). In the concert hall itself (opposite page, top) the acoustic ceiling canopy houses rows of adjustable downlights

Photos: Richard Payne, FAIA

Meyerson Symphony Center, Dallas

Lighting design: Jules Fisher & Paul Marantz Inc
Architects: Pei Cobb Freed & Partners

The $100-million Meyerson Symphony Center is the crown jewel of the Dallas arts district, a civic monument which both expresses a modernist architectural vision and echoes the warm, opulent concert halls of Europe. Fisher-Marantz's lighting design brief involved developing a family of architecturally sympathetic luminaires for the public circulation areas, as well as lighting the giant auditorium itself.

Due to the extensive glazing of the building, during the day the public lobbies are essentially daylit spaces. Curved lens-like skylights rise up from the lobbies to intersect the monumental limestone walls. The sunlight and shadows cast by these glazed structures are quite dramatic. During the evening, electric lighting transforms the lobbies into one large lantern, which acts as an inviting beacon for the Center's visitors.

The architectural lighting fixtures in the lobbies are arranged in rows that conform to the skylight lens shapes. A PAR 38 *(ch 2)* fixture was specially designed to provide a minimum profile when viewed against the skylights. Banks of incandescent *(ch 2)* wallwashers highlight the giant limestone arch and large cut-out circle of limestone that serves as the donor wall. Additional spotlights give accent lighting to several pieces of art which were specially commissioned for the lobby.

A family of custom-designed *(ch 4)* lighting standards, with a geometric, overlapping metal bar construction – and each using a quartet of fan-shaped diffusers in glass and onyx – are used to mark stairways in the lobby. They reappear as wall sconces in the inner lobbies and inside the hall. These ornamental luminaires offer a luminous continuity as one travels from the exterior through the various spaces inside.

The transition from the open lobby areas with their cool finishes of stone and glass, into the warm, rich interior of the performance hall itself, is striking. Warm, brown woods and upholstery, plus an orange-brown terrazzo floor are supplemented by walls adorned by panels, accented by softly backlit onyx panels. A delicate wooden lattice at the top of the hall stands in front of an uplit scrim.

The enormous 60-ton acoustic ceiling canopy hanging above the stage is home for banks of adjustable lighting, directed both at the stage and orchestra seats. Rows of recessed downlights *(ch 3)* to both sides wash the intricate glass and onyx panels. In the highest ceiling, the geometries of light are extended, using a radial pattern of backlit glass and a multi-layered dome. All the lighting in the hall and lobbies is controlled by separate dimmers *(ch 5)*, so that each of the individual lighting elements can be balanced against the others.

Imperial War Museum, London

Lighting design: Lighting Design Partnership
Architects: Ove Arup Associates
Exhibition design: Jasper Jacob Associates

In the mid-1980s the Imperial War Museum decided to cover its central courtyard and convert it into an additional spacious display area for some of its larger exhibits, including V-2 rockets, tanks and aircraft, spanning the two World Wars.

The main gallery area in the covered courtyard (left and above) showing the contrast between day and night. At night, filtered blue HID light is directed up onto the canopy to simulate the night sky while low-voltage PAR lamps on theatre lighting bars highlight the exhibits

Spotlights were positioned at acute angles to reveal the texture and form of the structure (top); modified Thomas PAR Cans were used, with narrow-beam low-voltage lamps (bottom)

the fragile, sensitive historical materials and means that the lights can be maintained without opening the cases.

Much of the ceiling on the lower floor is coffered concrete, designed to support the weight of heavy military equipment on the floor above. Special cruciform compression brackets were designed to support the spotlamps used to light the graphics and free-standing exhibits. Each fitting has a tapped transformer allowing different light levels to be set individually without dimmers *(ch 5)*.

The quantity of natural light entering the upper spaces presented difficulties when it came to devising a lighting scheme. On a bright day, with light levels up to 16000 lux *(ch 1)* at floor level, the areas under the side galleries appear very dark and need to be strongly lit. As the natural light fades, the situation is reversed. To offset the sombre effect of the synthetic roof-glazing after dark, filtered blue HID *(ch 2)* light is directed up into the canopy to represent the night sky and to provide an effective background for the suspended aircraft.

Because of the extreme variability of light levels, LDP utilized total electronic dimmer control. The system installed is entirely automatic, allowing for photocell *(ch 5)* and timeclock controlled dimming and switching within all the spaces, including the basement area. It requires no manual correction.

On the higher levels of the structure, hung with period aircraft, low-voltage PAR 36 and PAR 56 *(ch 2)* lamps were mounted on theatre lighting bars. With a throw distance of about 30 metres, these allow for the tight beam control required in such a space. The luminaires are hung like theatre lighting spots and plugged into adjacent three-channel lighting tracks *(ch 3)* to keep the system completely flexible.

The display lighting under the galleries is also a mixture of tungsten halogen *(ch 2)* and HID: for the lamps mounted within the exhibits, low-voltage *(ch 2)* dichroic *(ch 2)* reflector spots were used, fixed onto the structure using cable ties, so as not to cause damage. LDP was keen to light the underside of the aeroplanes hung above the central floorspace, but reluctant to resort to conventional uplighting *(ch 3)*. Original Second World War searchlights were adapted, by refitting them with tungsten halogen and metal halide floodlights .

Working alongside exhibition designers, Jasper Jacob Associates (JJA), Lighting Design Partnership (LDP) was appointed to light both the new covered courtyard and the other gallery areas in the museum. The area devoted to the First and Second World Wars consists of a lower ground floor with no natural light; while the upper galleried floors have an abundant supply of daylight, suffused through the new glazed barrel vault.

The lower floor consists of a stud-partitioned structure containing individual showcases for small-scale wartime artefacts. Within the cases screened fluorescent lighting provides general ambient illumination, while emphasis lighting and interpretative spotlighting *(ch 3)* is provided by fibre optic *(ch 3)* outlets in the perimeter of the cases. These were fed by light ducted from a remote source outside the case. This minimizes heat gain around

The Sainsbury Wing, National Gallery, London

Lighting design: Jules Fisher & Paul Marantz Inc
Architects: Venturi, Scott-Brown & Associates

The architectural design of the Sainsbury extension to London's National Gallery caused considerable controversy when it was opened in 1991. However, the way its collection of Renaissance art is exhibited drew more admiration than criticism, due in part to the carefully calculated mix of natural and artificial lighting.

The architects and trustees were anxious to capture some sense of Mediterranean light quality. Fisher-Marantz, too, wanted to avoid the usual over-controlled daylit gallery scheme, which precludes any variation in illuminance *(ch 1)*. On top of that, the technical requirements of the scheme were exacting: daylighting, whenever possible, with an average mean illuminance of 200 lux *(ch 1)*; a maximum ratio of different light levels across the hanging zone of 2:1; and extremely low ultraviolet *(ch 1)* levels, for conservation reasons.

To maintain colour consistency, tungsten PAR lamps *(ch 2)* were chosen for the public circulation areas and tungsten halogen *(ch 2)* point sources were used throughout to light the paintings. This entailed special air-conditioning provision, due to the heat gain involved.

Ambient daylight is provided by a series of louvred rooflights, with most of the direct light falling on the high, light grey painted walls above the hanging zone. The louvres are pre-set at a particular

The main lighting strategy was to avoid an over-controlled daylit scheme. Photocell-managed louvred rooflights (opposite page) provide gradually changing ambient light, mainly to the upper walls while the art works themselves are lit by tungsten halogen spotlights (bottom right). Elsewhere, 'cool' daylight-compatible downlights provide additional illumination (top right) while direct daylight from windows (left) is filtered to avoid ultraviolet ingress

Courtesy: Erco Lighting
Photos: Dennis Gilbert

angle each day – every two hours a photocell *(ch 5)* measures and averages the light levels for 15 minutes, and opens or closes the louvres accordingly. However, within that period, small shifts in daylight levels can be registered within the galleries.

Appearances apart, the spaces are never lit entirely by daylight – the roof space contains three distinct lighting components. Around the perimeter of each rooflight is an Erco multi-circuit lighting track *(ch 3)*; one set of Eclipse low-voltage tungsten halogen spotlights *(ch 3)*, with integral transformers *(ch 2)*, gives a base 60 lux on the paintings at all times. They are fitted with blue-tinted, pressed glass lenses, to provide cool, daylight-compatible illumination at 4100 degrees K *(ch 2)*.

A second set of photocell-controlled spotlights with plain glass lenses provides a warmer (3100 degrees K) light and is switched on only when daylight and the 'blue' circuit cannot produce enough light for comfortable viewing (125 lux). These are controlled and switched in three zones, and faded up

and down over 30 seconds, to avoid visual disturbance to visitors. To extend lamp-life *(ch 1)*, transformers are tapped to only 80 per cent of maximum output. For days when darkness falls before the gallery closes, rows of 3900 degrees K tubular fluorescents *(ch 2)* switch in, to provide daylight replacement. A set period before lighting-up time, the white-painted louvres close completely to act as reflectors for these sources. After closing, all the normal gallery lighting is replaced with high-pressure sodium *(ch 2)* security lighting, controlled to put almost all the light on the floor.

The very low specifications for ultraviolet demanded additional measures. All daylight is filtered, using a special double-glazing unit, which incorporates a sheet of laminate with a filtering interlayer. Four of the rooms and the staircases have conventional windows – on the stairs grey glass acts as a neutral density filter, while in the galleries the ultraviolet-absorbing interlayer is supplemented by translucent blinds *(ch 3)*.

The main pyramid structure is spotlit from within so that it appears as a transparent solid (left). Inside, the treads of the staircase (opposite page, top) are gently washed from behind. Within the subterranean spaces, downlights under the walkways (bottom) disguise the transition from natural to artificial illumination. The bulk of the lighting is provided by a range of fittings recessed into the concrete coffers (opposite page, bottom)

The Louvre Pyramid, Paris

Lighting design: Claude Engle
Architects: I M Pei & Partners

The underground extension of the Louvre museum, with its entrance hall capped by I M Pei's controversial glass and steel pyramid, is one of the most admired of President Mitterand's *grands projets*. Claude Engle's lighting design scheme had two main technical objectives: first, to light the Pyramid structure itself, without creating glare or veiling reflections from the 675 glass panels; and second to light the 50,000 square metres of underground gallery space, without giving the visitor the impression of being in a basement.

The Pyramid had to be lit so that it appeared as a transparent solid through which buildings and people could still be seen. The strategy was to light only the stainless steel framework below the glass, so that the eye reads the glowing lattice as a solid volume, yet no light spills onto the glass itself. A special luminaire was developed, a 100W 12V shielded tungsten halogen *(ch 2)* lamp, housed in extra narrow beam units, located in ducts around the inner base of the Pyramid. These light the structure evenly from top to bottom.

However, in the original mock-ups, reflection of the lights at the bottom of the glass blocked the view inside. Two special linear parabolic reflectors were designed, which redirect the image of the lamp above the viewer's head.

Lighting requirements below ground were equally demanding but far more varied. Most of the luminaires are recessed into the pre-cast concrete ceiling, in many cases at the centre of the distinctive coffered ceiling module which recurs throughout the building. A universal housing had to be designed, two years in advance, to take a variety of lamp and luminaire types.

In some areas, false ceilings left only a 150mm void; an entire series of wallwashers , downlights *(ch 3)* and adjustable accent lights was developed at this depth, including transformers . These were just some of the massive range of unique fittings required by Engle and his team. For example, there was the discreet but effective directional signage, comprising Erco pictograms on thick perspex, which are lit internally from compact fluorescent lamps *(ch 2)* concealed within their brackets.

An initial objective was to minimize the transition between natural lighting under the Pyramid and artificial lighting in the corridors and galleries around. Daylight is thrown onto walls up to 20 metres away from the Pyramid (and the two supplementary skylights). But the ceiling plane itself had to be lit to higher than normal levels to minimize surface contrast, without being obviously in use during daylight hours.

A special recessed fitting, utilizing two 18W TC-L fluorescents *(ch 2)* and with asymmetrical reflectors was designed and manufactured by Erco. This gave uniform illumination on two adjacent angled sides of

the coffer, while preventing any direct downlight. As the visitor moves away from the daylight source, near-natural light levels are maintained. For example, along the lower and upper walkways a flush recessed fluorescent downlight is used, supplemented with a rotate-and-tilt, mains voltage tungsten halogen lamp, to wash the pink-orange tinted walls evenly. Due to the narrower areas at the upper level the luminaires are spaced more widely, something the eye does not register.

The standard recessed fixture was also supplemented by a huge range of other custom-made luminaires for special locations including a decorative *(ch 3)* wall light, using a frosted glass disc for various wall recesses; a rotate-and-tilt wallwasher with darklight reflectors for use in plaster ceilings; and a PAR 38 *(ch 2)* spotlight version of the coffer luminaire for lighting the auditorium stage.

National Museum of Natural Science, Taipei

Lighting design: Lighting Design Partnership
Museum design: James Gardner Studios

**The £13-million National Museum of Natural Science, containing 9000
square metres of exhibition space divided into 15 galleries, covers the
whole of the natural sciences. All but two of the galleries exclude natural
daylight, offering an ideal black-box-type lighting control situation; all the
exhibits are replicas or models, so there was no conservation requirement.
However, as the exhibits are fixed, there was little future flexibility
requirement. As a result, the costs of multiple ceiling tracks
and/or multi-channel dimming capability could not be justified.**

*As all the exhibits are
replicas or models
(left) there was no
specific requirement to
design the lighting with
conservation in mind*

The main problem was to devise a flexible system to illuminate each exhibit to optimum levels, without the benefit of tracks and sophisticated dimmer units. The solution lay in the false ceiling, comprising 600-mm tiles supported on T-bars, which was used as an impromptu lighting grid. Selected tiles were strengthened with a plywood back plate and spotlights *(ch 3)* fitted at either the centre of the tile, or at any one of the four corners. Power to each individual luminaire was run off a single-circuit track hidden in the ceiling void.

The next problem was to create the necessary variety of beam intensities and angles. The main fitting used was a specially modified Light Projects projector, housing an Osram Superspot PAR 36 metal reflector lamp *(ch 2)*, which comes in 50, 75 and 100W versions and is available with 10, 30 and 60 degree beam angles.

Careful selection of lamps from this range offered considerable flexibility, but this was further enhanced by an integral tappable transformer in each of the 1500 luminaires. Four settings offered steps of 25, 50, 75 and 90 per cent of total light output. Where necessary, colour could be added by filters. A sculpture lens accessory, creating a lozenge-shaped beam, was also useful for lighting elongated objects, such as the vertical Chinese language signage.

The strategy adopted was dramatic, high-contrast, high-key illumination on the exhibits, with low ambient lighting levels, created purely from reflected exhibition light. The one gallery which presented particular problems was the large dinosaur hall, a 15-metre high space, whose throw distances did not permit a ceiling-mounted solution. Substituting the PAR 56 for the PAR 36, the spotlights were mounted on bars and winched up to the required position on pulleys. Original aiming and focusing had to be done from a large mobile scaffold tower.

For maintenance purposes, the bars can be winched down to the floor – a cut-off device disconnects the power automatically and restores it when the bar is back in position. To prevent disturbance of the critical beam focusing, the lamps are locked off at pre-set angles, indelibly marked on the fitting. With no centralized control system, and the project's dependence on precise focusing,

In the 15-metre high dinosaur hall (above and bottom) spotlights are bar-mounted and winched into position. Elsewhere in the lower height galleries the false ceilings were used as an impromptu lighting grid (left)

Lighting Design Partnership also devised a maintenance manual which details the settings of each lamp.

The dinosaur hall was the main area where daylight intruded, through windows offering a view of further dinosaur models outside. These windows had to be coated with gold film *(ch 3)* to prevent excessive solar gain and to avoid uncomfortably high levels of contrast *(ch 1)* for visitors. This technique had the additional benefit after dark of creating a large interior mirror-like surface, on which exhibits could be seen in duplicate.

Ambient lighting in the circulation area (left) is kept low to achieve maximum impact for the surrounding exhibits and to avoid veiling reflections

The 18th-Century Gallery, London Museum

Lighting design: John Johnston, Concord Lighting
Gallery design: David Stanfield

Concord's lighting design team has worked on many of the galleries within the London Museum. However, the 18th-Century Gallery exemplifies most of the challenges thrown up by the scheme and the integrated solutions which resulted from a close collaboration between lighting and exhibition designers from the beginning of the project.

The octagonal space consists of a central public circulation space, with a series of recreated room-sets arranged around the outside. These are interspersed with display cases containing many historical artefacts – textiles, manuscripts, prints and wooden materials – which presented major conservation problems. Ultraviolet *(ch 1)* light had to be virtually excluded, with overall light levels of about 50 lux *(ch 1)*. For that reason, and to give greatest flexibility and precise control, all the lighting is low-voltage tungsten halogen *(ch 2)*. The lamps are Philips 20W metal reflector lamps , which come in three different beam angles and offer good fade-off at the edge of the beam. The bayonet fitting is simple to change, and the plain glass optic filters out most of the potentially damaging ultraviolet rays.

Lighting in the central circulation space was kept subdued, to achieve maximum impact for the exhibits. A sprinkling of recessed downlighters *(ch 3)* in the ceiling casts pools of light sufficient for orientation. The brighter display cases and room-sets automatically draw visitors to them. This high ratio of showcase to ambient illumination also prevents distracting veiling reflections *(ch 1)*.

One room-set presented particular problems – a reconstruction of a prison cell in Newgate prison, complete with graffiti scratched into the walls. The room had to be lit to very low levels, to suggest daylight filtering into a subterranean space. Tracks for the small low-voltage spotlights were mounted vertically down the sides of the viewing window, behind the inner bulkhead.

Within the display cases, light levels were varied still further, depending on the sensitivity of the object. The shelves were tailor-made, with a front lip, under which was mounted a Concord low-voltage micro-track with dimmers *(ch 3)* linked to a remote transformer . Spotlights *(ch 3)* could be mounted out of sight beneath the shelf edge and angled down onto the exhibits.

Some of the walls between the room-sets feature full-length text panels, set into blank arched doorways. Low-voltage angled downlights mounted in the ceiling illuminate these panels. After consider-able experimentation these were positioned so that the upper edge of the illuminated scallop coincides exactly with the top of the curved arch.

Metal reflector lamps, mounted on a low-voltage micro-track behind the front shelf-lip allow great flexibility for the different exhibition cases (below and opposite page, right). Text panels set into blank doorways (right) are precisely lit by angled low-voltage downlights

Opus Sacrum Exhibition, Warsaw

Lighting Design: Lighting Design Partnership

Exhibition design: Franco Zeffirelli

In 1990 Lighting Design Partnership (LDP) was commissioned to design and supervise the lighting installation for Opus Sacrum in Warsaw, a prestigious exhibition of religious art and sculpture owned by the prominent US collector, Barbara Piasecka Johnson. Designed by Franco Zeffirelli, the temporary exhibition was mounted in five rooms of Warsaw's restored Zamek Palace.

Individual pictures and pieces of sculpture are given specific lighting treatments using up to four lamps from different angles to maximize the modelling (top)

The lighting scheme had to be entirely flexible, capable of being run and maintained easily by local non-expert staff, and had to use equipment shipped in from outside the country. The brief was for the best lighting scheme possible to enhance and complement the overall ambience and the objects on show while at the same time giving due consideration to the colour rendering *(ch 1)* of the paintings and their conservation requirements. In only one of the rooms, a long south-facing gallery, was natural daylight allowed in and this was controlled with solar film and fabric blinds *(ch 3)*. Elsewhere, three of the rooms were blacked out totally in order to concentrate the visitors' attention.

LDP's general strategy was to provide two lighting elements – even wallwashing to create a low ambient lighting level, plus framing projectors and spotlights *(ch 3)* to highlight the exhibits. To ensure good colour rendering and precise control, tungsten halogen *(ch 2)* was used throughout – energy efficiency was not a major consideration. In two of the blacked-out rooms, a 600-mm slot around the dropped ceiling allowed some of the spotlights to be hidden. In other rooms the wallwashers were mounted on the same tracks *(ch 3)* as the high-level low-voltage *(ch 2)* spotlights. In all cases wallwashers were dimmed to overall ambient levels of between 20 and 50 lux *(ch 1)* so that spotlights would operate to maximum dramatic effect. In several areas, particular paintings were mounted within their own partitioned 'shrines' and isolated in pools of light.

Paintings, sculptures and other objects were all given their own lighting treatment. Each painting, for example, was individually metered and Erco's multi-circuit track allowed the use of regulated lighting set-ups using integral dimmers *(ch 5)*. A set of remote dimmers permitted further detailed adjustment of the light levels. In addition to the precisely framed projectors, discreet additional spotlighting was often used within the frame, for added effect. Three-dimensional objects were often lit by three or four different lamps at different angles to give good modelling *(ch 1)*.

In all, the lighting scheme was a triumph of precise control, reliability and flexibility, particularly in the context of a country that had yet to come to terms with the dichroic lamp *(ch 2)*.

The general strategy was to provide a low level of ambient lighting using wallwashers, and then to use precisely controlled tungsten halogen projectors to highlight the exhibits (above). Certain pieces are isolated and emphasized in their own pool of light (left, and opposite page, bottom)

Nike Town, Portland, Oregon

Lighting design: Ramsby, Dupuy & Seats

Nike Town is the leading sports goods company's prototype retail store, a hybrid hi-tech showroom and multimedia exhibition, covering approximately 2000 square metres, designed to recreate the glories of fitness and sporting competition.

The lighting had to do more than illuminate products and displays. It had to contribute to the essential fantasy nature of the store and establish visual hierarchies by defining circulation paths and sales zones.

Much of the dramatic effect of the store is achieved through its all-black, stage-like aesthetic; almost all illumination is produced by direct spotlighting *(ch 3)*, with no direct ambient light .

This highly controlled, high-contrast strategy uses batteries of directional low-voltage PAR lamps *(ch 2)* housed in real theatrical cans . These are clamped to a surrounding, black-painted pipe grid, which has its own modular power strip; and each low-voltage fixture is available in a wide range of beam spreads and wattages, as well as incorporating built-in dimmers *(ch 5)*. All this allows quick, flexible relocation, refocusing and re-lamping, as the displays change.

At the entrance, customers who come in off the street have to wait in a black vestibule – 'the decompression chamber' – where the only light comes from slots in the floor.

A solid black door panel then slides away to reveal an illuminated fibre-optic *(ch 3)* tape recessed into the floor track. Customers are drawn into a dark cavernous space, spotted with pools of light over different displays – a slide projector wall, video monitors, a huge shimmering fibre optic Nike sign and life-size plaster statues of well-known athletes frozen in motion.

This is the so-called 'town square', around which are ranged the dozen or so product pavilions located on two levels, each for a different sport. Bishop's crook task lights *(ch 3)* and decorative sconces , echoing streamlined lighting fixtures, underline the 'town square' theme.

An automated 20-minute dimming cycle for various parts of the square gives a dynamic, constantly changing effect. The store is built on a one-metre-deep underfloor service void, into which is cut a series of lighting pits. These are railed-off areas located at the sides of some pavilions, which contain dramatic concealed wallwashing and display uplighting *(ch 3)*.

The product pavilion interiors are differentiated from the town square – light is allowed to spill onto

In the main 'town square' (opposite page, right) a dramatic effect is achieved by the use of the all-black, stage-like set, highly controlled narrow-beam PAR spotlights and wallwashing from below floor level. Within the product areas (above and opposite page, left) the merchandise is more brightly lit using low-voltage dichroic lamps and themed luminaires

Photos courtesy: Strode Eckert Photographic

walls, for example. To draw customers in, merchandise is brightly lit, using either track or pendant low-voltage dichroic *(ch 2)* fixtures (a whiter, more intense light than the PAR lighting in the square). Some shelves are backlit by uplighting through slots in the floor.

Luminaires here are appropriately styled for a given sport – a wing-like fixture for the Air Jordan basketball boot collection and optical fibre baselines set into the floor of the tennis pavilion, which change colour constantly. Novel and dramatic illumination is incorporated at every opportunity – for example, seats in dressing rooms are fitted with inflated plastic cushions, backlit from below by compact fluorescent lamps *(ch 2)*.

Ecology Gallery,
Natural History Museum, London

Lighting design: Maurice Brill Lighting Design
Interior design: Ian Ritchie Architects

The Ecology Gallery, opened in 1991, is a new exhibition component of London's Natural History Museum. The exhibition content was designed and lit by the in-house team; Ian Ritchie Architects was commissioned to design a striking, modern framework for the exhibition, within the shell of Waterhouse's gothic exhibition hall. The solution was a huge charismatic structure in glass and steel. This comprises two five-metre high, sand-blasted glass walls, which create a 'canyon' down the full length of the gallery, in which visitors are introduced to the exhibition. Returning through the upper levels, they criss-cross the canyon on three skeletal bridges.

The skeletal walkways bridging the central 'canyon' were subtly lit by hidden low-voltage spotlights to highlight the ribbed structure (left) and, in one case, the etched glass floor (above)

The two sand-blasted glass walls (right) were lit from behind, using modified narrow-beam fluorescent luminaires, so that they diffuse the light from top to bottom. Within the walls, etched caption panels were dramatically illuminated with hidden low-voltage spotlights (below)

were mounted within the glazing structure below the ceiling. To avoid cut-off at the top of the glass and to create sufficient luminance at the base of the wall, the front edge of the reflector was redesigned. A critical angle of tilt had also to be established, to achieve the desired effect.

The curved north-facing wall is lit with very cool colour temperature *(ch 1)* lamps, representing sky and water; the straight wall has warm colour lamps, to symbolize earth and fire. Here, an additional lava-flow element had to be added: a series of floor-mounted troughs containing two tubes, on two circuits, was randomly wrapped in a series of orange and red filters . A control system cross-switches the two sets of sources, creating a constant flickering effect. Where glazed exhibition dioramas have to be viewed through windows in the walls, the luminaires had to be heavily shielded, to prevent distracting veiling reflections *(ch 1)*.

Low-voltage spots *(ch 2)* were used sparingly but effectively: each of the three bridges has one hidden below, to gently highlight the prominent ribbed structure. On one of the bridges a glass floor etched with a leaf pattern is similarly picked out by the concealed lighting.

Both walls have a series of etched caption panels which had to be illuminated invisibly. Low-voltage spots, fitted with long cowls and egg-crate louvres to avoid stray light, were mounted on the steel glazing supports, to crosslight the lettering. Two-way mirror glass in front of the luminaires ensures that the sources cannot be seen by visitors. This project is a good example of how, in close co-ordination with an interior designer, it is possible to create a scheme which is at the same time appropriately mysterious, dramatic, and inexpensive.

Maurice Brill Lighting Design was asked to tackle the lighting design for these structures. To give the exhibition a degree of mystery, light sources had to be hidden; and in accordance with the ecology theme, they had also to be energy efficient. High-frequency fluorescent *(ch 2)* sources were chosen, for their low consumption and minimal heat output and their even light distribution.

The idea was to backlight the etched glass walls by grazing light down the internal faces, which act as a diffuser . The walls were positioned very close to the building's original columns, leaving only a 100-mm gap in which to locate the fixtures. It was difficult, too, to avoid throwing a shadow of the columns on the glass. Maurice Brill redesigned and modified special narrow-beam reflector troughs , each containing one 1.5 m fluorescent tube, which

Stansted Airport, near London

Lighting design: Claude Engle and Erco Lighting
Architects: Foster Associates

Sir Norman Foster's terminal building for Stansted Airport, 40 miles north east of London, has been acclaimed for its structural innovation and the calm, airy ambience of its interiors. Much of this success must be credited to the skilful integration of daylight control and artificial lighting. The main building itself is a large hangar, measuring 200 by 162 metres. Unusually, all the services are buried away in the undercroft, so the 12 metre high roof, supported on 36 tubular steel branching 'trees', could be used as a major light control feature.

Although all four sides of the terminal are glazed, light did not penetrate to the heart of the deep space. The solution was to incorporate a glazed rooflight into each of the 18 by 18 metre steel pyramidal roof sections. Below each of these is hung a micro-perforated metal sheet, which acts as a daylight reflector. These let in indirect daylight by reflecting it onto the underside of the steel-panelled ceiling, whilst diffusing glare *(ch 1)* from direct sunlight. The effect is to create an apparently translucent, floating roof, even though only three per cent of the roof surface is glazed. Average light levels of 180 lux *(ch 1)* are achieved at the floor, even on an average winter day.

To maintain similar light levels on darker days and at night, natural lighting was supplemented by series of specially designed uplighters *(ch 3)* – 96 inside, and 48 outside under the cantilevered canopies. These comprise custom-made asymmetric reflectors housing up to six 400W metal halide lamps *(ch 2)*, all concealed within the top of the 'tree trunks', well above eye level.

The powerful ceiling washlights, apparently the largest in the world, throw light diagonally up on to the ceiling, which spans 36 metres from 'tree' to 'tree'. In this way starkly contrasting light and dark areas are avoided, and the ceiling seems to glow like an artificial sky. A three-stage, photocell-controlled switching system *(ch 5)* allows them to be gradually phased in over time.

Direct and accent lighting elsewhere are equally well considered: for example, the canti-levered washlights, equipped with 36, 30 or 16W fluorescent lamps *(ch 2)*. Using a high specular reflector these evenly illuminate the 3.1-metre metal-clad walls of shops and service facilities, from an offset distance of 300 mm. The three-metre high ceiling of the enclosed retail area is equipped with 100W tungsten halogen *(ch 2)* downlights *(ch 3)*, for a warmer, more intimate feel. This is supplemented by grids of low-voltage track *(ch 3)* mounted flush to the ceiling, to allow retailers their own individual accent and spotlighting facilities. The shop entrances have been provided with special low-brightness fluorescent luminaires which give a 35-degree

The two main lighting elements inside the airport are the micro-perforated daylight reflectors in the roof and the lighting 'trees' which each house six 400W metal halide lamps. At night the fully glazed airport building (opposite page) seems to float on the horizon

cut-off from the ceiling in all directions. Another similar version, built into the door lintels, draws attention to each of the terminal entrances.

Lighting for the 200 check-in desks is very important. Each has its own local task light *(ch 3)* which is a substantially modified version of the Erco Cantax model, containing a 24W compact fluorescent lamp. A low-brightness louvre and asymmetric reflector means that an illuminance level of 500 lux is achieved at the desk – the work surface and staff are lit, without dazzling the customer.

Durbar Court, Whitehall, London

Lighting design: DPA (UK) Lighting Consultants
Architects: Property Services Agency (PSA)

In the mid-1980s the Property Services Agency (PSA) was asked to refurbish the Italianate, 19th-century Foreign Office building on Whitehall, designed by George Gilbert Scott and Matthew Digby Wyatt. Originally open, the courtyard had later been glazed over but had been allowed to deteriorate badly. The refurbished Durbar Court atrium space now provides a weatherproof venue for occasional receptions and official functions. As the space would be fully lit perhaps only two or three times a year, energy consumption and lamp-life were not major priorities.

Night-time views of the façades (above and opposite page) showing the gentle metal halide wash and the warmer tungsten dichroic treatment of the statuary at high level. At ground level multi-branch candelabra standards (left), using standard tungsten sources, complete the ensemble

DPA's lighting scheme had to complement the restored neo-classical façades. The plan had three main elements: general floodlighting of the walls, using a low-energy source with good colour rendering *(ch 1)*; warmer spotlighting *(ch 3)* of architectural features; and decorative *(ch 3)* period ambient lighting at ground level. The night-time appearance of the glazed ceiling was to be left dark. The walls are flooded to a comparatively low level (50 lux) *(ch1)*, using 70W metal halide *(ch 2)* luminaires. For maintenance purposes these are mounted on specially constructed catwalks below the atrium glazing. The chosen source has relatively good energy and lamp-life *(ch 1)* characteristics – 50 lm/W and 6000 hours respectively. The rear walls of the two open arcades at each end of the court also use the same source, mounted at low level behind the balcony balustrades. These are also sufficient to illuminate the terracotta ceilings above, without recourse to additional uplighting *(ch 3)*.

Semi-circular medallions around the top storey and statues in niches around the court are all given individual light treatment, using precisely focused, narrow-beam 50W dichroic, low-voltage *(ch 2)* spotlights *(ch 3)* mounted on the catwalk. This provides a warmer emphasis when seen against the cooler colour of the Portland stone. The long corridors along the south side of the court at ground- and first-floor levels were already fitted with Holophane pendant fittings in period style, incorporating 160W mercury blended *(ch 2)* lamps. These were retained and refurbished.

Decorative lighting at ground level, to enhance the festive ambience of occasional grand events within the court, was a problem. Photographs of the court decorated for Edward VII's coronation in 1902 showed a series of torchères lighting the stairs. DPA adopted the same technique and designed four multi-bracket candelabra-type fittings, 2.7 metres high, to stand on either side of two of the short staircases. Here, standard tungsten 150W GLS lamps *(ch 2)* were felt appropriate, to blend with the spill light from the ground-floor offices around the court, and to enhance the silverware on the dining tables.

The scheme won a citation in the 1987 International Association of Lighting Designers Awards.

By day, sunlight is the major light source, diffused through the sand-blasted tiles of the tripartite vault so that the mullions and mirrored squares stand out as silhouettes (above)

Courtesy: Carl Hillman Associates

First FA Bank, Orlando, Florida

Lighting design: Carl Hillman Associates

Architects: Morris Architects

Strong contrasts between daytime and night-time interior lighting can make a fascinating design theme. One spectacular example is provided by the main banking hall at the First FA Building in Orlando's duPont Centre. It is also a rare example of the deliberate use of uplighting onto a glazed ceiling.

The grand, tripartite vaulted space is directly accessible from the public plaza. At night the ornamental gates are closed, but the space still acts as a foyer to the tower lobby beyond and so has to remain attractively illuminated. The vaulted ceiling plays a dual role: translucent skylight by day and reflective ceiling at night. After rejecting an initial plan for night-time backlighting from above as technically unfeasible and illogical, the design team worked on the ceiling's potential for creating a dynamic interplay of day- and night-time opposites, in which light and dark were cleverly reversed.

Carl Hillman evolved the idea for a glazed inner ceiling, hung from the outer transparent roof. Special glass tiles, set in semi-reflective aluminium mullions, were evolved to simultaneously interrupt, transmit and diffuse daylight, while receiving and reflecting uplight from interior sources. The exterior silvered face of each tile was sand-blasted away, except for a floating square, which was left mirrored. The inside non-silvered face was also sand-blasted, but this time just the floating square, which overlays the mirrored square on the outside.

During the day, sunlight is the primary light source, supplemented by two rows of architect-designed torchères, with internal glass reflectors and phosphor-coated metal halide *(ch 2)* lamps. Daylight is diffused by the sand-blasted tiles, but the mirrored square patterns block natural light, so they (and the grid of mullions) stand out as dark outlines. At night, with uplight from the torchères as the main lighting source, the effect is reversed; interior incident light passes through the glass, but is reflected back from the mirrored floating square (and the surface of the mullions). These then appear as illuminated outlines on a darker background. At the same time the ceiling is given the appearance of architectural solidity, more appropriate to the ambience of a bank.

Augmenting the direct/indirect light from the torchères are two other lighting components. There are two inner rows of recessed, shielded PAR 56 *(ch 2)* accent lights for highlighting furnishings and architectural details, such as the gates; and a contin-uous row of closely spaced 60W incandescent *(ch 2)* reflector downlights *(ch 3)* around the perimeter, to define the edge of the ceiling and to give a warm wash to the sandstone walls.

By night, the effect is reversed (above) – incident light from the torchères picks up the mullions and mirrored squares so that they stand out as illuminated outlines on a dark background

Courtesy: Carl Hillman Associates

General view of the ground floor and altar (above right) showing the linear tungsten halogen uplighters mounted in the upper balcony bulkheads; and the custom-made 'eternal light' (above) designed by Box Products

Liberal Jewish Synagogue, London

Lighting design: Lighting Design Ltd
Architects: Koski Soloman & Ruthven

The Liberal Jewish Synagogue comprises a new interior behind an old façade, with seating for 1000 people in a broad U-shaped formation, on two levels. There is little natural daylight within the space. The lighting design brief was to create a flexible scheme which provides an appropriate, comfortable ambience for normal weekly services of possibly 20 to 30 people, as well as for festival services, when the building is full.

The solution was to treat the area towards the front of the ground-floor space as if it were a synagogue within a synagogue, with its own dedicated lighting scheme. A major component of this scheme is a series of floodlights *(ch 7)* recessed into the top of the wide balcony bulkheads at the upper level.

Three-hundred-watt linear tungsten halogen *(ch 2)* sources, mounted behind sand-blasted glass diffusers , uplight *(ch 3)* the unusual stepped ceiling above the seating at the front of the ground floor.

To avoid glare, these are only switched on when the upper gallery is not in use.

Within the ceiling is a skylight, shielded with wooden louvres . PAR 56 *(ch 2)* spotlights *(ch 3)* hidden behind them light the Bimah platform at the front of the space, while a series of 100W 24V double-focus downlights *(ch 3)* mounted around the louvres cast pools of light onto the congregation directly below.

The Ark wall, which provides the backdrop to ceremonials in the synagogue, is constructed of Jerusalem stone, with a heavily hewn lower portion which becomes smoother towards the top. Lighting from above, giving most light and shadow to the upper part of the wall, would have tended to flatten its texture. The Bimah platform was moved forward 200 mm so that a series of 200W tungsten halogen floodlights could be hidden behind it, to uplight the wall, with the initial hot spot just out of view.

Other details had to be specially lit. For example, cross-lighting was needed to improve the modelling *(ch 1)* of the altar. This is provided by PAR 56 spots hidden behind grills on either side of the platform.

The ornate doors housing the ceremonial Ark and set in the stone wall are a sculpture in themselves. During the day they are framed by cold cathode *(ch 2)* to give a sense of daylight creeping in. In addition, the mesh grid fronts of the doors are lit by two narrow-beam, low-voltage sources housed in a custom-made basket-like 'eternal light' hanging from the ceiling.

When the synagogue is in full use, the spaces under the gallery could have been depressing. Ceiling heights were too low for uplights, so the solution was to wash the perimeter walls (a combination of wooden panels, stone and marmarina plaster). Low-voltage directional fixtures were concealed behind the timbered air-conditioning bulkhead which runs round the walls – the light was softened and spread downwards with sand-blasted glass covers.

With all these elements and light sources, an easy-to-operate control system *(ch 5)* was important. This offered two main groups of scenes *(ch 5)*, for small and full congregation use, and within that a variety of moods for different times of the day or types of event. Various sections of the interior can also be switched off or accentuated independently.

The rear walls of the ground-floor space under the balconies (above) were gently washed with hidden low-voltage fixtures. The Bimah platform (right) is framed in its own pool of light, emanating from the louvred skylight and hidden spotlights around it

Cuenca Ravines, Cuenca

Lighting design: Philips Lighting

The ancient town of Cuenca, 150 miles west of Madrid, is poised on a rocky ridge between two steep river valleys, the Huecar and the Jucar. The town council wanted to make the scenic splendour of the Huecar visible by night, as an additional tourist attraction. Following the success of the scheme, the neighbouring Jucar valley was also lit.

The Huecar rock face and the town above it (below right) and opposite page, top) are lit by carefully shielded, twin-beam floodlights (below) which provide a contrasting combination of warm high-pressure sodium and cooler metal halide lighting. Floodlighting the distant crags of the Jucar Valley (opposite page, bottom) requires the use of powerful 1800W metal halide floodlights

Courtesy: International Lighting Review

The Huecar gorge rises almost vertically to the town of Cuenca 100 metres above. The irregularity and steepness of the terrain presented particular difficulties, never before tackled in Spain. The first step was empirical on-site testing of various lamps, to determine the best combinations for the type of landscape. The main floodlight chosen was a twin-lamp unit, containing a 400W metal halide *(ch 2)* source and a 250W high-pressure sodium lamp *(ch 2)*, in a range of beam widths. There were 30 of these, plus 20 smaller units, with a single 150W metal halide or high-pressure sodium source, for special zones or smaller features.

Each of the larger twin-beam units in fact produces three beams, each of a different colour: the golden-white of the high-pressure sodium and the cold white of the metal halide from the two side mirrors, and an approximate 3600 degrees K *(ch 1)* mixture of these from the centre. This colour difference was utilized in emphasizing the bumps and hollows in the rock face.

The aim was to locate the floodlights in such a way as to create as flat an illumination as possible in the zones furthest away from the observer, increasing the degree of relief in the foreground. This was achieved by manipulating the distance between luminaires, depending on their mounting height from the rock face.

The floodlights have been hidden from sight behind low stone walls, and those located close to the road are equipped with anti-glare louvres to ensure drivers will not be

blinded by stray light. Average power consumption of the scheme is 21kw/h.

Following the completion of the Huecar scheme, the decision was taken to light the wider, but less precipitous Jucar valley, on the other side of Cuenca. A series of additional problems had to be overcome. For example, the ideal location for floodlights was down at river level, but this was impractical, because of regular flooding. Finally, a decision was taken to simply light the rock walls visible to the town across the valley. However, the floodlight used for the Huecar project was insufficiently powerful and the cost of laying cables across the valley was prohibitive.

Fortunately the new Arena Vision floodlight had just been developed. Fitted with an 1800W metal halide lamp, the narrow-beam version could easily reach the far crags, 500 metres away, from the town side of the valley where there was adequate power supply. The cool colour temperature and rendering *(ch 1)* properties of the lamp also served to bring out the natural beauty of the ravine. Eighteen units were employed, five on the plateau and thirteen in the valley; five of the latter are aimed back at the city walls above. The two installations, on opposite sides of the town, can be switched on independently of each other.

Embankment Place, London

Lighting design: Lighting Design Partnership
Architects: Terry Farrell Partnership

Embankment Place is a monumental commercial development, built above London's Charing Cross station and containing 45,500 square metres of office space. Widely regarded as one of Terry Farrell's most mature and impressive post-modern creations, the building has a very powerful presence when viewed across the Thames and from the South Bank, but is largely invisible from the north. The brief was to produce a lighting scheme for the building, and principally for this prominent south-facing façade, which simplified its complex form at night without creating any light nuisance for the occupants.

Lighting Design Partnership (LDP) and Terry Farrell Partnership (TFP) decided that the main elements to be lit would be the two grand roof arches, which signify the span of the building over the railway tracks. It would have been easy to flood these with light, but this would have resulted in discomfort for occupants in the fully glazed offices below. A more controlled approach was adopted, using a series of narrow-beam luminaires to put light onto the arches in precise, overlapping areas. The diagonal chevrons on the glazed façade were picked out by spill light from the same luminaires.

Here, as elsewhere, cool white metal halide *(ch 2)* sources were chosen, so as not to add colour to the steel and granite façade. Only tiny details at the top of the building, such as the 'eye' windows and core capitals of the asymmetric towers were lit with warmer high-pressure sodium lamps *(ch 2)* to give contrast. A total of 28 250W narrow-beam metal halide lamps were used, mounted on the lower balcony and the roof-top catwalk.

One of the potential problems of lighting just the upper areas of this tall building was that the structure would appear to 'float'. To mitigate this effect, two pairs of lower, subsidiary columns closer to ground level were lit using the same fixtures; the grill-like balustrade of the lower curving balcony was also featured. A limited amount of light was also applied to the side walls, using narrow-beam metal halide fixtures flush-mounted between the tall windows. Originally these should have been cantilevered off the walls, but this interfered with the window-cleaning apparatus.

The other main lighting treatment concerned the main entrance tucked away at ground level on Villiers Street. To attract visitors inside, the decision was taken not to light the polished granite façade, but only the door openings, circular windows and outer lobby. The high outer lobby walls were washed from the ceiling, using a slightly warmer metal halide lamp, Metalarc from Sylvania. The curved entrance canopy over the doors was lit from behind an angled glass cornice, using white cold cathode *(ch 2)*.

The result is a building that many acknowledge now looks even better by night. Through selective, sensitive lighting of the total exterior the lighting load was kept down to a modest 24KW.

To give the building maximum visual presence on the Embankment (above and opposite page) without obliterating the detail, exterior lighting is used precisely and selectively. Inside the Villiers Street entrance (top), lobby walls are washed from the ceiling with metal halide

Courtesy: Terry Farrell & Company

Lloyds Building, London

Lighting design: Imagination
Architects: Richard Rogers Partnership

Richard Rogers' Lloyds Building, completed in 1985, is widely acclaimed as a hi-tech modernist masterpiece. As part of Lloyds' tercentenary celebrations in 1988, Imagination was asked to create a new exterior lighting scheme which would energize the building at night, to symbolize Lloyds' round-the-clock, worldwide operations. All the lighting equipment had to blend in with the structure and be sited on Lloyds' property to allow for adjustment and maintenance.

A balance had also to be achieved between close-up viewing from the narrow City of London streets, long-distance perspectives from London's bridges and the South Bank, and even aerial viewing (Lloyds is on the Heathrow flight path).

The design team started with a scale model of the building, which was experimentally lit in the studio. Later, particular types of lamp were taken out on site to test the building materials' response to particular sources.

Conceptually, the building was broken down into two main elements – the 65-metre-high, barrel-vaulted glass atrium on the south side and the hi-tech clusters of external pipes and service elements which cocoon the building. The strategy was to cover the main steel clad body of the building in a blue wash of light, to contrast with the warmer, amber-orange colour tones of the atrium lighting. This is provided by Osram GEC's special metal halide *(ch 2)* lamps, containing a touch of Indium, housed in Philips floodlight fixtures positioned around the building at ground level.

The amber-toned treatment of the atrium's steel skeleton was achieved with high-pressure sodium sources *(ch 2)* mounted on the flat roof. To enhance the view from the air, it was also lit from above by luminaires located on top of the service pods. SON DL *(ch 2)* units, positioned inside the atrium, light up the inside of the glass vault. The slightly diffusing glass specified by Richard Rogers helps give the glazing an added reflective, sparkly quality. To

highlight the silver service pipes on the outside of the building, very narrow beam spots were required, to skim the length of the pipe.

Francis Marine searchlights were chosen because of their high-quality optical parabolic reflector which offers a near-parallel beam. However, Francis had to replace its low-voltage tungsten halogen *(ch 2)* sources with white single-ended metal halide lamps, to meet the scheme's longer lamp-life requirement; and the fittings had to be custom-manufactured in stainless steel, rather than the original brass, to blend in with the building structure. All 500-plus fittings and a range of special brackets, were custom-made for the scheme in the same material.

The shape of the building was also emphasized by the inclusion of a number of point light sources. This is particularly important when the building is viewed from a distance. Boosted bulkhead lamps, using 250W SON lamps *(ch 2)* create the white outline of the front of the atrium, while a blue navigation beacon is located at each corner of the large service pods at the top of the building. The result is a scheme that has made Lloyds Building one of the city's major after-dark attractions.

An essential part of the lighting strategy is to light the atrium (above right and opposite page) with warmer sodium to contrast with the colder, blue-tinted illumination of the exposed steel building. Narrow-beam, metal halide spotlights are used to skim the exterior cladding (above left)

Courtesy: Imagination

To give the site a dramatic visual focus, the central rotunda (above) is lit more intensely than the flanking colonnades (left)

Courtesy: Luminae Souter and Douglas Salin (photographer)

Palace of Fine Arts, San Francisco

Lighting design: Ross De Alessi, Principal, Luminae Souter
Consultant architect: Michael Helm

San Francisco's Palace of Fine Arts, with its impressive neo-classical open rotunda and colonnade, is located in the city's residential Marina district. It was designed by architect Bernard Maybeck for the Panama-Pacific Exposition in 1915 and built for one year's use only. In 1967 it was more permanently reconstructed in steel and concrete. In the late 1980s Luminae Souter principal, Ross De Alessi, became involved in a scheme to relight the building. The design had to be aesthetically effective, energy efficient, vandal resistant, easy to maintain and, above all, the luminaires had to have no distracting visible presence by day.

The chosen lighting strategy was to accentuate the building's warm tones and reveal the architecture, while avoiding light spilling into the surrounding neighbourhood. For dramatic emphasis the rotunda, the centrepiece of the site, is lit more intensely than the flanking colonnades. The technique of grazing or washing light on the columns, statuary and sculpture panels, rather than flooding them – insisted on in the

Subtlety of effect is achieved by grazing the columns and capitals (right) using close-offset luminaires and by concealing sources behind ledges (below)

Courtesy: Luminae Souter and Douglas Salin (photographer)

original scheme by Maybeck – has been respected and recreated.

Around the colonnade and rotunda, asymmetric fixtures, housing 150 or 250W deluxe high-pressure sodium (HPS) *(ch 2)* sources, are used as footlights. Despite their 15,000 to 20,000-hour rating, they are all re-lamped every 6000 hours, to avoid colour deterioration. The footlight fixtures are located three to five metres out from the base, to ensure that the detailed capitals are lit. On the columns, they are located off-centre and staggered slightly, in order to better model *(ch 1)* the stonework. The luminaires are hidden out of sight in concrete vaults, which match the walls, and protected with a locking metal grid. Remote control gear *(ch 2)* is used on the rotunda fixtures to reduce their profile still further.

Remote gear is also used on the low-profile, asymmetric fluorescent *(ch 2)* sign-lighters, often mounted on narrow ledges, which illuminate the high-level sculpture panels, statuary and rotunda arches. All fluorescent fixtures are fitted with louvres and colour-fast, amber-tinted lenses to match the deluxe HPS sources; tri-phosphor lamps *(ch 2)* were used throughout.

Some incandescent *(ch 2)* sources were also used. Enclosed PAR 38 *(ch 2)* lamp holders, with 250W tungsten halogen *(ch 2)* spotlamps, give crisp, white backlighting to the rotunda columns (replacing 1000W tungsten fixtures in the original scheme). Enclosed PAR 56 oval beam spotlights *(ch 3)*, equipped with custom-made hoods to control glare *(ch 1)*, and housing 12V PAR 56 lamps, illuminate the Priestesses of Culture statuary inside the rotunda. All tungsten and tungsten halogen sources were dimmed to 85 per cent of maximum voltage, to prolong lamp-life *(ch 1)*.

A timeclock switches the scheme on from sunset to 11.30pm, but 12 of the HPS floodlights remain on all night, for security reasons. All accessible fixtures are mounted in tamper-proof, steel plate boxes with locking grates, custom-painted to resist salt corrosion. Total energy consumption is 44KW.

Completed in late 1990, the scheme is one of the most admired exterior lighting design projects in the USA and has won numerous awards, including the 1991 International Association of Lighting Designers Award of Excellence.

To minimize their daytime visibility, recessed mercury luminaires are used to illuminate the chapel (right), while recessed PAR 56 spotlights dramatically uplight the trees (below and opposite page)

Private House and Gardens, England

Lighting design: Lighting Design Partnership

The brief was to light the front façade of the 18th-century house, a nearby converted chapel, and the surrounding gardens which contain several magnificent old trees, some evergreen and some deciduous. The totally dark rural context meant that light levels could be kept comparatively low. There were some existing floodlights on one side of the house consisting of large bulky fittings which were replaced with more discreet fixtures.

The chosen strategy was to provide an exterior lighting system which would be invisible when not in use, so as not to spoil the view or interfere with daytime usage of the grounds. To this end cable routings had to be trench-dug and covered, and many of the fittings were recessed flush into the soil. Large conventional freestanding floodlight fittings were avoided.

To obtain the maximum range of beam types and dimming capability, tungsten sources were chosen – a selection of PAR lamps *(ch 2)* in the main. The large trees were uplit by 300W PAR 56 spotlights *(ch 3)*, with protective toughened glass front covers, recessed into the ground. This technique also minimizes glare *(ch 1)* for visitors using the gardens at night.

The main exception to tungsten-based sources is the 250W MBF (HP mercury) *(ch 2)* units, again recessed into the ground around the chapel. Their mercury-based, blue-tinged light blends well with the flint stonework, and with careful positioning four fittings were sufficient to wash the walls and tower evenly. Uplighting *(ch 3)* the building also helps reveal details, such as the cornice round the top of the tower, not normally apparent. However, as the wide-beam sources are very dispersive, the lamps had to be partially masked on the inside face of the lenses to prevent excessive backspill onto the trees.

To contrast with the cool, blue uplighting the blanked-out stained-glass windows of the chapel were backlit with warmer tungsten halogen *(ch 2)*; similar highlights were also added to the high-level Norman arches in the bell tower. Finally, the weather vane was picked out with two narrow-beam PAR 38 spots mounted behind the tower parapet.

The long façade of the house, facing down the main driveway, presented particular problems. Large floodlight boxes would have been visually obtrusive and sources close offset to the façade would have created scallops of light and accentuated the texture of the brickwork. The chosen solution was two groups of ten 12V 50W dichroic lamps *(ch 2)* positioned almost centrally at right angles to the wall to flood the façade evenly from virtually hidden fixtures. The dormer windows and the house's own bell tower were picked out in slightly warmer tones, again by PAR 38 lamps located behind the parapet wall. Four nearby garden sculptures are uplit by dichroic spots flush-recessed into the ground.

The entire lighting set-up is controlled by an Electrosonic System 12 *(ch 5)* which enables individual circuits to be switched on and dimmed from a number of different locations. Dimmer controls also allow balancing of the cool MBF and warmer tungsten sources. Dimming down the tungsten sources around the house has the added bonus of accentuating the mellow tones of the two-hundred-year-old brickwork, whilst extending lamp-life *(ch 1)*.

chapter 7

Exterior lighting

Exterior lighting is a large sub-division of lighting design. In this chapter we cover the principles and problems associated with it.

In this chapter we discuss only the lighting of buildings, monuments and their associated landscapes, often dubbed, erroneously, 'floodlighting'. Except indirectly we do not refer to street lighting, the lighting of utility areas (car parks, goods yards, and so on) or sports stadia lighting. These are specialized lighting sectors, which don't fall within the remit of the majority of architects and designers.

Done well exterior lighting can enhance a night-time environment and display a building's features to good effect. When an exterior lighting scheme is ill considered or executed, it doesn't just affect a building's owners and users, it can be both a blight on its urban or rural surroundings and an environmental nuisance.

As yet, unlike noise or litter, most exterior lighting is not controlled by planning or environmental law. Planners can regulate the brightness of illuminated advertising signs, but not the lighting of buildings. The only legal requirement on architects and designers is that the fittings should not interfere with or damage the exterior structure of listed buildings. There are signs that exterior lighting schemes could be given a legal framework within the next few years, putting a new premium on getting it right.

Functions and benefits

Apart from the simple aesthetic enhancement of a building's façade or the details of a landscape, exterior lighting can have a number of other functions and benefits. Generally, good exterior lighting can offer environmental and psychological benefits for its users; it can also help instill a feeling of civic pride in the population of a town or city. One sophisticated use of exterior lighting is to link together a disparate group of buildings, for example on a residential estate or business complex, into a coherent whole, by lighting them in similar ways and extending lighting to the areas between them.

On a city-wide or smaller-scale commercial level, night lighting can be used as a marketing device, to draw attention to an area, company or facility after daylight hours. This can involve the simple floodlighting of a façade or something far more ambitious – for example, Edinburgh City Vision, where the intention is to co-ordinate all forms of urban lighting to market the city as a financial and commercial centre. Within that remit, co-consultants Lighting Design Partnership and architects Morris & Steedman took as their more specific brief the use of exterior lighting to enhance users' appreciation of the whole city, to expose and reveal its structure and architecture, and within that to create local mood and detail.

The scheme is still in development; some of the underlying principles and relevant recommended techniques are touched on below.

Exterior lighting can be a way of extending the usage of premises into the evening; and it can contribute to real and perceived security. Buildings which are well lit are less liable to be broken into or vandalized. An example of where several of these functions come together is the lighting of petrol stations and their forecourts. Here, good lighting plays an important marketing role, enabling the petrol station to function after dark, and instills a feeling of security into its users (particularly women customers).

Problems and pitfalls

Alongside the positive benefits of night-time exterior lighting, architects and designers must take on board a range of potential, and actual problems. Principal amongst these is light spillage or light pollution. When using powerful, broad-beam sources of light in an otherwise dark environment, the potential for a large proportion of that light to go where it is not wanted, is enormous. When this happens, it can be both a nuisance to neighbours and passers-by and a waste of energy.

Two of the most common mistakes in exterior lighting contribute directly to this problem. First there is a tendency to use too powerful a source (or sources), to put too much light onto a relatively small area of a building. As well as being a potential brightness nuisance within surrounding areas, this is also counter-productive in terms of highlighting a building's features. When blitzed with light in this way, architectural features are often lost or washed out and become invisible from a distance.

In addition, when only one or a limited number of sources are used from one direction, particularly if that coincides with the viewer's dominant line of sight, the resulting effect can be 'flat', with extremely poor modelling *(ch 1)* of the building. Much more subtle, effective techniques can be

Unsympathetic exterior lighting can result in glare, excessive contrast and poor rendering

Artist's impression of part of the Edinburgh City Vision lighting plan

Exterior lighting, for example of petrol station forecourts, requires attention to issues of safety, function, and commercial marketing

Courtesy: Concord Lighting

A common application of opal spheres in a pedestrian area. Although relatively inexpensive, as much light is lost upwards as reaches the ground

*Close offset lighting
of a building can
emphasize texture
but disguise
architectural form*

*Effective exterior
lighting can be
achieved without
'flooding' the entire
façade*

achieved using light more sparingly, and preferably angled across the viewer's line of sight. In general, if the building's features aren't to be washed out, it shouldn't be lit from the dominant viewing angle.

A closely associated mistake is the use of luminaires with too broad a beam, so that there is spillage around the sides of the object or building. For example, slender columns and monuments are commonly lit with broad beam floodlights, when much narrower beam luminaires, using less light, but concentrated onto the object, would be more appropriate.

Floodlighting

The use of the term 'floodlighting' for all exterior lighting symptomizes the problem. Floodlighting is usually regarded as throwing as much light as possible at the face of a building. Context is rarely considered. For example, a building standing alone against a dark background will require much less light than one located amongst other lit buildings, each with its own sources of competing light (such as interior lighting seen through windows).

This combination – too much light from too few, powerful, broad-beam luminaires – is probably the most common exterior lighting design fault. There are far more effective strategies, which lighting designers have been refining for several years. Where the budget allows, the use of a larger number of lower-wattage sources, each with appropriate beam spreads, can achieve a controlled, subtle effect, and will waste far less light. To follow Mies van der Rohe's dictum, in lighting as in architecture, 'less is more'. Narrower beams mean tighter control, and tighter control means less potential light spillage.

Such an approach also means that light can be applied from a number of different positions, which avoids heavy shadows and

gives better modelling. By gently incorporating light and shade, the building's form and detail can be better brought out. The whole building façade doesn't always have to be flooded with light; the highlighting of particular details, while relying on a gentle spill of light to suggest the rest of the building's structure, can at times be far more effective; not all the features of a building are necessarily equally worthy of attention.

In some cases the best strategy may be to enhance the building, by subsuming the lighting to the architecture. The building may not appear lit because the lighting is made an integral part of the structure. The use of overtly decorative luminaires, with totally concealed functional sources, is one way of achieving this effect.

The reflective qualities (reflectance) *(ch 1)* of a building also have a strong bearing on its perceived luminance and so on how much light it requires. This often receives little attention in exterior lighting, yet pale limestone walls could appear dazzlingly bleached out if lit with the same quantity of light as, say, red brick. This deserves greater attention where several different materials, with different reflectances, are used in one building. In chapter 1 we include a list of standard CIBSE reflectance factors for some of the main types of wall finish. It should be remembered, however, that grime and discolouration due to urban pollution and weathering can further reduce reflectance.

Light pollution

Light pollution is not something that only affects neighbours, astronomers and passers-by, it can also be a nuisance for users of the building being lit. This is particularly an issue in hotels, which use night-time illumination, as a means of marketing. For residents, there is nothing more ugly, or irritating, than glare from a row of 1000W floodlights directly visible

Rather than 'washing' the building, lighting has been used here to emphasize the main architectural features

At the Savoy Hotel, London, close offset lighting creates a dramatic effect while avoiding light spillage into guest rooms

from a hotel bedroom window, particularly if a guest is trying to sleep. Lower-powered lamps, sensitively positioned, with controlled light distribution – louvred or shielded, if necessary – could minimize this annoyance.

Alternatively, floodlights can be positioned close to the building, at an acute angle to the walls, so that they are below the cut-off viewing angle from the windows. However, not only will any protrusions, such as cornices and window-sills, be more heavily shadowed, any imperfections in the wall material will be accentuated.

At the Savoy Hotel in London, Lighting Design Partnership, which has long been aware of the implicit contradiction between guest comfort and a hotelier's marketing needs, employed a series of narrow-beam luminaires fixed almost flush to the wall so that they threw light up the building between the clear glass windows. This achieved an interesting effect with no light interference to the impressive river views.

Colour matching

Another consideration with exterior lighting concerns the choice of lamp source, its colour temperature, colour rendering, lamp-life and wattage *(ch 2)*. The type of source should be matched, as far as possible, to the materials and type of building. Too often, however, solely for reasons of energy-efficiency, buildings, regardless of their qualities or position, are bathed in an overall orange-tinted light, either high-pressure sodium or, worse, low-pressure sodium *(ch 2)*. If the building is located near sodium street lighting, one way of making it stand out from its surroundings is to use lamps of a contrasting colour temperature (metal halide or mercury, for example).

As part of the Edinburgh City Vision plan, specific colour temperature lamps are planned for different areas of the city. The rambling, winding streets of the old town

Two contrasting approaches: the often over-used uniform wash of high-pressure sodium (right), and an imaginative mix of light sources for different features (below)
Courtesy: Philips

are to be deliberately lit largely with warmer high-pressure sodium lamps, to complement the older stucco and stonework, to create a sense of intimacy and to hint at former, historic types of lighting once used there, such as candles and oil lamps. Across the city in the Georgian new town, with its disciplined, grid-like street plan, cooler mercury and metal halide sources *(ch 2)* are to be employed, in order to emphasize the formality and austerity of the architecture, and to contrast strongly with the warmer residential interiors, as glimpsed from the street. These proposals extend to both street lighting and the direct illumination of building exteriors.

In the same way that a range of smaller sources in different positions can be used for maximum effect, in many cases a mix of perhaps two lamp types, with different colour qualities, can offer an interesting contrast, or be used as an effective means of emphasis.

Costs of exterior lighting

The cost of installation, maintenance and running of exterior schemes can be high. Often clients find out too late that they cannot justify the running costs of an exterior lighting scheme and so leave it switched off most of the time. The result may be a 'black hole', where something less ambitious (and less costly) might at least have given some effective night-time presence. Off-peak, night-time electricity can be much cheaper than peak-time power, so users should explore the possibilities of off-peak tariffs with the electricity companies.

Some control systems *(ch 5)* can reduce running costs, whilst adding variety to the scheme. If, for example, tungsten lamps *(ch 2)* are used, simple dimming can increase lamp-life *(ch 1)* and thus reduce running and maintenance costs. Pre-set control systems can offer several possible 'scenes', which might be used at different times of the day or week. For example, there might be a basic level for use during the week and a full-on setting for, say, the weekend, when the facility needs to make most impact or attract most users.

Luminaire location

Exterior-quality equipment needs to be made to a higher standard than interior models, to withstand extremes of weather, ingress of water, and so on. The BSI has devised an Ingress Protection (IP) system (see Appendix 3) of rating luminaires for their waterproof capabilities, which should always be consulted. When used in coastal resorts, salt corrosion can be a problem; many of the metal luminaires available are unsuitable for such environments.

Where to position the luminaires needs careful thought and not just in terms of their lighting effect. They should not simply be located where there is a convenient ledge or canopy on which to mount them. They should be positioned with due sympathy for the building's fabric, as well as practical considerations (such as cable routes), and be concealed as far as possible.

Trees and shrubs around a building can be used creatively. If luminaires are situated between planting and the building, they are not only concealed from the viewer, but the plants can also be thrown into attractive silhouette against the lit façade. Lakes, ponds or other stretches of water can also be exploited effectively. Where the lit building is viewed from across the water, its reflections can make it doubly attractive. But beware, unsheilded light sources reflected in water are simply twice as annoying.

Access to luminaires is important. In urban environments, for example, if luminaires are too easily accessible, the opportunities for vandalism can be increased. If they are not easily accessible,

then maintenance standards may be compromised. One obvious step is to consider longer-life lamps in luminaires which are likely to be difficult to re-fit.

Consider what the luminaires will look like during the day. Large, ugly fixtures may work well in the dark, but create a visual blot during daylight hours. An increasingly popular way of concealing equipment is to bury it in the ground, so that it is virtually invisible during the day and far less tempting to vandals. A limited range of standard luminaires is available for this purpose.

In general, the size, weight, and in some cases style, of luminaire should be considered in relation to the building it is mounted on or in front of. It should be as small as possible in relation to the desired light output. Decorative equipment is available, but its use should be considered carefully. It is too easy to specify a period-style fitting without assessing its true appropriateness to the building.

The Victoria and Albert Museum, London – lighting historic buildings may require the use of custom-designed fixings in order to avoid damage to the fabric

An effective way of minimizing the daytime visual impact of luminaires is to recess them below ground level

chapter 8

Lighting and the environment

In recent years environmental and ecological concerns have risen close to the top of our political and social agendas. The issue of energy conservation, in particular, has become pressing, due to fears of air pollution, the increase of greenhouse gases and possible destruction of the ozone layer.

Lighting has been drawn into the debate over care of the environment. Out of the cluster of ecological questions surrounding lighting, most attention has focused on energy consumption. Lighting consumes energy. In Britain and the USA at least, this is in the main produced through burning fossil fuels, a process which pollutes the atmosphere and may contribute to the 'greenhouse effect'. Such resources are finite and need to be conserved, at least until reliable sources of renewable energy come on stream.

The problem for the lighting business is that lighting is one of the most visible and obvious users of electricity, despite the fact that individual lamps consume a very small amount of energy compared with many electrical appliances or an entire air-conditioning system. According to Electricity Association estimates, lighting as a whole comprises around 15-16 per cent of our national consumption of electrical

power. Within modern commercial buildings, such as office blocks (see Eastop and Croft 1990), lighting could constitute 30 per cent of total energy consumption; but it is obviously a much smaller percentage of total operating costs, when staff wages are included, for example. Lighting's share of the energy cake also depends on whether air-conditioning systems are installed; in most air-conditioned buildings lighting could constitute less than ten per cent of electrical power consumed.

In other words, lighting is a minor, if significant, factor in the production of greenhouse gases. But just as other users of energy are, more or less enthusiastically, giving increasing attention to energy conservation, the coming years will see a growing emphasis on energy-saving design. Already, proposals for taxes on energy are under consideration within the European Commission; the diminution of fossil fuels will also inevitably push up costs, as more users compete for less energy. Some forecasters suggest that energy prices will have to rise fivefold in the next 30 years, if people are to be compelled to take sufficient steps to reverse global warming.

So while lighting design has always been concerned with controlling light, both quantitatively and qualitatively, to achieve a given effect as efficiently as possible, today there is an added and growing environmental dimension which has to be taken on board.

Energy efficiency and user comfort

The issue of lighting and its relation to more general environmental and ecological questions is complicated. There are fundamental, and potentially insoluble, problems in balancing the requirements of users for a comfortable, aesthetically pleasing local environment and broader energy conservation and global ecological considerations. It's a fact that people are the major asset (and expense) of any company; even at the most basic financial level, labour costs can easily constitute between 40 and 50 per cent of overall costs of a business. To get costs into perspective, according to our own calculations the annual lighting costs per person in an average office are equivalent to between two and four hours' salary. If staff are demotivated through inadequate working conditions, their efficiency may deteriorate and output may decline on a scale far greater than the gains that may accrue from the installation of more energy-efficient (but less user-friendly) lighting, for example.

Poor lighting can be a major, but unrecognized, cause of worker dissatisfaction and inefficiency. For example, it can cause workers to make more mistakes, or to take more time to read written material, and to work slower. Employees' health may even be affected; badly designed, poorly specified lighting can cause stress and is often associated with glare, eye strain, migraines and other features of what is known as 'sick building syndrome'. Paradoxically, an energy-efficient approach to workplace lighting, which pays little or no attention to user comfort, could turn out to be both ugly and ineffective. Such a design strategy, far from saving money, may in the long run be more expensive.

This contradiction was encountered recently by Greenpeace, in its British headquarters in London, designed by architects Fielden Clegg. The architects opted for an extensive uplighting *(ch 3)* scheme, using metal halide *(ch 2)* sources, in many of its deeper office spaces. While such a lighting strategy is effective in terms of the working environment created, it is not the most efficient in terms of energy conservation. On those grounds alone, direct lighting, possibly using fluorescent lamps *(ch 2)* should have been the chosen solution. However, it is pleasing to note that the staff environment was considered more important than merely minimizing energy consumption.

Another example of the complexity of this issue is the exterior lighting of buildings at night *(ch 7)*. One could argue that such lighting is completely wasteful. But on local amenity and aesthetic grounds, it has to be acknowledged that many of our streets and town centres are visually enhanced, during night-time hours, by judicious, well-designed exterior floodlighting *(ch 7)*. There may be added commercial advantages; night-time lighting may entice people in and so extend a facility's usage.

There is evidence that well-lit streets, car parks and estates can reduce crime (see Painter 1988 and Philips 1990). Power failures in major cities in the USA, including New York, have resulted in rises in opportunistic crime and social disturbance.

Greenpeace's offices in north London – a light and airy interior achieved by uplighting fabric sails. A successful combination of user-friendliness with efficient light sources
Photo: Michael Evans

Exterior lighting of buildings – a waste of resources or an acceptable enhancement of the night-time environment?

An increasing awareness of the benefit of natural daylight has led to its greater use and control within commercial buildings

Courtesy: Erco

Despite our deep-seated environmental concerns, we (like Greenpeace) find it impossible to adopt a totally dedicated energy-conservation position on lighting design. In our opinion, energy efficiency should never be seen as the principal measure of good lighting design if it compromises functional and aesthetic effect. While important, it has to be balanced against other factors.

One estimate by Sweden's National Energy Administration claimed, at the 'Right Light, Bright Light' conference (Stockholm 1991), that energy consumption by lighting could be halved without sacrificing lighting quality. The problem with such optimistic predictions is the determination of the criteria by which lighting quality can be judged; an engineer's criteria would probably differ from a designer's, for example.

There are many steps that architects, designers and lighting designers can take to make their schemes more energy efficient, without necessarily compromising their aesthetic appeal. With a little knowledge, certain obviously wasteful lighting strategies can be avoided. In the 1980s there was an over-specification of relatively inefficient low-voltage tungsten halogen dichroic lamps *(ch 2)* for all purposes, many of them inappropriate. If designers and architects had better understood their functions and limitations, aesthetics and energy conservation might have been better served.

Planning with daylight

Several new (and not-so-new) techniques and technologies are available which offer energy-saving potential. The most obvious technique is the greater use of the cheapest, most abundant source of light available to us all, daylight. For many years offices and other commercial spaces have been built in a way that limits or even excludes daylight. In deep-plan buildings, exterior light rarely reached the innermost spaces and in many cases it was even seen as a nuisance, particularly in relation to the use of visual display terminals. It was regarded as a hindrance to full environmental control, where air-conditioning was specified – glazed curtain-wall buildings often suffer particularly from heat gain on sunny days.

Today, environmentally conscious reassessments of building design are recognizing that daylight, and natural fresh air, are important commodities and should be exploited. Glazed atria are a common architectural feature, to bring daylight into the centre of deep buildings. There's a trend away from air-conditioning and intense artificial lighting – both of which have been seen as contributors to sick building syndrome – towards the re-introduction of large windows, which open to admit fresh air.

Daylight has to be controlled, like all other forms of light, if it is not to become a nuisance, particularly on bright, sunny days. In chapter 3 we discuss the wide range of devices and control systems available, from the relatively cheap and simple internal blind, through to hi-tech, computer-controlled heliostats which follow the line of the sun and reflect daylight deep into the interior of the building.

Fielden Clegg's Greenpeace building, mentioned on page 185, employs an interesting variation on this theme. The building suffered from excessive solar gain on its south elevation, coupled with lack of natural light in the centre of the building. Horizontal steel slatted louvres, which can be tilted at different angles, were fitted about a third of the way up the exterior of the tall windows; these shade areas close to the windows, while reflecting light deep into the building from their upper surfaces. Horizontal fabric 'shelves' work in a similar way inside the building.

Elsewhere in Europe, even more

sophisticated ways of controlling and harnessing sunlight to replace or supplement conventional power have been tried. The ING Bank in Amsterdam, designed by a team led by Dutch architects Alberts and Van Huut, for example, is regarded as one of the most energy-efficient, environmentally friendly buildings yet devised. There, the windows on the south face of the building are used as solar energy collectors; heat is transferred to the cooler side of the building and stored in large water tanks where it is given off throughout the day. Natural light is enhanced by the use of light-reflecting and dispersing materials in the window openings, so that artificial light is required for only 30 per cent of office time.

Improving performance and lamp-life

At ING Bank and elsewhere, artificial lighting is still necessary, and here too there have been important developments. For example, the new generation of lower-energy lamps, such as compact fluorescents *(ch 2)*, could in many cases replace less efficient incandescent sources. Such sources, which can offer good colour rendering *(ch 1)* and, because of their small size, relatively easy optical control, can be up to four times more energy efficient than an equivalent incandescent *(ch 2)* source, if used correctly. They can also have up to eight times longer lamp-life. Such gains are dependent on the efficiency and appropriateness of the luminaire, its application, optical performance and the control gear *(ch 2)* employed. When wrongly specified or utilized, the result can be (and often is), a far greater proportional reduction in lighting levels than in energy saved.

The US Environmental Protection Agency (EPA) has estimated that replacing a 60W incandescent source with a 16W compact fluorescent lamp will avoid the emission of 300 lbs of carbon dioxide,

An effective daylight control device at the Greenpeace building, designed by Fielden Clegg. A series of external horizontal louvres shields the lower part of the window while reflecting light into the building from their upper surfaces

Photo: Michael Evans

The ING Bank, Amsterdam – an energy-efficient building that combines careful daylight control with the heating and cooling system

Courtesy: Pentagram Design

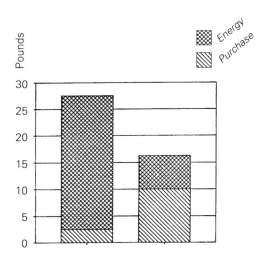

Figure 1 Comparative purchase and running costs of incandescent (left) and fluorescent lamps (right)

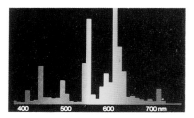

Spectral composition of a modern fluorescent lamp, in which both efficiency and colour quality have been considerably improved

Courtesy: Osram

1.4 lbs of sulphur dioxide and 0.8 lbs of nitrogen oxide from a typical fossil-burning power plant every year. It would also save about $21.5 (about £12.00) per lamp per year in fuel costs.

Even amongst fluorescent sources, there are substantial performance differences; 26mm-diameter fluorescent tubes, for example, are more efficient than old-style 38mm tubes. The latest electronic control gear for fluorescent lamps can cut up to 20 per cent of power consumption, as well as getting rid of the potential nuisance, or even danger *(ch 2)* of hum and flicker. While such controls are currently expensive, improved manufacturing techniques and their greater use may bring down the price. As energy prices rise, the equation may become increasingly attractive. There are low-loss versions of conventional wire-wound inductive control gear which are more efficient than their predecessors.

The choice of luminaire can have a significant impact on efficiency. Appropriate lamps, in well-designed and correctly specified reflectors, which deliver the right amount of light where it's needed will always be more energy efficient. Yet designers and architects rarely look at how well luminaire reflectors perform, or study a luminaire's photometric data, to ensure the optimal use of the client's resources.

In 1990 Concord Lighting refurbished the lighting at Heathrow Airport's Terminal 1. The company claims that the replacement of the original Frederick Gibbard-designed lighting – four 40W fluorescent tubes in each ceiling panel – with one modern 100W Metalarc (metal halide) luminaire, achieved a 24 per cent reduction in energy consumption, with an 11 per cent increase in light output. Maintenance costs were reduced and the whole public environment looks 'brighter and cleaner'.

Matching the lamp and luminaire correctly is important. It's no use simply putting an energy-efficient compact fluorescent lamp into an inappropriate fixture, for example one originally designed to take an incandescent reflector lamp (a common mistake). The result will generally be both ugly and inefficient. This sort of error most often arises during retro-fitting, which is one reason why an energy-efficient scheme demands regular, consistent and informed maintenance. Other forms of regular maintenance, such as periodic cleaning of reflectors and lenses is also vital to maintain their effectiveness.

One problem, of course, is that attractive, stylish luminaires and reflectors for energy-efficient lamps such as fluorescent, have often been limited, so designers or architects have declined to use them on aesthetic grounds. New types of luminaire are constantly coming onto the market and we hope that this expansion of the range will widen their appeal.

Switches and controls

A major part of designing an energy-efficient lighting scheme involves all the issues of what could be called light optical control, to deliver the right kind of light exactly where it's required – the correct choice of lamps, luminaires and associated optical devices such as louvres, lenses, reflectors and diffusers. Equally important is operational control (switching). There's no better energy-conservation measure than turning off a lamp or appliance. Unfortunately, as discussed in chapter 5, the manual on/off switch can present problems in a large, commercial environment. Where do you locate it? Who does the switching? How many luminaires are affected?

Recent years have seen the development of more sophisticated automated control systems – such as ripple

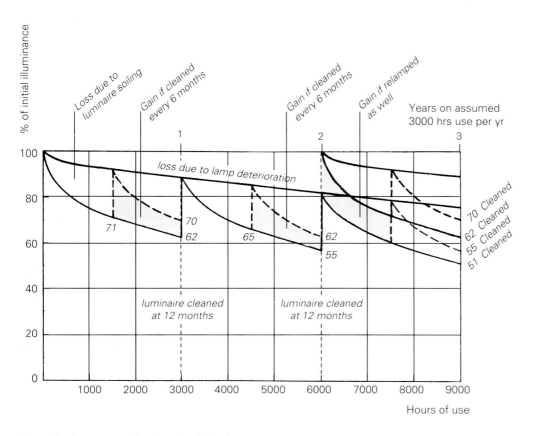

% of initial illuminance

Loss due to luminaire soiling

Gain if cleaned every 6 months

Gain if cleaned every 6 months

Gain if relamped as well

Years on assumed 3000 hrs use per yr

loss due to lamp deterioration

70 Cleaned
62 Cleaned
55 Cleaned
51 Cleaned

71

70
62

65

62

55

luminaire cleaned at 12 months

luminaire cleaned at 12 months

Hours of use

Figure 2 The comparative effects of good maintenance on an installation's efficiency over a notional three-year period

Courtesy: Electricity Association

Automated control systems, which ensure that lamps are operational only when required, can make a significant contribution to an energy-saving strategy

switches, dimmers, timers, and proximity detectors – which can play a central role, both in creating an attractive, efficient working environment and in saving energy *(ch 5)*. Dimmer systems, for example, aren't only potential power-saving devices. In some cases they can also prolong lamp-life and so conserve manufacturing resources. At the same time, the more sophisticated dimmer systems give the designer a chance to control an interior ambience over time, while more perfectly matching lighting levels to user needs. In retail and leisure environments, intelligent control systems can go further, to set different scenes and create different lighting ambiences, depending on the time of day and possible changes of use (for example, in a restaurant, from breakfast to lunch and dinner).

The possibilities of automatic control systems to enhance interior design to better fit users' needs, while also possibly saving energy, are considerable. At the moment they tend to be expensive and can be complex and bulky – thus they are commonly seen as appropriate only for large-scale commercial environments. As technology develops, control systems will come down in size and price and will probably be used more, even possibly for general domestic interiors. Twenty years ago manual dimmers and presence-sensing security switching systems were unheard of; now they're commonplace.

Dealing with lamp disposal

Energy isn't the only ecological question to impinge on lighting design. A broader environmental audit, necessary under the 1991 Environmental Protection Act (EPA), will have to look well beyond mere lumens per watt *(ch 1)*. Unless specifiers can show that they have designed a scheme for maximum energy efficiency across its total lifespan, and have instructed the client in approved lamp disposal techniques, they

Simister's Lampcracker disposal system

Marlin's Matrix downlight system – interchangeable components can offer extended life to an installation

are liable to prosecution under the terms of the EPA. To date how many designers or architects can vouch for the environmental friendliness of their schemes?

Perhaps part of the problem is that many designers and architects have little knowledge of lamp manufacturing processes and the potential toxicity of the materials employed. Ironically, energy-efficient lamps can be the worst offenders: ballasts for discharge *(ch 2)* lighting and transformers for low-voltage systems *(ch 2)*, for example, can involve metals, copper wire, plastics, tars and other potentially toxic elements in their production.

While fluorescents may be energy efficient in use, both lamp and luminaire can require high-energy inputs during manufacturing, due to their large size and complex construction. At the moment, this is redeemed by energy savings during operational life. Both fluorescents and HID metal halide *(ch 2)* sources contain sub-stantial amounts of mercury and cannot be legally dumped on a landfill site. With the tightening up of anti-dumping laws under the 1991 EPA, disposal costs of these kinds of lamp could rise considerably.

Sodium lamps *(ch 2)* are also efficient in energy terms, but if broken and then exposed to water, they produce corrosive caustic soda. GE Lighting, for example, have issued disposal guidelines, which specify, amongst other things, that no more than 20 lamps should be broken into one container at the same time. But how many specifiers/managers currently either know or follow these guidelines?

In the case of large commercial installations, the problems are obviously multiplied. Because of the fall-off of lamp efficiency (light output) over time, in order to maintain intended lighting levels most lighting designers will often recommend a complete lamp re-fit after a specific period,

regardless of how many lamps have actually failed. This can be more cost-effective than individual lamp replacement, but a number of factors have to be considered to establish the optimum maintenance regime for a given installation. If managers/users do not heed this recommended replacement cycle, they can waste energy and ruin the intended effect.

Mass disposal can present a considerable problem. Several disposal devices are available to help here. Lampcracker, for example, developed by Simister Engineering, is a disposal machine for discharge lamps, which, it is claimed, can safely crush any type of lamp and dilute and filter its dangerous components. While final disposal is a problem, waste materials can at least be handled and transported in a compact, safe form. Such devices could become a commonplace service fixture in large retail or leisure environments.

The old-fashioned GLS tungsten lamp is one of the relatively environmentally-friendly sources, with a low-energy production process and none of the toxic materials associated with discharge lamps. However, as we explained in chapter 2, they have other major disadvantages – not least their low efficiency and intrinsic failure rate at only 1000-2000 hours. Both these features carry environmental penalties – higher consumption of carbon-based fossil fuels, with its inherent emission problems, increased amounts of packaging, more frequent transportation requirements.

To date, no one appears to have undertaken a comprehensive environ-mental audit of different forms of lighting, from the manufacturing process, through consumption to disposal/recycling, which considers all of these contradictory features. Until this happens, it will be difficult for specifiers and users to balance the features in an informed way. At the moment all they have to go on is the price of the product. Ultimately this may not reflect the true environmental cost.

New sources are coming onto the market which are either more energy efficient, have a longer lamp-life, and/or are less onerous in construction; for example, Sylvania's SMFL (sub-miniaturized fluorescent lamp) source, which emerged from research into miniaturized backlighting for laptop computer screens. This small hot and cold cathode lamp *(ch 2)*, about the size of a pencil, has a rated life of 20,000 hours (compared with a replacement cycle of around 7000-10,000 hours for standard fluorescent lamps).

Another innovation is the Philips QL inductive lamp, which is instantly dimmable and has moderate efficiency. However, with no filament, it has a rated lamp-life of 60,000-80,000 hours.

Recycling

Recycling used lamps and luminaires is an important environmental consideration. Unfortunately, the simple replacement of new filaments in worn-out incandescent lamps is not yet a feasible option, but the recycling of glass and metals used in lamps is. Britain has a very poor record on this front. A directory of manufacturers using recycled materials could be compiled to help 'green' specifiers.

Luminaires which allow different components, such as bezels , lamp holders , and reflectors, to be replaced, rather than having to junk the whole unit, are already available. While the parts are not recyclable *per se*, flexibility of this sort is one move away from total disposability and could mean the extension of component life. Marlin's Matrix system is a good example of the trend – demountable reflectors can be replaced or changed, while retaining the same housing, to update it or modify its function. Other companies, for example Zumtobel, offer a similar range.

Low-voltage lighting *(ch 2)* is one area where this modular approach could be very beneficial. Where a dichroic effect is required, it is environmentally beneficial to specify capsule lamps with a separate dichroic reflector *(ch 2)*, rather than integral reflector lamps *(ch 2)*, each with its own energy-hungry dichroic coating. However, at the time of writing (1992), company pricing policies belie this. Another option would be to simply use a cheaper metal reflector lamp.

Insufficient consideration has been given to the wholesale recycling of luminaires; the phenomenom of viable luminaires being scrapped, rather than re-used elsewhere, is particularly prevalent in Britain with its tradition of 'spec' building, where tons of brand-new fluorescent luminaires are routinely stripped out and then replaced.

Whilst some manufacturers already offer a leasehold system for purely commercial reasons, the principle could be adopted on environmental grounds. One day we might have a thorough-going leasehold, rather than purchase, system for lighting, so that lamps and luminaires automatically revert to the supplier/ manufacturer, for recycling. Such an approach needs pushing hard within a design culture which for years has been geared to instant disposability and renewal. It remains to be seen whether the Environmental Protection Act – which specifies that by the end of the 20th century 50 per cent of materials used in a design scheme must be recyclable – will have sufficient powers to bring about this change.

CIE guidelines for lighting design for energy conservation

- Analyse the task in terms of difficulty, duration, criticalness and location, to determine the lighting needs throughout a space, taking into account the visual differences among people due to age and other factors.

- Design the lighting to provide the necessary illumination on the task in accordance with current recommendations.

- Select the most efficient lamps appropriate to the type of lighting to be specified, taking into account the need for colour rendering.

- Select luminaires that are efficient, having light distribution characteristics appropriate for the tasks and the environment, and not producing discomfort glare or serious veiling reflections.

- Use the highest practical room surface reflectances, so as to achieve the best overall efficiency of the entire lighting system.

- Integrate the lighting with the heating and air-conditioning systems, as dictated by climatic conditions, to save energy for cooling and heating purposes.

- Provide a flexible lighting system, so that sections can be turned off or the lighting reduced, when not needed.

- Co-ordinate, when appropriate and when the space permits, daylighting with the electric lighting but ensure that this does not introduce glare or other brightness imbalance in the environment.

- Establish an adequate maintenance programme for periodic cleaning of the luminaires and room surfaces and for lamp replacement.

chapter 9

Lighting designers and how to work with them

Many of the schemes featured in chapter 6 were designed by independent lighting design consultants. In this chapter we explain what lighting designers do. We offer advice on how to choose a lighting designer and how to get the best out of them on a project.

Many types of expert, from architects and interior designers to electrical engineers, manufacturers and equipment suppliers, claim to offer professional lighting design. In our opinion, compared with the genuine independent lighting design consultant, all have distinct disadvantages. The architect or interior designer will certainly be independent, and their terms of appointment often specify that they are paid to design the lighting. But few will have had substantial training in the discipline and, with the exception of the postgraduate course at The Bartlett, University College London, few British architecture and design courses lighting design. In general, only the largest practices can afford to include a full-time lighting design specialist on their staff. With today's proliferation of light sources, luminaires and other equipment, architects and interior designers rarely have the time to keep in touch with developments.

Design or engineering?

While architects and designers may have a vision of what they want from the lighting scheme in aesthetic terms, they may not know how to achieve it. Often, they will leave it to electrical engineers to specify and execute the project, some of whom claim to offer specialist lighting design as part of their service.

Consultant electrical engineers are technically proficient in electrical installations; they design the lighting circuits and are indispensable to the project team. But, generally, they are not specialists in the functional, psychological and aesthetic aspects of lighting.

Engineers should plan the installation but not the lighting effects. In any building project they also have the other aspects of electrical engineering to work out, such as cable management and power distribution. As with architects, they are hard-pressed to keep up with developing technologies in construction, without immersing themselves in the additional demands of another specialism.

The result is likely to be that engineers may tend to follow the book, in terms of the codes and regulations. Taking such an approach can result in functional but uninspired, standardized schemes.

Lighting design services, which are offered by manufacturers or distributors, often on an apparently 'free' basis, can be tempting, particularly if budgets are tight. They can lead clients to expect similar free services from genuine lighting consultancies.

While the practitioners may indeed be trained, manufacturers' design departments are inclined to take a product-led approach to design, with little or no involvement during installation. It is quite possible that the designer will not visit the scheme or meet the architect. Instead, he/she will simply receive the brief from their local sales person.

Sales people may be tempted to 'over-specify' in order to sell more of the company's product, and specification will inevitably be limited to the company's own ranges. For commercial reasons specification of another company's products will not be possible, and if the available luminaires are not appropriate, the scheme will be compromised.

In the long run, the cost of these so-called 'free' services is built into manufacturers' prices. In this way every customer pays, whether they have used the service or not. It would perhaps be better to reduce product costs and charge a fee for an improved, comprehensive service.

Another risk relates to design responsibility. In the event of problems who will be liable – will it be an 'unpaid' supplier or manufacturer, or the designer or consultancy as the employed professional?

There are also 'independent' lighting design companies which are tacitly tied up with particular manufacturers – in some cases co-funded by them – and who are inevitably limited in the range of products they will specify. Again, apparently low fees may be subsidized by resulting higher product prices.

While genuinely independent lighting consultants may design, procure and supply products, particularly on fast-track projects, they should never make a profit out of supply. Otherwise, consideration of 'their' margin on particular products may over-ride the client's best interests.

The role of the lighting designer
A common misunderstanding is that a lighting designer is someone who primarily designs lighting products. Designers from Mario Bellini to Philippe Starck have worked on luminaires at one time or another. But that doesn't make them lighting designers – in our sense of the term this is someone who *designs with*

light. While designing luminaires can be one part of the work of a lighting designer, it does not define or encompass his/her total skills or knowledge.

Lighting design consultants are not mechanical, electrical or lighting engineers, though they have to to be conversant with these specialisms. They do not simply calculate lumens and lux *(ch 1)*, though that is part of their responsibilities. Nor are they fixture sales people, though the selection or design of fixtures is generally part of the service they provide.

A lighting designer's field of specialization is the design, manipulation and control of light, and the independent designer earns a fee solely for the time spent providing that service. There is no bias towards particular products and there should be a clear agreement with the client on the exact service and fee.

Broadly speaking, the lighting designer's job comprises three parts: first, in close collaboration with the client and/or architect or designer, to create a lighting scheme that will present the interior or exterior as its designer envisaged, and/or will answer the client's objectives. This might involve concept rendering, or drawing up plans to show fixture locations and how they are controlled.

Second, the lighting designer has to specify the equipment and provide other relevant details such as special fixings or mounting requirements which might not be obvious from the plan. The lighting designer might also assist in the analysis of bids and tenders on large projects.

Third, the lighting consultant has to commission and review the completed installation and sometimes has to monitor its performance during the early days or weeks of operation (the post-occupancy evaluation).

All three stages of this process may have a different emphasis from project to project. Unfortunately, some clients try and

How to choose a lighting consultant

- *Recommendation: has the lighting consultant been recommended by someone else in a similar line of business?*
- *Experience: does the lighting consultant have experience in the appropriate project type?*
- *Independence: is the lighting consultant free of all commercial allegiances?*
- *Payment: is the lighting consultant to be remunerated only on a fee basis?*
- *Workload: does the lighting consultant have the time and resources to meet your deadline?*

make do with the first stage alone – the 'concept only' deal – on the assumption that they can source the products and oversee the implementation. This can be a false economy and can end in disappointment; designs change and what was designed in the abstract at the outset may differ markedly to the needs of the completed scheme. Designers or architects may need to change the colour scheme, which could affect all the reflectances *(ch 2)*. The whole lighting scheme may then have to be modified and possibly re-specified, if desired effects or lighting levels are to be achieved.

In some cases the lighting designer may find that no standard product meets the exact requirements of the project. In such cases they may either produce designs for a 'special' *(ch 4)*, or tailor an existing product. They should also be responsible for ensuring compliance with British, European or other relevant standards.

Who pays lighting designers?

Lighting designers, like any other independent consultants, work on a fee basis. At least in the British context, the issue of who employs them can vary from project to project.

Sometimes lighting consultants are hired directly by far-sighted clients to work as equals alongside the other members of the team from the beginning of the project. This is without doubt the most satisfactory arrangement, in terms of results and in establishing the credibility and standing of the profession. It is also the best set-up for resolving any future disputes about design liability.

Because lighting consultancy is still a young and relatively poorly recognized specialism, compared with, say, acoustic or landscape design, and because few clients appreciate its potential contribution, many are unwilling to hire lighting consultants

directly, as a distinct part of the project budget. Where architects and interior designers recognize their lack of expertise in this area, they may sub-contract the work to the lighting designer, within their own fee structure. This can often lead to lighting design fees being squeezed. The lighting designer's position as a sub-consultant also means he/she may not be given acknowledgement by the full team.

Lighting design – a science or an art?

Because of limited full-time educational courses in lighting design, many lighting designers in Britain have taken a non-academic route into their professions; many came out of theatre and stage design. Alternatively, they first worked as lighting engineers or product designers, often within one of the large lighting manufacturers.

Due to their varied training and experience, independent lighting design consultants can have widely differing approaches to lighting design. At one extreme there are those who see lighting design as a technical science, something that can be done on the drawing board or computer, using photometric tables, diagrams, codes and standards. Schemes produced according to this philosophy will tend to be technically correct and competent rather than inspired.

At the other extreme, some lighting designers see their practice as a creative art, relying principally on intuition. In the words of US lighting designer, Gerry Zekowski (in Lee Watson 1990), 'Illumination engineering is only a small part of lighting design. Lighting and the environment are an interactive human perceptual phenomenom that cannot be evaluated by simple pass/fail scores'.

We see lighting design as lying somewhere between the two extremes. While knowledge of technical codes and standards is necessary, and while a great deal can be done in diagrammatic form, much of the best work has an unpredictable, intuitive and creative element. Experimentation and empirical testing will always play a crucial role. It is important, too, to recognize that even the best designers don't always get things right the first time – continual reassessment and re-adjustment are vital and unavoidable parts of the lighting designer's job.

The lighting designer's essential skills are usefully summarized in the judging criteria used by the International Association of Lighting Designers (IALD) in selecting schemes for its annual awards. These criteria – listed below – could usefully be applied by anyone attempting a lighting design scheme.

Evaluating a lighting design proposal

- *Is the lighting solution appropriate for the activities of the space?*

- *Is there a satisfactory level of illumination for the specific tasks performed in the space?*

- *In addition to providing the correct quantity of light, have the more subtle aspects of viewing comfort been addressed, such as glare and contrast ratios?*

- *Does this project reinforce the architectural concept?*

- *Does the design reinforce the natural mood of the activity or situation to create a sense of well-being?*

- *Are the lighting elements (such as fixtures and coves) integrated well into the architectural framework?*

- *Has the appropriateness or inappropriateness of the design to its cultural or geographic context been considered?*

- *Does the project exemplify technical expertise?*

- *If energy conservation was an issue, was the solution successfully executed within the limitations?*

- *If the budget restrictions were an issue, was the solution successfully executed within the limitations?*

- *If colour or unusual lighting effects were considered, were they executed successfully?*

- *Does this project exemplify high aesthetic achievement?*

chapter 10

The future of lighting

Lighting and lighting design are in a continuous and accelerating process of change, with growth in new sources, luminaires, control gear and control systems permitting many new design possibilities. How do we see the future of lighting, in the medium term of, say, the next two decades, and even further into the 21st century? What might be the processes and technologies that will inspire and engage the lighting designer of tomorrow? While some of these predictions are admittedly little more than speculation, most are extrapolations from existing technologies and techniques, either already available on a small scale or known to be in the pipeline.

We have already seen in chapter 2 that all currently available light sources are far from perfect – selecting lamps is a continual trade-off between efficiency, lamp-life, colour temperature, colour rendering, colour stability, and cost. There are considerable improvements to be made in the area of lamp efficiency; for example, the theoretical maximum efficiency of lamps is around 600 lm/W *(ch 1)* compared with current maxima of 200 lm/W (and that only in the case of low-pressure sodium) *(ch 2)*. To achieve that output, such lamps, if they were developed, would have to convert all the electrical energy into visible light, with no wastage, either as ultraviolet or infra-red. In other words they would run entirely cool, thus eliminating one of the other major problems with current lamp technology, heat. While such a lamp is a futuristic fantasy, even on the timescale of 15 or 20 years, current environmental concerns about the depletion of finite energy resources and the possibility of the greenhouse effect will focus research and development on lamp efficiency. Most of this research and development work will concern discharge lamps *(ch 2)*, which will certainly become cheaper, more user-friendly, available in lower wattages and be far more amenable to dimming *(ch 5)* and optical control.

Metal halide lamps *(ch 2)* are available in versions as small as 35W (offering around the same lumens output as a 100W tungsten lamp). In terms of efficiency, the technical development of standard filament lamps has probably gone almost as far as it can. However, there remains the possibility of special infra-red coating for the inside of the bulb, a spin-off from space research and development. This would reflect infra-red (heat) back towards the filament, thus maintaining its optimum temperature, while using less energy – 60 per cent say some estimates.

There may be further developments in the applications of tungsten halogen lamps *(ch 2)*. Low-voltage *(ch 2)* versions are beginning to enter the domestic sector, but the necessity for transformers and high currents remains a major bugbear. The 1990s could see the introduction of mains-operated tungsten halogen lamps of a similar size and performance to their low-voltage cousins; already we have 240V 100W PAR 30 *(ch 2)* tungsten halogen sources, which were unheard of in the 1980s.

Elsewhere in the domestic sector, rises in energy costs and growing environmental awareness could see the widespread replacement of GLS lamps *(ch 2)* with energy-saving compact fluorescents *(ch 2)*, which will become smaller, cheaper and more efficient than versions available now. Within 20 years the intrinsically poor efficiency of GLS tungsten lamps (little changed in over 80 years) will probably see them go the way of the vinyl disc. For personal health and comfort, and as a way of minimizing the SAD syndrome , full spectrum fluorescent lamps may be increasingly demanded. But it shouldn't be forgotten that, with current technology at least, there is an intrinsic contradiction between expanding the spectral composition *(ch 1)* of any lamp, and its efficiency. Improved colour rendering *(ch 1)* always results in reduced light output.

The perfect lamp of the future will have an infinitely long lamp-life *(ch 1)*, thus obviating re-lamping and maintenance considerations. The appearance of entirely new sources, such as Philips QL Inductive lamp, with its claimed 60,000 hour lamp-life, sets the bench-mark here, though its current size, offering only limited optical control and average efficiency (around 60 lm/W) will have to be improved if it is to make inroads into the mass market for more conventional sources. A similar, cheaper version of the same technology,

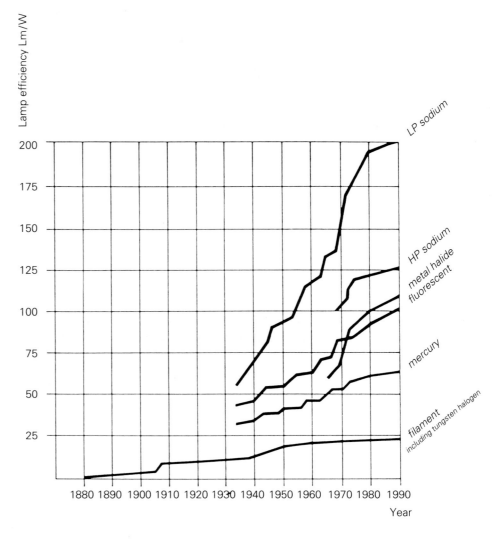

Figure 1 Schematic diagram showing the growth in lamp types and their efficiencies over the last century

Philips QL Inductive lamp, which uses a magnetic coil in place of a traditional filament

called the E-Lamp, was launched by Intersource, a US company, in 1992. Like the QL lamp, it uses a small electro-magnetic coil in place of a filament or electrodes; this generates ultra-high frequency radio signals which vapourize mercury inside the lamp. As in fluorescent lamps, ultraviolet light then causes a phosphorescent coating on the tube to glow. Whether the intrinsic problems of such a system – miniaturization of components, control of temperature and radio interference – have been solved is something that has not been independently verified. Intersource claims it will be selling the lamp to domestic consumers at between £6 and £12 in 1993.

The ideal lamp will have to be flexible. At the same time as being a very small point source (offering optimum optical control) it will be adaptable from a pin spot to general floodlight source, with infinitely variable light output. Lamps will be simple to handle and fit, with one universal cap for all types and no control gear.

The role of electronics

Such a vision is for the long term. In the short term, control gear is one component ripe for increasing sophistication. The replacement of electromagnetic coils (a technology with its origins in the late 19th century) with unmistakably late 20th-century electronic, digitalized systems, could have repercussions over the next two decades. Universal, programmable ballasts will be able to operate with all types of discharge lamp; and they will be small enough to be integrated neatly into the lamp holder, in much the same way as with some existing PL compact fluorescent fittings.

The flexibility of lamps could be extended by these 'intelligent' lamp holders, which will do away with the need for separate control gear. Electronic ballasts can ensure controlled voltages, so discharge lamps will be potentially more stable, longer lasting with a more constant colour. Colour temperatures *(ch 1)* of the same lamp may even be variable, from cool to warm, depending on the needs of the particular scheme.

The dimmability of discharge lamps will be increased, too. Integral dimmers may enable the same source to be used as a 10W mini-lamp or as a powerful 1000W lamp for floodlighting, simply through precise, programmable control. From a situation of proliferation of lamp types in the 1980s and 1990s such intrinsic flexibility could see a simplification of lamp ranges in the 21st century.

The future of fittings

In addition to integral control gear, there could be other innovations in luminaire design. Robotized fittings could become the norm; at the moment they are restricted to costly specialist products, such as the Vari-Lights or Goldenscans, often used in entertainment venues, or the limited versions of the same technology offered by Philips and Hoffmeister. Brightness adjustment, focusing, panning and tilting could all be achieved by remote control, either through a hand-held unit, like the ones currently used for TVs and videos, or via a dedicated data highway, or directly through its mains voltage supply cable. Such luminaires, equipped with long-life lamps, would be a boon in hard-to-access locations where manual adjustment presents problems.

The intelligent luminiare will become commonplace, capable of being equipped with photocell/proximity detectors *(ch 5)* and their own timers, which will sense when they need to be switched on. Thorn Lighting already sell a fluorescent luminaire which incorporates a photocell and presence detector.

Due to refinements in glass technology, fibre optics systems *(ch 3)* will

undoubtedly improve in efficiency and operational range. Currently there are limits to the length of fibre runs, but they could in future operate efficiently over far greater distances. This would enable light to be piped around a building. Sunlight, for example, could be collected by reflectors and lenses on the roof and directed inside the building to where it is needed. Light-boxes for such systems will improve in efficiency too, and become much smaller and cooler running, so eliminating two of their biggest current disadvantages.

Other forms of sophisticated daylight control *(ch 3)* will see enormous refinements in coming years, as the maximization of natural lighting becomes a major building design priority. Sun-collecting heliostats *(ch 3)*, which are currently expensive and at an early stage in development, could become commonplace. Light-activated glazing, which darkens and lightens according to outside light levels will be another automated way of making optimum use of natural light, while avoiding its potential disadvantages – heat gain, glare, and so on. Again, light and/or heat could even be collected and directed to particular parts of the building. This technology has been explored in a rudimentary way in the ING Bank building in Amsterdam *(ch 8)*.

Changing the form of luminaires

Why should light fittings be confined to their present limiting forms? One possibility is to make whole room surfaces into light and/or heat radiators – luminescent walls or ceilings, structured and powered rather like a computer screen. The brightness could be controlled, perhaps by the use of a laser light pen, so that particular zones glow at various brightnesses to order.

Such a system will require, from the outset, close integration of lighting planning into new buildings. Eventually, though, buildings may be built with just a single

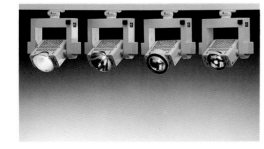

Hoffmeister's RC robot spotlights can be adjusted via remote electronic control

power circuit, with a large number of simple, all-purpose electrical outlets, into which any appliance, including luminaires, can be plugged. The particular lamp, or other appliance, will then be addressed individually – for example, switched on/off or dimmed.

Set-ups like these will make lighting infinitely flexible and moveable, with far less need for dedicated, complex wiring circuits. Universal, interchangeable connection systems – a situation that some European companies are already moving towards with their Euro-track – would be a *sina qua non* of such developments.

The increased flexibility and portability of lighting will be achieved by lighter, less bulky fixtures, requiring fewer raw materials, so their physical structure may undergo changes too. There will be a far greater use of new thermo-plastics, possibly with power-carrying circuits printed or moulded into the body itself, where necessary. As with many other products, luminaires will become 100-per-cent recyclable. A system of leasing, rather than buying luminaires from manufacturers *(ch 8)*, may help to ensure that this process is controlled.

Innovations in control systems

Control will be the watchword of lighting design in the future, both to minimize energy consumption and to create pleasant and personalized working and leisure environments. At work, ambient and task lighting combinations *(ch 3)*, tailored to the individual's precise needs, will be demanded. The transformation of the conventional office organization, in which workers no longer have a dedicated desk, but 'plug in' to a common pool of workstations (the free address or office-as-car-park scenario, as it is known) will demand new lighting solutions. The smart card will probably be the key here: when logging in, this could power up the

computer with a worker's particular files, allocate a phone extension, and set precise lighting levels. As well as all the other information such cards might carry, they could incorporate personal physiological data, such as body size (to adjust the seating) and visual acuity (to tailor the lighting levels).

Desktop task lighting will become increasingly portable, cool running and have instant, hands-off adjustability; voice-activated controls could be a common feature of future work-places within the next 25 years.

The message is that lighting control developments will have to move in two directions simultaneously: towards greater individual, personal control and adjustment of lighting; and also towards greater integration of lighting into overall computerized building management systems. These are not necessarily in conflict. Computerization could maximize the degree to which lighting fits individual requirements.

In the commercial sector, computerized lighting control will no longer stand alone, but will be part of a building's comprehensive alarm, air-conditioning and security programme. A similar level of integration – the so-called 'smart house' scenario – may take longer to establish itself on the domestic scene. Eventually it will become the norm to make a simple phone call, from inside or outside the home, to switch on the heating, activate the lighting, record a TV broadcast, or override an existing command.

Lighting systems in retail outlets, which are subject to constant change, will be more computer-driven. For example, particular lighting scenes could be programmed for different departments. If departments are moved, instead of having to manually reset all the lighting, computers could amend the designation of lamps, so scenes are re-set in other parts of the

In future lighting systems in retail projects will be increasingly computer-controlled to offer both design flexibility and energy savings

Pressure towards the improvement of night-time environments will mean the greater use of better exterior lighting

building. Such modifications will become simple to execute. As we suggest in chapter 5, computerized control systems are already becoming more user-friendly.

Exterior lighting

Another area that could change dramatically is the night-time lighting of streets, buildings and exterior spaces *(ch 7)*. Pressures towards the improvement of the urban environment, and mounting evidence of the contribution that better night-time lighting can make to crime prevention, will mean that it is used more extensively. At home, too, cheaper, more energy-efficient and controllable systems will see the increased lighting of patios and gardens.

However, all this won't necessarily be done well. Changes in the quality of exterior lighting will be harder to achieve. With the advent of improved sources, we should see the phasing out of low-pressure sodium lamps *(ch 2)* on all roads regularly used by pedestrians. Whether we'll see the sort of dual lighting set-ups outlined in the influential Edinburgh Lighting Vision report *(ch 7)*, with high-level louvred lamps for the roadway itself, and lower-level, more human-friendly lighting over the pavements, remains to be seen.

Because of the fundamental role exterior lighting plays in the environment, its interrelationship with architecture, and the growing problem of light pollution, exterior lighting has to be brought under formal planning control. The challenge for lighting designers in this changed situation will be how to work within a framework (recommended maximum luminance levels and reduced spill light, for example) without producing standardized results.

Improving professionalism, increasing responsibility

Planning control is one of many changes that will be forced on lighting designers in the near future. At one level the lighting

designer's role – his/her part as a valued member of the architecture and design professions – will be revalued and given an enhanced status. Part of that process will be the establishment of officially recognized qualification standards for the profession.

We should see a greater degree of lighting design input to construction schemes at an early stage. For that reason, amongst others, lighting consultants will require a greater awareness of regulations, as they impinge on the lighting design area. They will require skill to achieve interesting results within the reduced energy limits that will probably be forced on all of us in the next 20 years.

Lighting designers will need a knowledge, too, of the accelerating development of light sources and their applications. In many ways their job will become more technological; knowledge of computers and their software will become essential, though not, it is hoped, at the cost of the creative, artistic aspects of lighting design.

Finally, as a function of the increasing complexity of both their technologies, and the demands made on lighting design by the world around them, lighting design professionals will have to become more concerned about the end-user (rather than making their own private statements) and more far-sighted about the effects and implications of their work on the rest of society. It is a big challenge, but one that specialists working in this vital area of design will have to meet, if they are to survive and prosper.

Glossary

A

accent lighting Often used as a synonym for spotlighting; a technique of creating areas of more intense illumination on objects or surfaces.

adaptation The physiological adjustment of the human eye (and optical system), enabling it to respond to widely differing amounts of light or colour. 'Dark adaptation' is particularly important in enabling the eye to function at night *(ch 1)*.

additive mixing (light) The technique of overlapping (mixing) different colours of light to produce a new colour (eg blue and yellow to make green). Fluorescent lamps use the same principle; different phosphors on the inside of the glass tube create distinct colours which blend together to create the final colour appearance.

air-handling luminaire A dual-function luminaire for use in air-conditioned buildings; usually in the form of a ceiling-recessed fixture linked with the air-conditioning system so that air is extracted through the luminaire. Can also include air supply slots *(ch 3)*.

ambient (background) lighting Overall illumination, often to low levels, with localized 'boosting' via task or accent lighting.

amp Abbreviation of 'ampere', a unit of electrical current. Used to denote the capacity of an electrical wire or cable. Using the analogy of water supply, the equivalent of the width of bore of the pipe. A high capacity permits a large flow of energy.

anode The positive electrode in a discharge lamp (see *electrodes*).

apparent brightness Subjective impression of how bright an area appears. The technical term is luminosity.

arc Luminous discharge of electrical energy across the gap in an electrical circuit or between an anode and cathode (the electrodes) in a discharge lamp.

asymmetric reflector A reflector specially designed to distribute light differentially in a specific direction or directions (eg a ceiling-mounted downlight used for wallwashing).

B

backlighting A technique of lighting an object so that it is between the viewer and the source, with the result that the object is seen in relief or silhouette.

background lighting See *ambient lighting*.

baffle Device attached to a luminaire to limit spill light. In spotlights and downlights, multi-groove baffles are the concentric black grooves on the inside of the cowl.

ballast (choke) A component of the control gear of a discharge lamp which limits the current flow. Traditional wire-wound electro-magnetic ballasts are now being replaced by solid-state electronic versions.

barn doors A device derived from the theatre, where hinged 'doors', attached to the front of a luminaire, can be adjusted to vary the beam spread and prevent glare.

batten A simple luminaire for fluorescent lamps.

'batwing' light distribution A pattern of light distribution (eg from a ceiling-mounted fluorescent, louvred luminaire) designed to give a wide, even illuminance on the working plane.

bayonet fitting (BC) Standard type of lamp base with two lugs, used for tungsten sources (see Appendix 2).

beam The spread of direct illumination from a directional source such as a spotlight.

beam angle The measurement of the width of a beam. The angle describes the limits of the beam where the light intensity *(ch 1)* is 50 per cent of maximum.

BESA box Standard electrical connection box approved by the British Electrical Standards Association used for terminating a circuit at a luminaire. Usually used in conjunction with a conduit. Can be recessed or surface-mounted.

bezel Visible outer ring or rim of a luminaire, which covers the junction with the wall or ceiling surface.

birdie A small, low-cost, low-voltage spotlight, derived from theatre styling, typically with a square colour filter frame mounted to the front of the unit.

blended lamp A dual source lamp, incorporating a high-pressure mercury discharge source and an incandescent filament in one bulb *(ch 2)*.

brightness See *luminance*.

British Standards (BS) Advisory and regulatory standards of construction, safety and manufacturing quality applied to all electrical products. To be superceded by European Norms (EN).

bulb Common, but erroneous, synonym for a tungsten filament lamp. 'Bulb' refers only to the glass envelope of the lamp.

burning position See *operating position*.

BZ (British Zonal) A little used method of classifying symmetrical light distribution patterns of different luminaires (typically, BZ1 is a very narrow beam, BZ5 a broad beam, BZ10 is a diffuse, omni-directional source).

C

can Term for the normally cylindrical housing of a reflector lamp.

candela The standard unit of luminous intensity, abbreviated as 'cd' *(ch 1)*.

capsule lamp Generic term for small low-voltage lamps.

cathode One of the two electrodes of a discharge lamp (see *electrode*).

chroma Subjective estimate of the amount of chromatic colour present; a low chroma implies a pastel colour. Also an index of saturation of colour (see *Munsell system*).

chromaticity diagram Graphic representation, using two-dimensional coordinates, used to define colour.

CIBSE Chartered Institution of Building Services Engineers.

CIBSE Codes A series of recommendations for lighting design (including illuminance levels) in different types of establishment, providing useful industry guidelines to good lighting practice.

CIE (Commission Internationale d'Eclairage) An international body which plays a role similar to CIBSE.

coiled coil Term used to describe the double coil construction of the filament of an incandescent lamp.

cold cathode lamp Also known erroneously as 'neon'. Custom-made low-pressure discharge lamps, often in elongated lines or other shapes. Contains neon or argon gases, which emit a coloured, glowing light via an electrical discharge *(ch 2)*.

colour appearance The apparent colour of light emitted by a particular light source *(ch1)*. See also *colour temperature*.

colour rendering The effect of a particular light source on the visual appearance of a coloured surface *(ch 1)*. See also *colour rendering index*.

colour rendering index (CRI) Indexing measure of how colours under a particular light source compare with the same colours viewed under a standardized illuminant *(ch 1)*. The index ranges from 0 (poorest colour rendition) to 100 (best).

colour temperature An objective measure of the temperature of a 'full radiator' (black body) with the same colour appearance as a particular light source, measured in degrees Kelvin *(ch 1)*. Technically known as 'correlated colour temperature'.

compact fluorescent Small fluorescent lamps, often with their own integral control gear, some of which can be directly substituted for less efficient incandescent sources.

contrast Subjective experience of comparative brightness between two luminances (brightnesses), seen simultaneously or successively. Too high a degree of contrast can lead to *glare*.

control gear The ancillary components of a discharge lamp, comprising ballast (choke), starter, ignitor, capacitor etc, which regulate the electrical energy flowing into the lamp.

control systems (lighting) Manual or automated equipment for controlling the switching and dimming of a series of luminaires *(ch 5)*.

'cool beam' lamp A type of reflector lamp incorporating a dichroic reflector, which reflects only a reduced proportion of infra-red radiation (heat) within the lamp beam. See also *dichroic reflector*.

cowl or cowling A shield device, often comprising an extension of the lamp housing, designed to control the spread of light.

critical angle Angle of incidence at which a ray of light will be totally reflected from a surface.

current See *amp*.

cut-off angle Terms used to define the angle above which no light is emitted from a luminaire.

D

darklight reflector Specular reflector which creates a controlled spread of light, used in 'low-brightness' luminaires (ie it creates a dark appearance outside the beam).

data highway Dedicated cable used to transmit electronic-coded control signals, usually at low voltage.

dichroic filter Colour filters utilizing the selective reflective properties of multi-layered coatings to produce a single saturated colour.

dichroic reflector (cool beam) Separate or integral reflector for lamps, with a multi-layered, selective reflector coating. This dissipates a large proportion of the infra-red radiation (heat) through the back of lamp, while producing an intense white beam.

diffuse or diffused lighting Light which emanates evenly in all directions, with no evident vector (direction).

diffuser Translucent or frosted screen covering a light source, so that light is distributed evenly.

diffuse reflection Light reflection scattered evenly in all directions (eg light reflected from a white matt surface).

dimmer Regulating device attached to a luminaire or lighting circuit to vary the intensity of a light source.

direct lighting Lighting where most of the light reaches the working plane directly from a luminaire, rather than being reflected off walls or ceiling.

directional lighting Lighting designed to illuminate an object or room primarily from one direction (eg spotlights).

disability glare Glare caused by excessive contrast that impairs the ability to see detail *(ch 1)*.

discharge lamp A lamp in which light is produced directly or indirectly by an electric discharge through a gas or vapour *(ch 2)*.

discomfort glare Glare that causes visual discomfort, but does not necessarily impair the ability to see detail *(ch 1)*.

downlighter Luminaire that casts most of its light downwards, either vertically or at a relatively narrow angle to the downward vertical *(ch 3)*.

downlighting The technique of lighting a space primarily from high-level sources (downlighters) directed down onto the floor or work surface.

E

Edison screw (ES) Type of threaded lamp base manu-factured in a number of sizes. See Appendix 2.

efficiency/efficacy See *luminous efficiency*.

electrode The two poles of a discharge lamp (anode and cathode) across which the electric current arcs to excite the lamp's gases.

emergency lighting Ancillary system of lighting, often battery-powered, designed to maintain a lower, functioning level of light to permit evacuation of a building, in the event of a mains' power failure *(ch 3)*.

emitter A coating added to, for example, the cathodes of fluorescent tubes, to aid the emittance of electrons.

European Norm (EN) European-wide advisory and regulatory standards of construction, safety or manufacturing quality applied to electrical equipment, superceding British Standards (BS).

F

fibre optics System of transmitting light beams from a remote light source down thin glass rods or tubes *(ch 3)*.

filament Thin, coiled wire (usually tungsten) component of an incandescent lamp which heats up and emits light when electricity is passed through it.

filter A piece of translucent gel or glass which, when placed in front of a white light source, cuts out selected spectral emissions. For example, ordinary plain glass acts as a filter to some ultraviolet radiation, while a coloured gel cuts out all light waves except those of the desired colour.

fitting Usually used synonymously with *luminaire*.

flicker The rapid variation in light intensity of a lamp (100 cycles a second) caused by the standard 50Hz alternating current. This can be a nuisance, even a health hazard; high-frequency ballasts, which operate at 25–40kHz to obviate this problem *(ch 2)*.

floodlight (floodlamp) Any luminaire which emits a broad beam of light.

floodlighting Often used loosely and erroneously to refer to all types of exterior lighting. More precisely, the technique of using broad-beam luminaires to illuminate large vertical or horizontal surfaces *(ch 7)*.

fluorescent lamp Low-pressure discharge lamp, in which most of the light is produced when ultraviolet radiation emitted by the discharge excites a coating of phosphors on the inside of the glass tube *(ch 2)*.

focus (or focal point) The point at which light rays meet, after reflection or refraction.

foot candle A US unit of illuminance, equal to one lumen per square foot or 10.76 lux *(ch 1)*.

framing projector (profile spot) A spotlight (often theatrical) with attachments that allow accurate control over the shape and focus of a beam.

frequency The number of cycles of an electromagnetic wave which pass a certain point in one second, measured in *hertz*. The shorter the wavelength of light, the higher the frequency.

G

general lighting Lighting designed to illuminate the whole of an area without provision for special local requirements.

glare Discomfort or impairment of vision, caused by too high a contrast between two luminances (brightnesses) within the visual field. See also *discomfort glare*, *disability glare*.

glare index Numerical index, indicating the degree of discomfort glare.

gloss factor Degree of specular reflectivity of a (painted) surface (eg 20 per cent gloss).

GLS General lighting service lamp. The commonest type of tungsten filament lamp, used mainly in domestic interiors.

gobo A patterned screen device, either stationary or rotating, located in the light beam of a projector or spotlight, to throw patterns or other images onto a surface.

H

halogen lamp See *tungsten halogen lamp*.

hertz Cycles per second, abbreviated as Hz (see *frequency*).

HID High intensity discharge source; a term covering several types of high-pressure discharge lamps *(ch 2)*.

high-frequency ballasts/control gear Electronic components which boost the switching cycle of discharge lamps from 50Hz to 25000Hz or more and thus eliminate lamp flicker *(ch 2)*.

housing Professional term for the part of the luminaire which holds and encloses the lamp source.

hue The subjective impression of colour or tint, eg blue or green (see *Munsell system*).

I

ignitor Component used in a discharge lamp (or its control gear) to provide a high-voltage impulse, to begin its operation.

illuminance The amount of light (luminous flux) falling on a surface, expressed in lumens per square metre or lux *(ch 1)*.

illumination General term for the process of lighting an object or space.

incandescent lamp A lamp source which produces light when electricity is passed through a thin filament (usually tungsten) so that it incandesces (glows) brightly.

incident light Light which falls on an object or surface.

indirect lighting Lighting technique whereby most of the light reaches the working plane by reflection from other surfaces, particularly walls and ceiling, rather than directly from the source.

ingress protection (IP) rating A classification of luminaires, according to how well they withstand dust and/or water ingress. Ratings range from IP 00 (no protection) to IP 68 (totally protected from dust and long-term submersion in water). See Appendix 3.

initial lumens Luminous flux of a lamp after 100 hours of operation (see *lighting design lumens*).

integral reflector A lamp which incorporates its own reflector (eg low-voltage metal reflector lamps and PAR lamps).

L

lamp Any artificial light source. Often colloquially and erroneously used to refer to the whole lamp and luminaire combination.

lamp base or cap The mechanical component of the lamp which attaches it to the *lamp holder*. See Appendix 2.

lamp holder The receptacle within a luminaire into which the lamp base or cap is fixed.

lamp-life (rated lamp-life) Manufacturers' stated operational life, at which (usually) 50 per cent of lamps are expected to fail under test conditions. Different manufacturers use different test conditions and degree of lamp mortality *(ch 1)*.

lens Concave or convex piece of glass at the front end of a luminaire, which focuses or spreads the light beam.

light Visible electromagnetic radiation with wavelength between 380 and 730 nanometers.

light box The major component of a fibre-optics lighting system, containing transformer, control gear, light source, lens, filters etc, which is located remotely and to which the light-transmitting fibre-optic strands are connected.

light loss factor (LLF) Standard allowance made in lighting calculations for light depreciation due to lamp ageing and luminaire and surface soiling.

light source The point of origin of any kind of light, artificial or natural.

lighting design lumens Conventional value for the average flux output from a lamp, throughout its life. Often taken as the flux at 2000 hours of use.

louvre A screening device of vertical or horizontal slats or blades, usually made from plastic or aluminium, which cuts off the light beam at certain angles and prevents spill light.

low-brightness louvres A particularly efficient louvre system, usually used on fluorescent downlighters in VDT-intense environments, which controls the light spread of a luminaire and has a limited 'low-brightness' appearance.

low-voltage lighting Light systems where the voltage has been stepped down from 240V to a 'safer' 12V or 24V, using a transformer. This makes it possible to produce an intense light beam from a much smaller lamp. The Institution of Electrical Engineers (IEE) classifies voltages between 50V and 1000V AC as 'low voltage' and anything below 50V AC as 'extra low voltage'.

lumen The standard unit of luminous flux. Abbreviated as lm *(ch 1)*.

lumen depreciation The fall-off in light output of a source over time. Most pronounced in discharge sources.

luminaire Often erroneously known as 'fitting'; the entire apparatus for housing a lamp, incorporating the lamp holder, lens, reflector and so on. The luminaire protects the light source, provides a connection to the power supply, and often directs the flow of light.

luminance (photometric brightness) The physical measurement of the stimulus which produces the sensation of brightness. Measured in candelas (cd) per square metre *(ch 1)*.

luminance factor Ratio of luminance of a reflecting surface, viewed in a given direction, to that of a perfectly uniform (white) diffusing surface identically illuminated.

luminosity The subjective assessment of luminance, colloquially expressed as 'brightness'. For example, the moon has a certain luminance; by night its luminosity is high, by day it is low.

luminous flux The amount of light emitted from a light source, measured in lumens *(ch 1)*.

luminous efficiency/efficacy The ratio of light output of a lamp to the electrical energy it consumes (including energy consumed by the control circuit), measured in lumens per watt (lm/W) *(ch 1)*.

luminous intensity A measure of the brightness of a light source, measured in candelas (cd).

lux Lumens per square metre, the standard unit of illuminance.

M

maintenance factor Ratio of the average illumination for an installation in service to the average illumination when it is a new installation.

matt surface A non-lustrous surface that reflects incident light totally evenly in all directions.

mercury lamps A type of discharge lamp where light is produced by exciting vapourized mercury *(ch 2)*.

metal halide lamp High-pressure mercury vapour lamp in which various halides have been added to the discharge gas to broaden their spectral composition and increase their efficacy *(ch 2)*.

metal reflector lamp Usually a small, low-voltage tungsten halogen lamp, often used in exhibitions and display projects, which incorporates its own metal reflector *(ch 2)*.

metal vapour lamp Generic term for a range of discharge lamps which use metallic additives which vapourize in the discharge process. Sodium and mercury lamps are probably the best-known examples *(ch 2)*.

modelling The technique of lighting an object from several directions, to emphasize its form and perspective *(ch 1)*.

monochromatic Light of a single wavelength. Low-pressure sodium lamps *(ch 2)* are virtually monochromatic.

multi-circuit A type of lighting track which contains more than one power circuit so that individual luminaires or sets of luminaire can be controlled separately.

Munsell system System of surface colour classification using uniform colour scales of hue, value and chroma.

N

nanometre (nm) One thousand millionth of metre; a unit used to measure wavelengths of light *(ch 1)*.

neodymium filter Rare earth element fused into the glass of incandescent lamps, which has the effect of removing some of their yellow colour. Used in food displays and galleries, for example.

neon lamp See *cold cathode*.

O

offset distance The distance between, for example, a floodlamp or wallwasher and a wall surface.

opaque Dense, non-translucent or non-transparent material.

operating position Permissible orientation of a lamp, for optimum operating effectiveness (eg horizontal, base up, universal). See Appendix 1 for abbreviations.

optics Generic term referring to the lenses and focusing systems of luminaires.

P

PAR lamp Parabolic aluminized reflector lamp. A lamp with a sealed beam and an aluminized parabolic rear surface, which acts as an effective integral reflector. Their robust, thickened glass construction means they are resistant to thermal shock and can be used outdoors *(ch 2)*. The number – for example PAR 56, PAR 38 – indicates the diameter of the lamp in eighths of an inch (ie a PAR 56 is seven inches in diameter).

peripheral vision Unfocused areas of sight at the margins of the main visual field.

phosphors Metallic elements, coating the internal surfaces of lamps, which produce visible light when excited by ultraviolet rays emitted by the discharge process (eg fluorescent lamps).

photocell Component of a control system, which detects and measures the light within a space and dims or switches off the lighting automatically.

pin spot Generic term for very narrow-beam spotlights.

planar illuminance The amount of light falling on a plane. Also called 'horizontal illuminance'.

plant health lighting Lighting incorporated into a scheme to compensate plants for shortfalls in daylight. Metal halide lamps are most commonly used.

point source Theoretical lamp with an infinitely small area of light emission, facilitating precise optical control.

projector Term derived from the theatre to describe a type of luminaire with good, controllable optics, allowing precise light distribution (see *framing projector*).

Q

quartz-halogen lamp Alternative name for tungsten halogen lamp, derived from the use of a heat-resistant quartz envelope around the filament *(ch 2)*.

R

rack Assembly for modular control components (eg dimmers) mounted on a chassis.

rated life See *lamp-life*.

reflectance A measure of how effectively a surface will reflect light, ie the ratio of lumens falling on it to lumens reflected off it *(ch 2)*.

reflectance index Classification of the comparative reflectance of

different materials or surfaces, expressed as a decimal fraction of one, or as a percentage *(ch 1)*.

reflection Incident light which bounces back off a surface.

reflector A surface, often of mirrored glass or polished metal, shaped to project the beam from a light source in a particular direction. The reflector may be an integral part of the lamp or part of the luminaire.

reflector lamp Any lamp with its own integral reflector (see *dichroic lamps* and *metal reflector lamps*).

refraction The perceived bending of light rays as they pass obliquely from one medium to another (eg from air to glass or vice versa).

re-strike time The time required for a discharge lamp to reach 80 per cent of full light output, after being switched off.

retro-fitting The replacement of failed or inefficient lamps or luminaires after the initial installation either piecemeal or *en masse*. Careful attention is needed to re-lamp appropriately.

run-up time The time required for a discharge lamp to reach 80 per cent of full light output from cold, after first being switched on.

S

SAD (seasonal affective disorder) The name given to a psychological and/or physiological malaise experienced by some people in northern latitudes, during the short, sunless days of winter.

safety glass An additional protective cover of strengthened glass in luminaires using HID and tungsten halogen sources, to prevent lamp glass being scattered in the event of its explosion.

saturation Subjective assessment of the amount of colour in light

beams, compared to their brightness. Pastel colours are not saturated; pillar-box red is.

scalar illuminance A theoretical calculation of the average illuminance, from all directions, on the surface of an infinitely small sphere.

scalloping Technique of lighting a wall, which emphasizes the repetitive pattern of brighter pools of light on the darker wall surface.

sconce Originally a wall-mounted, bracket candlestick, now used to describe any decorative, wall-mounted luminaire.

semi-matt A surface that both scatters incident light uniformly and reflects a proportion of it directionally.

semi-specular reflector A specular reflector with some light-diffusing properties (eg the surface of satinized alluminium louvre in a low-brightness luminaire).

shade A device used in some types of luminaire to hide the light source and diffuse or colour the light emitted.

shadow Area within the visual field with a lower illuminance than its surroundings, due to light being blocked by an intervening object.

'sick building syndrome' A group of interconnected symptoms (eg migraines, allergies, eye strain, psychological depression) affecting some workers, which often occurs in sealed, air-conditioned, artificially lit office buildings.

sidelighting Technique of lighting from one side of an object, across the line of sight, to emphasize the form or texture of an object. See *modelling*.

sodium lamp Metal vapour discharge lamp, using vapourized sodium, creating an orange-tinted light. Available in low-pressure and high-pressure versions *(ch 2)*.

SON lamp A particular type of high-pressure sodium lamp *(ch 2)*.

spacing to height ratio (SHR) Ratio of the spacing between the centres of adjacent luminaires to the height above the working plane.

spectral composition The unique combination of spectral colours of a light source which determines its colour appearance and colour rendering properties *(ch 1)*.

spectrum The full range of constituent colours of visible light, created when white light is passed through a prism.

specular reflection The reflection of light from a mirror-like surface.

specular reflector A reflector that does not diffuse light falling on it (ie non-matt).

spill light Stray light from a tightly controlled, narrow-beam source, which incidentally illuminates nearby objects or surfaces.

spotlight Tightly focused, narrow-beam directional luminaire *(ch 3)*.

spread lenses Lenses which create a wider, diffuse beam of light.

standard service illuminance Recommended CIBSE illuminance levels across the life of a lighting installation, averaged over the relevant area.

starter Device within the control gear of many fluorescent lamps, which initiates the discharge process.

stroboscopic effect Optical illusion whereby the rapid 50Hz flicker of a discharge lamp can make a moving object seem to slow down or remain stationary. Caused by the close correspondence of the frequency of flicker and the movement of the object. It can be dangerous in industrial locations, and certain

frequencies may trigger fits in epileptic subjects. The installation of high-frequency ballasts will mitigate the problem.

subtractive mixing (light) The use of filters to remove some wavelengths of a light beam and so change its colour (eg a blue filter which removes all other colours from white light, so that it appears blue). See *additive mixing*.

T

T-lamp Singled-ended tubular tungsten lamp.

task (or local) lighting A dedicated, personalized luminaire for close, controllable illumination of a work surface *(ch 3)*.

terminal block An electrical component within a luminaire, where the power cables are connected; can be integrally fused.

thermal shock Sudden exposure to high or low temperatures, which can have a damaging effect on incandescent lamps in particular.

torchère A decorative luminaire which takes the loose form of a medieval torch-bracket.

track Combined mechanical support and power distribution system, usually in the form of aluminium extrusions attached to or supported from walls and ceilings. A variety of luminaires can usually be simply attached to them *(ch 3)*.

transformer Device for reducing the working voltage of a lighting system from mains voltage (240/220V in Europe, 120V in the USA) to 12V or 24V. See *low-voltage lighting*.

translucent Light-transmitting material with a diffusing effect.

transmittance Ratio of trans-mitted light to incident light.

transparent Clear light-transmitting material.

Tri-phosphor fluorescent lamps An advanced generation of fluorescent lamps, with a mix of three types of rare earth phosphors coating the inside of the glass tube, which gives a broad spectral composition *(ch 2)*.

trough General term for a rectangular luminaire housing.

trunking System of long, box-like enclosures used mainly to contain wiring and/or suspend light fittings.

tubular fluorescent lamps The conventional form of fluorescent lamp, now available in a wide range of lengths and diameters.

tungsten halogen lamp Refinement of the tungsten lamp, in which a trace of halogen is added to the envelope gas. This helps re-cycle the vapourized tungsten, extending the lamp's life and enabling it to glow hotter, so it emits a 'whiter' light *(ch 2)*.

tungsten lamp Oldest available form of incandescent lamp, in which electricity is used to heat up a coiled (tungsten) filament to emit light *(ch 2)*.

U

ultraviolet radiation (uv) Electro-magnetic radiation beyond the violet end of the visible spectrum, which can damage painted and dyed colours. The plain glass envelope of most lamps filters out some of the ultraviolet radiation. It is important in fluorescent lamps, where most light is created when ultraviolet radiation from the discharge process excites light-emitting phosphors on the inside of the glass *(ch 1)*.

uplighting A technique of indirect lighting where light is directed upwards so that most of it reaches the working plane indirectly after being reflected off the ceiling and walls. Produces a soft, diffuse light effect with little glare.

utilization factor Ratio of the amount of light (luminous flux) falling on the working plane to the amount of light emitted from the lamps (total flux).

V

vector illuminance Term defining the magnitude and direction of the flow of light.

veiling reflections Glaring, high-luminance reflections from a glossy surface, such as a visual display terminal, which totally or partially obscure task details.

visual field The full extent of what can be seen in a given direction, when our head and eyes are at rest.

visual task acuity Measure of the eye's ability to distinguish the details of a particular task.

volts/voltage Measure of the potential difference that drives the electric current through a circuit. Using the water-pipe analogy, it is equivalent to the pressure in a pipe. Abbreviated as 'V'. See *low voltage*.

W

wallwashing A variant of downlighting (or occasionally uplighting) where the vertical wall surface is gently and evenly illuminated from top to bottom.

watts/wattage The standard unit of electrical energy. Abbreviated as 'W'.

wavelength The distance between two corresponding points on successive electromagnetic waves.

wire system A development of the low-voltage track system *(ch 3)* which uses two tensioned bare

wires to support the luminaire and carry the current, usually at 12V.

working plane The horizontal, vertical or inclined plane in which a particular visual task is performed. Conventionally assumed to be 0.85m above the floor, unless otherwise indicated.

Appendices

Appendix 1
Guide to lamp prefixes and codes

This is a selection of the main lamp prefixes and codes and what they stand for. Different manufacturers often use different designations for products with broadly similar properties.

Filament lamps

GLS	General lighting service
TH	Tungsten halogen
PAR	Followed by lamp nominal diameter in eighth inch. Pressed glass aluminized reflector filament lamp with an internal reflector coating
PAR-E	PAR lamp with increased efficacy
R	Followed by number, nominal diameter in mm (previously in eighth inch). Blown glass with an internal reflector coating
K	Linear and tubular tungsten halogen
M	General display and miscellaneous filament lamps

Tubular flourescent lamps

MCF	Switch start lamp (also used for tubular fluorescent lamps in general)
MCFE	Starterless lamp. Silicone coat. (Also suitable for switch start operation)
MCFA	Starterless lamp. Earth strip. (Also suitable for switch start operation)
MCFR	As MCF with internal reflector
T5	⅝ inch (16mm) nominal diameter
T8 (TLD)	1in (26mm) nominal diameter
T12 (TL)	1½ inch (38mm) nominal diameter

Low-pressure sodium lamps

SOX	U-shaped arc tube. Single-ended
SOX-E	SOX with increased efficacy

High-pressure sodium lamps

SON	Diffuse ellipsoidal outer bulb. Single-ended
SON-EXTRA	Twin arc tube. Single-ended
SON-T	Clear tubular outer bulb. Single-ended
SON-T COMFORT	SON-T with improved colour rendering
SON-TD, SONL	Clear tubular outer bulb. Double-ended
SON-R	SON with internal reflector
SON-H	SON for use on mercury control gear
SON-DL/SON COMFORT	SON with improved colour rendering
SON-S, SON PLUS, SON-XL	SON with increased efficiency
SDW-T 'WHITE' SON	Tubular outer bulb. Single-ended

High-pressure mercury lamps

MB	High-pressure mercury with outer bulb
MBF (HPL-N)	High-pressure mercury with phosphor coating
MBFR (HPL-R)	MBF with internal reflector
MBFSD (HPL Comfort)	MBF with improved colour rendering and efficacy

High-pressure mercury blended lamps

MBTF (ML)	Combination of MBF lamp and filament lamp
MBTFR (MLR)	MBTF with internal reflector

Metal halide lamps

MBI (HPI)	Diffuse ellipsoidal outer bulb. Single-ended
MBIF	MBI with phosphor coating
MBIL	Linear arc tube. Double-ended
MBI-T (HPI-T)	Clear tubular outer bulb. Single-ended
MHD	Compact. Double-ended
MHN-T	Tubular outer bulb. Single-ended
MHN-TD (HQI)	MBIL low wattage (cool)
MHW-TD (HQI)	MBIL low wattage (warm)
CSI	Compact source with internal reflector

Compact fluorescent lamps

These are the hardest to keep track of; there is a plethora of new types, shapes and wattages. These are the major types. In many cases different wattage lamps have different suffixes after the main type letters.

PL/PLL	Twin tube. No integral gear or starter
PLCE	Two or four tube. Electronic Integral control gear
PLC	Four tube. No integral control gear or starter
SL	Stubby energy-saving replacement for GLS lamp. Integral control gear
SLD	Spherical version of SL. Integral control gear
2D	Distinctive double-loop shape. Two-pin version = without integral gear/starter. Four-pin version = with integral starter

Lamp operating positions

/U	Universal (not usually marked)
/V	Vertical
/H	Horizontal
/BD	Base down
/BDH	Base down to horizontal
/BU	Base up
/BUH	Base up to horizontal
/BUS	Base up, with internal starting device

**Appendix 2
Common lamp caps**

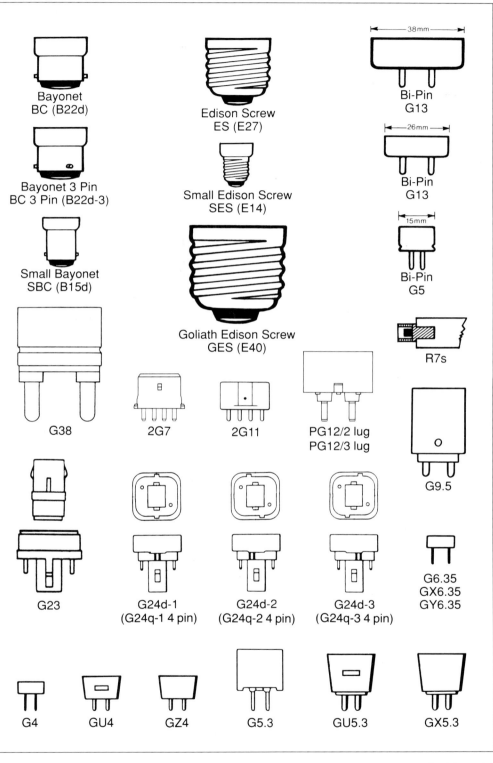

Appendix 3

Ingress Protection (IP) corresponding to some commonly used descriptions of luminaire types and the symbols which may be used to mark a luminaire in addition to the IP number

Commonly used description of luminaire type IP Number* Symbol which may be used in addition to the IP classification number

Description	IP Number	Symbol	
Ordinary	IP20**	no symbol	
Drip-proof	IPX1	●	(one drop)
Rain-proof	IPX3	▣	(one square)
Splash-proof	IPX4	⚠	(one drop in triangle)
Jet-proof	IPX5	⚠⚠	(two triangles with one drop in each)
Watertight (immersible)	IPX7	●●	(two drops)
Pressure-watertight (submersible)	IPX8	●● ▪	(two drops followed by an indication of the maximum depth of submersion in metres)
Proof against 1mm-diameter probe	IP4X	no symbol	
Dust-proof	IP5X	◈	(a mesh without frame)
Dust-tight	IP6X	◈	(a mesh with frame)

*Where X is used in an IP number in this Code, it indicates a missing characteristic numeral. However, on any luminaire, both appropriate characteristic numerals should be marked.

**Marking of IP 20 on ordinary luminaires is not required. In this context an ordinary luminaire is one without special protection against dirt or moisture.

Appendix 4

Recommended standard services illuminance levels for different interiors or activities

Standard service illuminance (x)	Characteristics of the activity interior	Representative activities interiors
50	Interiors visited rarely with visual tasks confined to movement and casual seeing without perception of detail	Cable tunnels, indoor storage tanks, walkways
100	Interiors visited occasionally with visual tasks confined to movement and casual seeing calling for only limited perception of detail	Corridors, changing rooms, bulk stores
150	Interiors visited occasionally with visual tasks requiring some perception of detail or involving some risk to people, plant or product	Loading bays, medical stores, switchrooms
200	Continuously occupied interiors, visual tasks not requiring any perception or detail	Monitoring automatic processes in manufacture, casting concrete, turbine halls
300	Continuously occupied interiors, visual tasks moderately easy, ie large details > 10 min arc and/or high contrast	Packing goods, rough core making in foundries, rough sawing
500	Visual tasks moderately difficult, ie details to be seen are of moderate size (5-10 min arc) and may be of low contrast. Also colour judgement may be required	General offices, engine assembly, painting and spraying
750	Visual tasks difficult, ie details to be seen are small (3-5 min arc) and of low contrast, also good colour judgements may be required	Drawing offices, ceramic decoration, meat inspection
1000	Visual tasks very difficult, ie details to be seen are very small (2-3 min arc) and can be of very low contrast. Also accurate colour judgements may be required	Electronic component assembly, gauge and tool rooms, retouching paintwork
1500	Visual tasks extremely difficult, ie details to be seen extremely small (1-2 min arc) and of low contrast. Visual aids may be of advantage	Inspection of graphic reproduction, hand tailoring fine die sinking
2000	Visual tasks exceptionally difficult, ie details to be seen exceptionally small (<1 min arc) with very low contrasts. Visual aids will be of advantage	Assembly of minute mechanisms, finished fabric inspection

References

Boyce, P R (1979) Users' attitudes to some types of local lighting. *Lighting Research and Technology* 11(3).

Boyce, P R (1981) *Human Factors in Lighting.* Applied Science Publishers.

Eastop, T D and Croft, D R (1990) *Energy Efficiency for Engineers and Technologists.* Longman.

Jeavons, P M and Harding G A (1975) *Photosensitive Epilepsy.* Heinemann.

Painter, K (1988) *Lighting and Crime Prevention: the Edmonton Project.* Middlesex University.

Philips (1991) *Philips Lighting Application Guide: Urban Lighting.*

Poulten, E C, Kendall, P G and Thomas, R J (1966) Reading efficiency in flickering light. *Nature* 209.

Shepherd, A J, Julian, W G and Purcell, A T (1989) Gloom as a pyschophysical phenomenon. *Lighting Research and Technology* 21(3).

Wilkins, A J *et al.* (1989) Fluorescent lighting, headaches and eyestrain. *Lighting Research and Technology* 21(1).

Bibliography

The literature on lighting design (as opposed to lighting engineering) is limited. The following titles represent a selection of the most useful publications. Some publications may be out of print, and some are US publications which may not be easy to find in British bookshops or libraries.

Caylen, M A and Marsden, A M (eds) (1983) *Lamps and Lighting.* Edward Arnold/Thorn. Dated but highly detailed reference textbook.

CIBSE (1984) *CIBSE CODE for Interior Lighting*
An important survey of CIBSE codes and other standards for interiors, what they mean and how to calculate them. There are also several other CIBSE publications on lighting for specialized interiors such as hospitals, museums and sports facilities.

Electricity Association (1986) *Interior Lighting Design.*
Rather technical, and bristling with diagrams, but a well-indexed explanation of lighting terminology.

Kellogg Smith, Fran and Bertolone, Fred (1986) *Bringing Interiors to Light.* Whitney Library of Design.
US-oriented and very technical in part. Includes some interesting and detailed case studies.

Lighting Industry Federation, (1990) *Lamp Guide 1990.*
An extremely useful pamphlet guiding the specifier through the maze of lamp names, forms and capabilities. Regularly updated.

Phillips, Barty (1987) *Christopher Wray's Guide to Decorative Lighting.* Webb & Bower. Catalogue-like survey of decorative lighting from Art Nouveau to contemporary luminaires; aimed principally at the domestic market.

Pritchard, D C (1990)*Lighting.* Longman.
Probably the cheapest and most up-to-date textbook to the technical aspects of lighting design.

Sorcar, Profulla (1987) *Architectural Lighting for Commercial Interiors.* John Wiley.
US-oriented, mono-illustrated, but comprehensive.

Sudjic, Deyan (1985) *The Lighting Book.* Mitchell Beazley.
Although aimed at the residential market, it contains some useful ideas. Well-illustrated with examples.

Watson, Lee (1990) *Lighting Design Handbook.* McGraw-Hill. Heavily concentrated on theatre lighting, but also covers architectural and other areas of lighting design. Good on general creative lighting issues.

Addresses

This compilation of addresses includes:

- *selected trade associations, designers' organizations, standards bodies and other institutions relevant to the lighting industry. Where necessary we explain the organization's role or function*

- *lighting design consultancies whose work is featured in this book*

- *manufacturers and suppliers whose products are illustrated or mentioned in this book, or who have otherwise supplied material. In the case of most overseas manufacturers, we list their agent or distributor in Britain.*

Organizations, associations, educational establishments and other bodies

The Bartlett
University College London
22 Gordon Street
London WC1H 0QB
071-387 7055
Its MSc course offers one of the few formal education courses in lighting design.

British Standards Institute (BSI)
2 Park Street
London W1
071–629 9000
and (0908) 221166

Building Research Establishment
Garston
Watford
Hertfordshire WD2 7JR
(0923) 664664

Building Services Research Information Association (BSRIA)
Old Bracknell Lane West
Bracknell
Berkshire RG12 4AH
(0344) 426511

Chartered Institution of Building Services Engineers (CIBSE)
Delta House
222 Balham High Rd
London SW12 9BS
081–675 5211
Publisher of comprehensive lighting codes and standards for engineers and designers.

Chartered Society of Designers (CSD)
29 Bedford Square
London WC1B 3EG
071–631 1510

Decorative Lighting Association (DLA)
Bryn House, Bryn
Bishop's Castle
Shropshire SY9 5LE
(059) 84658

Electricity Association
30 Millbank
London SW1P 4RD
071–834 2333

Institution of Electrical Engineers (IEE)
Savoy Place
London WC2R OB1
071–240 1871

Lighting Forum
c/o 29 Bedford Square
London WC1B 3EG
071–631 1510
Association of companies (designers, manufacturers and suppliers) interested in the lighting industry. Affiliated to the CSD.

Lighting Industry Federation (LIF)
Swan House
207 Balham High Road
London SW12 7BQ
081–675 5432
Trade association of British–based lighting manufacturers and suppliers. Publishes useful series of booklets, including the Lamp Guide *(see Bibliography).*

Institute of Lighting Engineers (ILE)
Lennox House
9 Lawford Road
Rugby
Warwickshire CV21 2DZ
(0788) 576472

International Association of Lighting Designers (IALD)
18 East 16 Street, Suite 208
New York NY 10003
(212) 206 1281
European contact: IALD
PO Box 70
London WC1X 8XP
Probably the most respected international association for architectural lighting design consultants. Membership is limited to individuals who are independent professionals working within the lighting design field.

Royal Institute of British Architects (RIBA)
66 Portland Place
London W1
071–580 5533

South Bank University
Borough Road
London SE1 0AA
071–928 8989
One of the few educational establishments to offer a lighting design course.

UK lighting design consultancies

DPA (UK) Lighting Consultants
24 High Street
Bovingdon
Hertfordshire HP3 OHH
(0442) 832021

Imagination
25 Store Street
London WC1E 7BL
071–323 3300

Lighting Design Ltd
Zero Ellaline Road
London W6 9NZ
071–381 8999

Lighting Design Partnership (LDP)
45 Timber Bush
Leith
Edinburgh
Scotland EH6 6QH
031–553 6633

Maurice Brill Lighting Design
48 Chilton Street
London E2 6DZ
071–613 0456

US lighting design consultancies

Carl Hillman Associates
118 East 25th Street
New York NY 10010
(212) 529 7800

Claude R. Engle
100 Potomac Street, Suite 202
Northwest
Washington D.C. 23337
(202) 337 0702

Cline Bettridge Bernstein
30 West 22nd Street
New York NY 10010
(212) 741 3280

Howard Brandston Lighting Design
141 West 24th Street
New York NY 10011
(212) 924 4050

Jerry Kugler Associates
155 Avenue of the Americas
New York NY 10013
(212) 255 6716

Jules Fisher & Paul Marantz Inc
126 Fifth Avenue
New York NY 10011
(212) 691 3020

Luminae Souter Lighting Design
555 De Haro Street, Suite 400
San Francisco
California 94107
(415) 861 1422

Ramsey Dupuy & Seats
239 Northwest 13th Street
Suite 301
Portland
Oregon 97209
(503) 224 8132

Manufacturers and suppliers

Andy Thorton Architectural Antiques Ltd
Ainleys Industrial Estate
Elland
West Yorkshire HX5 9JP
(0422) 375595

Architectural Metalworkers
Victoria Works
101–103 Hitchin Street
Biggleswade
Bedfordshire
(0767) 317272

Arteluce/Flos
The Studio
120 High Street
South Milford
Leeds LS25 5AQ
(0977) 685101

Artemide
17–19 Neal Street
London WC2H 9PU
071–240 2552

Axis Lighting Ltd
Merse Road
North Moons Moat
Redditch
Worcestershire B89 9HH
(0527) 584583

Banafix Solar Control
Banafix House
Amersham Road
Chesham
Buckinghamshire HP5 1NF
(0494) 778866

BBI Lighting
23 Parkside
Coventry CV1 2NE
(0203) 551444

Beta Lighting Ltd
383/387 Leeds Road
Bradford BD3 9LZ
(0274) 721129

BLV Lighting
31 Glynswood
Chinnor
Oxfordshire OX9 4JE
(0296) 399334

Box Products
21 Conduit Place
London W2 1HS
071–724 9389

Chelsom Ltd
Heritage House
Clifton Road
Blackpool
Lancashire FY4 4QA
(0253) 791344

Christopher Wray
600 Kings Road
London SW6
071–736 8434

Colt International
New Lane
Havant
Hampshire PO9 2LY
(0705) 451111

Concord Lighting
174 High Holborn
London WC1V 7AA
071–497 1400

Crescent Lighting
Unit 8 Rivermead Industrial Estate
Pipers Lane
Thatcham
Berkshire RG13 4NA
(0635) 878888

Crompton Targetti Ltd
PO Box 74
Doncaster DN2 4ND
(0302) 323941

Designed Architectural Lighting (DAL)
10 Bowling Green Lane
London EC1R 0BD
071–251 8459

Edison Halo
5 Delaware Drive
Tongwell
Milton Keynes MK15 8HG
(0908) 617617

Electrolite Ltd
Entrance C Rembrandt House
Whippendell Road
Watford
Hertfordshire WD1 7PN
(0923) 816099

Electrosonic
Hawley Mill
Hawley Road
Dartford
Kent DA2 7SY
(0322) 222211

Erco Lighting
38 Dover Street
London W1X 3RB
071–408 0320

Eurotec Optical Fibres
Shaw Lane
Ogden Road
Doncaster DN2 4SQ
(0302) 361574

Fibre Lite (UK) Ltd
Executive Centre
Midland House
Halesowen
West Midlands B63 3HY
021–585 6078

Futimis Ltd
Futimis House
11 Mead Park
River Way
Harlow
Essex CM20 2SE
(0279) 411131

GE Lighting
Lincoln Road
Enfield
Middlesex EN1 1SB
081–366 1166

GFC Lighting
Westminster Business Square
Durham Street
London SE11 5JA
071–735 0677

Glamox Electric (UK) Ltd
Glamox House
California Lane
Bushey Heath
Hertfordshire WD2 1EZ
081–950 0046

GTE Sylvania Ltd
Otley Road
Charlestown
Shipley
West Yorkshire BD17 7SN
(0271) 595921

Hitech Lighting plc
Tower House
Lea Valley Trading Estate
Edmonton
London N18 3HR
081–884 3333

Hoffmeister Lighting
Unit 3 Preston Road
Reading
Berkshire RG2 0BE
0734 866941

iGuzzini
Unit 3
Mitcham Industrial Estate
185 Streatham Road
Mitcham
Surrey CR4 2AP
081–646 4141

Illuma Lighting Ltd
24–32 Riverside Way
Uxbridge UB8 2YF
(0895) 272275

INTO Lighting Design
49 High Street
Wimbledon Village
London SW19 5AX
081–946 8533

JSB Electrical plc
Manor Lane
Holmes Chapel
Crewe
Cheshire CW4 8AB
(0477) 37773

Lampways
Allenby House
Knowles lane
Wakefield Road
Bradford
West Yorkshire BD4 9AB
(0274) 686686

LDMS
191 High Road
South Benfleet
Essex SS7 5HY
(0268) 755511

Levolux Group Services
Levolux House
Ashville Road
Gloucestershire GL2 6EU
(0452) 29794

Light Projects
23 Jacob Street
London SE1 2BG
071–231 8282

Lightworks Contracts Ltd
Eye Airfield Industrial Estate
Eye
Suffolk IP23 7HN
(0379) 870435

Lutron
6 Sovereign Close
Wapping
London E1 9HW
071–702 0657

Luxo/Thousand and One Lamps
4 Barmeston Road
London SE6 3BN
081–698 7238

Marlin Lighting
Hanworth Trading Estate
Feltham
Middlesex TW13 6DR
081–894 5522

Microlights
Elcot Lane
Marlborough
Wiltshire SN8 2BG
(0672) 515611

Miyakawa Europe Ltd
Unit 9 Barrington Industrial Estate
Leycroft Road
Beaumont Leys
Leicestershire LE4 1ET
(0533) 358818

Optelma Lighting
14 Napier Court
The Science Park
Abingdon
Oxfordshire OX14 3NP
(0235) 553769

Osram GEC
PO Box 17
East lane
Wembley
London HA9 7PG
081–904 4321

Par Opti Projects Ltd
Unit 9 The Bell Industrial Estate
Cunnington Street
Chiswick Park
London W4 5EP
081–995 5179

Philips Lighting
City House
420–430 London Road
Croydon CR9 3QR
081–665 6655

Reggiani Lighting
12 Chester Road
Borehamwood
Hertfordshire WD6 1LT
081–953 0855

Siemens UK
Siemens House
Windmill Road
Sunbury–on–Thames
Middlesex TW16 7HS
(0932) 785691

Staff/Brendel Lighting
Hampshire International
Business Park
Crockford Lane
Chineham
Basingstoke
Hampshire RG24 0WH
(0256) 707007

Strand Lighting
Grant Way
Syon Lane
Isleworth
Middlesex TW7 5QD
081–560 3171

TBL Fibre Optics Ltd
(now EuroTech Fibre Optics)
Mill Green Industrial Estate
Geldard Road
Leeds LS12 6HE
(0532) 440066

Technical Blinds Ltd
Old Town Lane
Woburn Town
High Wycombe
Buckinghamshire
(06285) 30511

Thorn Lighting
Elstree Way
Borehamwood
Hertfordshire WD6 1HZ
081–905 1313

Unilock HCP Ltd
Perimeter House
Napier Road
Castleham
St Leonards–on–Sea
East Sussex TN38 9NY
(0424) 852755

Zumtobel
Unit 5
The Argent Centre
Pump Lane
Hayes
Middlesex UB3 3BL
081–573 3556

Index

Acknowledgements

While we take full responsibility for the contents of this book we would like to thank the many people who have helped in its preparation. First there are all the companies and consultancies, too numerous to mention by name, who generously provided information about their products and projects, plus extensive photographic material. Their names and addresses are included in the Addresses section (pages 218–20).

We would especially like to thank Elaine Bishop for her invaluable efforts in sourcing and chasing up photo material; Doug Brennan, Mark Sutton-Vane, Andre Tammes and Jan Woods at Lighting Design Partnership for their help and co-operation; Janet Turner at Concord Lighting for the use of the company's photo library; Molly Rubinstein at Erco Lighting for her constructive suggestions; Julie Sheppard for keying in the address lists; John Baker of the Electricity Association for information from his published lecture on Energy Management, delivered at the 'Design for Offices' conference in 1989; and Mike Jankowski at Marlin Lighting.

Carl Gardner
Barry Hannaford